"I'd like to turn people
on to the fact
that the world is form,
not just function
and money."

Claes Oldenburg[1]

MAN CREATES ART CREATES MAN

Duane Preble

distributed by

CANFIELD PRESS   ·   **SAN FRANCISCO**

A Department of Harper and Row, Publishers, Inc.

New York   Evanston   London

To my students,
whose interest and ideas
helped create this book

Contents

1   Saul Steinberg

Introduction

The general ugliness pervading much of today's man-made environment seems to indicate that many of us have not realized the potential of our own visual capacity. Although art museums have record attendances, sales of art works increase, and much space is devoted to the arts in popular magazines, paradoxically artists still find themselves and their work isolated from people in everyday life. Vulgarized versions of the work of today's artists enter the commercial world of buying, selling, and consuming almost overnight. Yet the general public, continuing to be limited in its concept of what art is, still feels it can most comfortably enjoy "works of art" that were created generations and centuries ago for other times and other places. It will take considerable effort to close the gap between art and life.

Because art is sometimes vague and indefinite and seemingly related to nonessential things, it is assumed that the creation of art is not significant work.

The necessity for hard labor and frugality that accompanied the settling of the continent of North America strengthened the puritan ideal of constant work and sacrifice as a way of life. Idleness was sinful. Nonutilitarian art forms were considered a frivolous commodity associated with the devil. Much of this attitude remains with us today. Calvin Coolidge summed it up when he said,

"The chief business of America is business."[2]

Grant Wood's AMERICAN GOTHIC, painted in 1930, touches America's foundations. His strong visual comment has been modified to sell potato chips. Here is art borrowed and distorted, atop a pile of environmental chaos — as we continue business as usual.

A technologically explosive society needs the integrating rewards of art experience. The arts and the sciences can work for man in different ways. Science looks for and finds factual answers to questions related to our physical world. The arts help to answer our emotional and spiritual needs, and can help to shape our physical environment as well. Art is created by fusing skill, knowledge, intuition, and emotion with materials. Works of art are facts because of their physical existence; they must also possess inner life or spirit. Works of art have a unity of spirit and matter and remain *alive* no matter when or where they were created. For this reason art may live in the present for anyone who becomes engaged in its appreciation.

The visual arts range from drawing to environmental design, from making pots to making films. It would be impossible to cover inclusively this vast field of human endeavor. Although this book is written to give a broad understanding of these arts, its intent is to go beyond the usual art appreciation approach by including works and

1

2 Grant Wood
AMERICAN GOTHIC
1930. Oil on beaver board.
29⅞ x 24⅞".

concepts that relate to the environment.

All of the visual arts are environmental:
they exist in and help define human living
spaces. Aesthetic awareness and design ability can help to deal with the expanding environmental crisis. Art can be a tool for understanding and averting potential disaster
— and for making survival worthwhile.

Included here are many areas of artistic endeavor that fall under the following general
definition:

A work of visual art may be anything man-
made in which visual appearance is a primary consideration in its creation.

This book can only serve as an introduction to the visual arts. Ultimately the journey is your own.

3 Duane Preble
101 NORTH
San Francisco, 1971

MAN CREATES
ART
CREATES MAN

Why art?

To evoke in oneself a feeling one has experienced, and having evoked it in oneself, then by means of movement, line, color, sounds or forms expressed in words, so to transmit that feeling that others experience the same feeling — this is the activity of art.

Art is a human activity consisting in this, that one man consciously, by means of certain external signs, hands on to others feelings he has lived through and that others are infected by these feelings and also experience them.

Leo Tolstoy[1]

THE NECESSITY FOR ART

Art, like life itself, does not have to be defined or understood to be enjoyed. It must simply be received.

Art is not something out there. It grows from a capacity that we all possess. If you have ever experienced something intensely and have shared that experience with others, you have been where art begins.

Is it a necessity for us to give physical form to things we feel and imagine? Must we gesture, dance, draw, speak, sing, write, carve, paint, and build? I think we must.

Sharing experience is necessary for all of us. Studies have shown that an infant will not survive and develop as a healthy human being if denied interaction with another human being, even though provided with every

other necessity of life. We know how important it is to communicate an idea to someone else. If the idea is important to us and we succeed in making it known to another person, we feel satisfied and strengthened by the success. If we fail to get the idea across, we are frustrated and diminished.

Much of our communication is verbal from the time we learn to speak. Yet any single means of communication has its limitations. This is certainly true of visual communication. Still, many things can only be or are best "said" visually.

Artists have learned to make the subjective interaction between themselves and the world into something physically real. By so doing, they share their experience with others.

Art gives form to human experience. It can represent, interpret, clarify, and intensify those moments of life that are significant and complete in themselves. The entire range of human thought and feeling is the subject of art.

Art, science, philosophy, and religion are all disciplines that search for and demonstrate human concepts of reality. They are names for a continuous search for ultimate reality.

Works of art are physical manifestations of

ideas or experiences. In this sense it is difficult to draw a line between what we normally call works of art and all other physical manifestations of thought and feeling.

THE CONCEPT "ART"

A *work of art* is an objective manifestation of an idea formed with human skill through the use of a medium. Any medium can either limit or expand experience, depending on the way it is used. Television is a medium with great potential for the artist, but this potential is rarely realized. Television has a diminishing effect on the minds and hearts of people who watch it for hours daily. When a medium is used so that it contributes to experience, that particular use of the medium becomes art.

To most people *art* means something done by an artist, and an *artist* is a painter or sculptor. This conception of art acts as a limitation. Almost anything that we do can be art. Art is something done so well that it takes on more than ordinary significance.

art (ärt), n. 1. the quality, production, or expression of what is beautiful, appealing, or of more than ordinary significance.[2]

Creative works are produced by individuals, and they are enjoyed by the individual people who make personal contact with them. *No teacher or critic can tell you what to like.*

There are no absolute standards for judging the quality of works of art. If a work contributes to your experience, then it is art for you. It has quality valuable to you. Each person must ultimately judge the quality of any work for himself. Likes and dislikes change with time, as we change. We may like something very much at one time and find later that we have outgrown it.

People who live with works of art find that some of them gradually become less interesting. A painting may eventually seem to sink into the wall because it is no longer worthy of a glance. Some works do the opposite. Maybe they were not the most exciting objects at first, but as they are lived with they become more and more significant to the life around them. They have a presence about them, which acts as a vital force on those who respond to them.

Works of art that continue to contribute to the experience of many people over a long period of time are considered masterpieces because of their lasting contribution to human life.

The word "art" is being used here in a very general way. If we understand that no clear line needs to divide what is thought of as art from other human activities, we can then identify what are usually called "the arts" without erecting walls around them.

5 D. A. Bermann
ARTS AND CRAFTS FESTIVAL
1972

6 James Thurber

"He knows all about art, but he doesn't know what he likes."

When someone speaks of "the arts" in our culture he is usually referring to dance, drama, music, literature, and the visual arts. These arts are unique types of human activity, each producing forms perceived by our senses in different ways. Yet they grow from a common urge to give physical form to ideas, feelings, or experiences. It is an urge shared by all artists to go beyond functions, facts, and explanations. The arts could be thought of as attempts to fill or bridge the gap between the world we know and can measure and that much bigger universe whose presence we feel but cannot seem to comprehend consciously.

This book focuses on the visual arts. Since much common ground is shared by the arts in general, the word "art" as used here can be taken to mean either the arts or the visual arts, depending on the context in which it is found. It may refer to the most important art of all — the art of living.

We are living at a time when hard boundaries are dissolving, between the arts themselves and between the arts and other human activities. The Balinese say "We have no art. We do everything as well as we can."

FUNCTIONS OF ART

How does art function? That depends on how we allow it to function for us. Art can advertise, celebrate, clarify, communicate, decorate, discover, educate, enhance, entice, express, heal, inspire, integrate, intensify, interpret, narrate, organize, protect, record, refine, reveal, transform, and visualize, among other things. It can also arouse, attack, deceive, humiliate, incense, obscure, and terrorize. For some, art is merely an investment opportunity or property acquired for prestige.

Above all, works of art reflect us. As we look at ourselves in great works of art, the experience can be either terrifying or inspiring, or both. Art experience may give the joy of discovery that is also found in scientific research, or the awe-inspiring feeling described as religious experience. Through confrontation with works of art we can discover dimensions of ourselves that were hitherto unknown. Some of these dimensions may be very disturbing. In the ugliness and distortion of some of the images of man we may recognize negative and destructive aspects of ourselves. Yet through the form of the works themselves, we can also realize the potential for positive growth and change.

When works of art affect us they become part of us. Goya's THE THIRD OF MAY 1808 (see page 156) was created more than 150 years ago from Goya's own experience, yet this painting continues to offer his experience to us.

Art gives sensible form to human values, giving them force and momentum of their own through aesthetic appeal.

Art intensifies our involvement with life, making experience more vivid by stimulating our capacity to feel and respond.

Art is magic because it can heal our doubts by merging the known and the unknown in beneficial harmony.

There is a yearning now for art experience. During the year in which this book was written, I personally witnessed one clear example of this search. My family and I made a futile effort to see a special exhibition of paintings by van Gogh held in San Francisco during January of 1971. After standing in line for two hours we gave up. Those who waited up to four hours often got only quick glimpses of the paintings as they passed through the museum, along with hundreds of other visitors. Frequently as many as 20,-000 visitors a day pressed through the galleries. During the six weeks that this exhibition was held, over 400,000 people came to see the work of a lonely man who sold only one painting while he was alive.

This experience demonstrated to me again our overwhelming need to desanctify art in order to get it back into daily life. Most of the people standing in line were waiting to see **ART.** Perhaps we could have spent our time more wisely by simply living with art.

Much of the art being produced today is created by young people. Art is no longer found only in galleries and museums; it is entering the home and the street once more. The art developing today is an integral part of new life styles.

7

NAVAJO SAND PAINTING

From between the fingers of the medicine man
Colored sand flows steadily,
Out of the hand of the Singer, tirelessly chanting,
Flows blue and white and brown, flows yellow and
    black and red,
Covering the hogan floor with patterns,
Meaningless to unbelievers,
While the sick girl, surrounded by silent watchers,
Sits facing toward the East,
Awaiting, with quiet confidence, the Sing's sure
    end.
"There will be dancing to-night." she tells herself,
"And I shall dance with the others!"
"There will be feasting to-night." she says in her
    heart,
"And laughter and talk around the fires of my
    people;
And I shall be a part of it!"

                            Elizabeth-Ellen Long[3]

AWARENESS

Of all our planet's resources, the most precious is human awareness; each new device, instrument or technique that increases our receptivity to the stimuli of our natural environment also creates new avenues for the solution of ancient problems whose solution under the pressure of growing population cannot much longer be delayed. What we mine is the mind of man; what we extract are new dimensions of human experience.

Don Fabun[4]

Art helps us to see. It sharpens and rewards our senses.

The word "aesthetic" or "esthetic" was introduced into the English language to replace the phrase "sense of beauty" with a single word. Aesthetic means, simply, concerned with sensory perception. The opposite of aesthetic is anesthetic.

Our senses are continually bringing in information. From the flow of sensory data we select what we need in order to live. It would, of course, be impossible and undesirable for us to be aware of everything coming in through our senses. Our concern is with the extension of perceptual possibilities. These possibilities are under our selective control. Each of us sees differently according to our personal experience. A realtor, geologist, and landscape architect looking at a scenic view will see it differently for subjective reasons.

Meaningful reactions to works of art require personal participation. The experience and words of others can help to increase understanding. But the contact itself must be of our own making. Enjoyment of art is ultimately a personal thing. Each of us recreates the life of a work of art by putting together the parts for ourselves. This process of mentally reconstructing the work for our satisfaction takes effort and time.

Our response to things is all too often based on mental prejudice or preconception, rather than on direct awareness of forms and situations.

To see is itself a creative operation, requiring an effort. Everything that we see in our daily life is more or less distorted by acquired habits, and this is perhaps more evident in an age like ours when the cinema, posters, and magazines present us every day with a flood of ready-made images which are to the eye what prejudices are to the mind. The effort needed to see things without distortion takes something very like courage.

Henri Matisse[5]

Most of us have limited ideas of what beauty is. Even so-called good taste is a limitation because it bypasses direct perception. We judge what is beautiful not so much by what we feel, but by what is commonly accepted as beautiful: flowers, sunsets, waterfalls, human form as defined by the fashion of the day, etc. We reject things that other cultures consider beautiful because they do not fit our mold.

Can we set aside these limitations long enough to begin realizing other possibilities? Evaluating our terms may help. The idea behind the word "beauty" is bigger than might be expected. We use beauty to refer to things that are simply pretty. Pretty means pleasant or attractive to the eye, whereas something beautiful has qualities of a high order capable of delighting the eye *and* the aesthetic, intellectual, or moral sense. Something that is beautiful may be appealing to the mind and heart because it is true or right or real, but perhaps may not be visually pleasant at all. The opposite may also be true. Some things can be visually pleasant, but false or untrue in meaning or content, and thus are not beautiful. "Beautiful doesn't necessarily mean good looking." (Louis Kahn.)[6]

In twentieth-century Western culture beauty has been associated with women. Women are considered to possess more personal beauty than men, and women have been given the responsibility for "beauty" in society.

8 "A few times every century, a great beauty is born. I am not one of them. But what nature skipped, I supplied—so much so that sometimes I cannot remember what is real and what is fake."—Princess Luciana Pignatelli.[7] Photograph by Anne Zane Shanks, 1971.

There seems to be considerable difference of opinion about what constiutes personal beauty.

Beauty is Princess Pignatelli's business. In the book called THE BEAUTIFUL PEOPLE'S BEAUTY BOOK she offers to others what she has learned in her search for beauty. The Princess has been rebuilding her own body for some time. She has had silicone injections to fill out her cheeks, plastic surgery to lift her upper eyelids, her nose has been bobbed, and her breasts treated with cell implants. She has had treatments by mysterious processes she calls "diacutaneous fibrolysis" and "aromatotherapy," and she looks forward to eyelash implants. Such exaggerated concern about physical appearance is not new to our age.

9   A tribesman admires the result of hours of primping. Photograph by Jack Fields, 1969.

Many people assume that the primary function of art is to please the senses. If this is true, then ugliness has no place in art.

Four artists chose to push ugliness to its limits. Although the four works are similar in many ways, their similarities emphasize their differences. Each work is a unique expression created from very different points of view. The works range in date from the eighth century to the twentieth.

10   Leonardo da Vinci
CARICATURE
c. 1490. Detail. Pen and ink over red chalk.

12   CARICATURE FROM CEILING
OF HORYU-JI, NARA, JAPAN
8th century

13   Pablo Picasso
HEAD (study for GUERNICA)
1937. Pencil and gouache.
11⅜ x 9¼". See illustration 242.

11   Al Capp
PANEL FROM LI'L ABNER, UGLY WOMAN CONTEST
1946

All living things are expressive. Art is an extension of the natural expressive quality of the human body.

In his excellent study on art and visual perception, Rudolf Arnheim summarized the present state of our awareness when he said: "We are neglecting the gift of comprehending things by what our senses tell us about them. Concept is split from percept. . . ."[8]

In learning to cope with the world we have learned to conceptualize almost everything that we perceive. (The process is brought to a final crescendo by higher education.) We place the unique elements of our experience into general classes or categories, and give names to such categories in order to think about them and to communicate our ideas about them to others. The system built up by this process of classification is called a "cognitive system." Such a system provides a framework for our perception, which includes our basic values. Each of us has his own cognitive system, yet we share a common, more general cognitive system with others in our society. We could not get along without such classification, yet labeling and categorizing ignore the unique qualities of events and emphasize those qualities believed to be held in common. It is important to recognize that each of us has developed "a distinctive way of looking at the world *that is not the way the world actually is* but simply the way our group conventionally looks at our world."[9]

Every culture has a cognitive system that keeps it functioning. Yet major human problems are caused by the fact that almost every individual (and group) believes that his way of seeing things is the way things actually are.

We expect others to change to fit our cultural patterns. As a culture we feel that women's legs can be bare in public, but their breasts must be covered. In Yap, a South Pacific Islands territory with a culture of its own (now part of the United States Trust Territory of the Pacific), the legislature has recently considered two bills. The first would make it a crime for anyone to wear a miniskirt. The second would ban all bras, blouses, bikini tops, etc., making toplessness mandatory — even for tourists and missionaries. Bare breastedness is a traditional Yapese custom. It is equally traditional for women to cover their legs. This is just one of many cultures that seeks to maintain its own traditional standards under the pressures of foreign influence and rapid cultural change.

When we are limited to concepts and do not renew our consciousness with direct perception, we reach a dead end. When we look at things only in terms of labels, we miss the thing itself. We see "tree," "chair," "obscene," "beautiful," not this tree, this particular chair, this unique object, person, or situation. When we think that we thoroughly *know* what the world is like, we may be most cut off from it. We frequently confuse and limit what comes in through the senses with words and concepts. A state of growing awareness can be reached only when the mind works in harmony with the senses. To do this the mind must be open enough to receive what the senses bring in.

From infancy our awareness grows as we grow. As children we are taught what is good and bad — taught to reject some things and to accept others, thereby limiting our perception. We become prejudiced. We accept the standards and values of our culture and confuse them with objective experience.

We are guided in our perceptions by the people we emulate. We become aware to the degree that we are shown awareness by the awareness patterns of our relatives, teachers, and friends, and by the friendliness or hostility of our surroundings.

We have to learn to use our senses. The eyes are blind to what the mind cannot see. As we mentally discover new possibilities of seeing we increase our perception of the visual world.

14

his first real contact with people who could see. While he bumped into things in his walker, and felt for almost everything as a blind person does, it soon became apparent that he was not blind. Joey simply had never learned to use his eyes. After a year of working with specialists, and playing with sighted children, his visual responses were normal. Those who worked with him concluded that Joey was a bright and alert child. The combined disabilities of Joey and his parents had prevented normal perceptual awareness from developing.

"Looking" implies opening our eyes in a purely mechanical way, taking in what is before us in order to move about. "Seeing" is an extension of looking. This means that we not only did the looking, but also went beyond the looking and enjoyed seeing things for themselves. In the world of process and function a door knob is something to be looked at in order to grasp and turn it, not something to be seen for itself. When we get excited about the bright clear quality of a winter day, the rich color of a sunset, or the shape and finish of a door knob, we have gone beyond what we *need* to perceive and have enjoyed the perception itself. This is very much a part of what art is concerned with.

It is important for us to become conscious of what our senses tell us. We make choices based on sensory responses, yet we do not realize the basis of our choice. For example, a person sitting in a room with dark walls might get up and move to a lighter space without realizing what prompted the need for a change.

Joey, a New York City boy with blind parents, had cerebral palsy as a baby. As he grew older he learned to get around the apartment in a walker. Because of his own and his parents' disabilities Joey was largely confined to his family's apartment. His mother thought he seemed to have normal intelligence, yet clinical tests showed him to be blind and mentally retarded. At age five Joey was admitted to a school for children with a variety of disabilities. This was

As we become aware of common sensory-related decisions — aesthetic decisions — then we can begin to open up an entirely new world of sensory awareness. Ordinary things become extraordinary when seen in a new way. "Art is the demonstration that the ordinary is extraordinary." (Amédée Ozenfant.)[10]

CREATIVITY

. . . a first-rate soup is more creative than a second-rate painting.

Abraham Maslow[11]

After all, what is art? There is no way of defining art except from the inside. Art is the creative process and it goes through all fields. Einstein's theory of relativity — now that is a work of art! Einstein was more of an artist in physics than on his violin.

Art is this: art is the solution of a problem which cannot be expressed explicitly until it is solved.

Piet Hein[12]

Imagination is more important than knowledge.

Albert Einstein[13]

Imagination is the source of creativity. It is impossible to think without mental images. The making of these mental images is called imagination. Imagination involves the ability to form images in one's mind that are not actually present to the senses and especially to combine images of former experiences, thus creating new images not known by experience.

Art is involved with the making of actual images or forms. But the creation of an actual image must be preceded by a mental image. In the visual arts these mental images are visual; in music they are audible.

We all possess the potential to be creative. What does it mean to be creative? Without creative people there is no art.

To be creative is to be able to put things together in original ways in order to produce new things of significance. Simply making things or doing is not enough. Nor is it enough to make something unique. Being creative is being able to bring into being new things of value.

An artist (or creative person) must be a dreamer, a realist, and a skilled workman. The creative process requires the ability to manipulate freely and consciously the ele-

ments of perceptual experience. This includes a dynamic process of both awareness and action. Creative experience involves the open encounter of the person with the world.

Most of us have never been asked to be creative. Yet creativity can be developed. We can learn to improve ourselves and our world. We can deliberately seek new relationships between ourselves and our environment. To think of creativity as limited to those with (inborn) talent is a great mistake.

The abilities characteristic of creativity can be developed. These abilities include:

• the ability to wonder, to be curious
• the ability to be enthusiastic, spontaneous, and flexible
• the ability to be open to new experience, to see the familiar from an unfamiliar point of view
• the ability to confront complexity and ambiguity with interest
• the ability to take advantage of accidental events in order to make desirable but unsought discoveries (called serendipity)
• the ability to make one thing out of another by shifting its functions
• the ability to generalize in order to see universal applications of ideas
• the ability to synthesize and integrate, to find order in disorder
• the ability to be intensely conscious yet in touch with unconscious sources
• the ability to visualize or imagine new possibilities
• the ability to be analytical and critical
• the ability to know oneself, and to have the courage to be oneself in the face of opposition
• the ability to be persistent, to work hard for long periods, in pursuit of a goal, without guaranteed results.

To create is essentially to put two or more

15 Simon Rodia
WATTS TOWERS
Photograph by Duane Preble, 1971

known things together in a unique way, thus creating a new thing — an unknown thing. There are as many ways to do this as there are creative people. The need or desire for a thing or condition not yet existing is certainly where the creative process begins. Formulation of the problem is probably as important as the solution.

The ability to produce original ideas has little to do with measured intelligence. Although it is a fairly common ability in children, it is rare in adults.

The Watts Towers of California are the creative work of a poor Italian tile-setter named Simon Rodia. He worked for thirty-three years creating these fantastic towers out of steel rods, mesh, and mortar. They grew from his tiny triangular backyard like Gothic spires. He lovingly covered their surfaces with bits and pieces of broken tile, melted bottle glass, and other colorful junk that he

gathered from the vacant lots of the poor neighborhood where he lived. His statement of purpose reads as follows:

I no have anybody help me out.
I was a poor man.
Had to do a little at a time.
Nobody helped me.
I think if I hire a man
he don't know what to do.
A million times
I don't know what to·do myself.
I never had a single helper.
Some of the people say
what was he doing . . . some of the people
think I was crazy
and some people said
I was going to do something.
I wanted to do something
in the United States
because I was raised here you understand?
I wanted to do something for the United States
because there are nice people
in this country.
                              Simon Rodia[14]

Children's play often seems frivolous and unproductive to adults, yet it is a most fertile activity for growth, particularly for the growth of imagination. As adults we seldom call our activity "play" even when our fooling around has no other goal than plain fun. But fooling around or "toying with possibilities" is a very important part of the creative process.

How we feel about all of this is important not only to our own lives, but also to the lives of our children. Is it too late for you to further develop your own imagination? How can you help children who are influenced by you to develop their creative imaginations?

Creativity — the urge to inquire, to invent, to perform — has been stifled in millions of school children, now grown up, who did not get above rote learning, or at least did not stay above it.[15]

Creative imagination is necessary not only to create things oneself, but also to fully enjoy the creations of others. An art appreciation course needs to be a remedial course in this society at this time because our educational system has generally failed to nurture the development of creative imagination. From nursery school to graduate school opportunities to develop sensory awareness and creativity are rare. What passes for complete education often promotes absorption and retention of information at the expense of creativity. Teachers often ignore and even attack evidences of creative imagination in their students because their own imaginations are underdeveloped and their classrooms are overcrowded.

For all people, especially very young ones, mental and emotional growth depend on the ability to bring together experience of the world outside oneself with experience of the world felt within. Therefore, opportunities for creative expression are extremely important to us, not so that some of us will become professional artists, but for the general mental and emotional health of ourselves and society. Art helps a child (and a

16   Nell Dorr
Untitled
1958

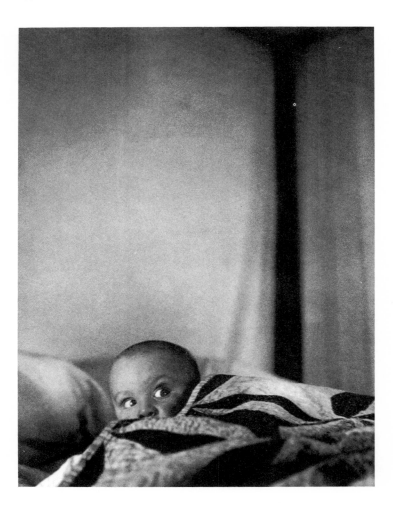

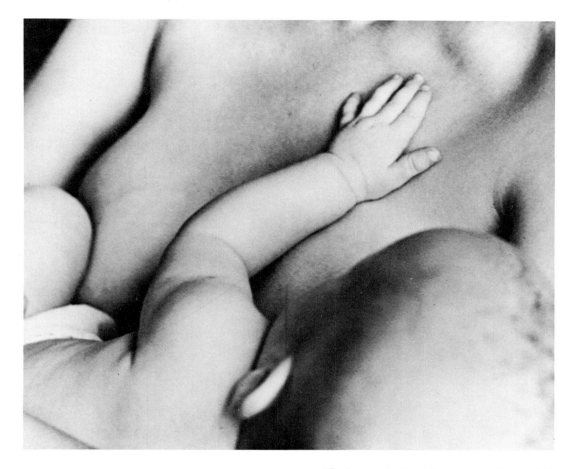

17 Wayne Miller. MOTHER AND BABY. 1948

mature person) discover his world and relate himself to it. Until we are able to express our feelings and experiences, we do
not really know what they are. By expressing them we objectify them. We take them
out and look at them. This process provides
for the integration of personal experience
and the apprehension of reality. It allows us
to meet the world with more self-assurance.

Most of the abilities listed as being characteristic of creative people are found in all
children (except the severely retarded) during the first few years of life. What happens
to this extraordinary capacity? John Holt,
author of How CHILDREN FAIL, answers:

What happens is that it is destroyed . . . by the
process that we misname education — a process
that goes on in most homes and schools. We

adults destroy most of the intellectual and creative capacity of children by the things we do to
them and make them do. We destroy this capacity
above all by making them afraid — afraid of not
doing what other people want, of not pleasing, or
of making mistakes, of failing, of being wrong.
Thus we make them afraid to gamble, afraid to
experiment, afraid to try the difficult and unknown.[16]

Children naturally reach out to the world
around them from birth. They taste, touch,
hear, see, and smell their environment, becoming part of it through their senses.

All forms of expressive communication are
part of that reaching out. When a child is
confronted with an experience that indicates
to him that his experiment was of question-
able value, he soon stops reaching so far.

18 This bird shows one
child's expression
before he was exposed
to coloring books.

When our own limitations, prejudices, and
fears are passed on to children through stereotyped projects such as workbooks and coloring books, the results can be disastrous,
and we rarely notice. The accompanying sequence tells the story.

seven birds

Color seven birds blue.

Then the child had to color a workbook illustration.

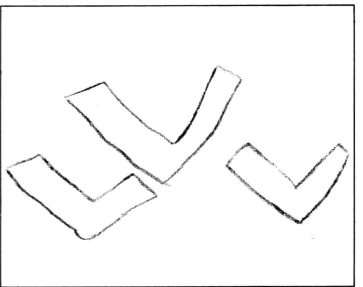

After coloring the workbook birds,
the child has lost his creative
sensitivity and self-reliance.

19 Drawing by a six-year-old
WALKING IN THE GRASS AFTER THE RAIN

Stereotyped images surround us in overwhelming quantity today. As Matisse has pointed out, ready-made images are to the eye what prejudices are to the mind.[17]

Children in the past had fewer toys. What toys they had were often simple. As the child played the toy was able to fill almost any role invented for it. Can this be said of the true-to-scale, real-life replicas of stereotyped people and things that children are given to play with today? These toys, along with coloring books, regimented school "art projects," and uncontrolled television watching, act as a giant wet blanket on the developing imaginations of the young.

Art education provides one fertile means for nurturing creative potential. What is important is to provide children with the opportunity to give their ideas and emotions an honest, tangible expression. Children, and adults even more, need a great deal of encouragement to be able to express themselves without fear or hesitation. These are ideas ably expressed by Susumu Hani in his film CHILDREN WHO DRAW PICTURES.[18]

How does it feel to go walking in wet grass just after it rains? John shares the feeling with us eloquently.

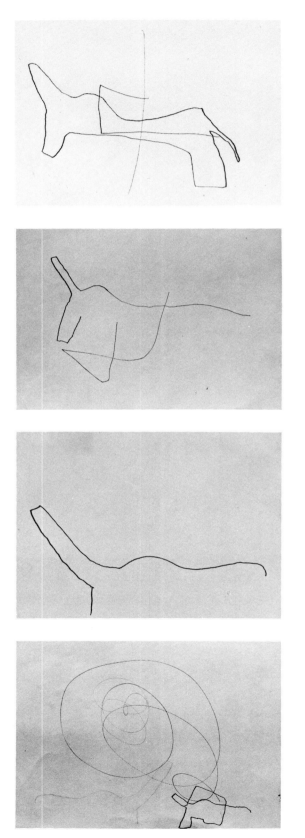

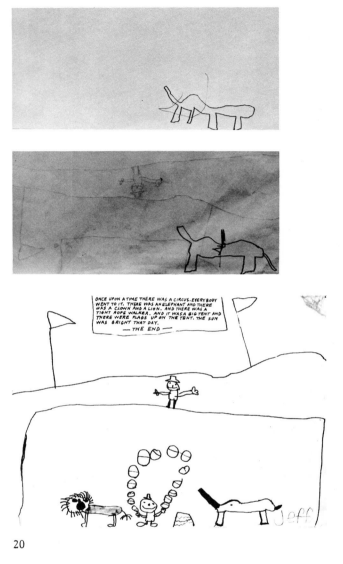

ONCE UPON A TIME THERE WAS A CIRCUS. EVERYBODY
WENT TO IT. THERE WAS AN ELEPHANT AND THERE
WAS A CLOWN AND A LION. AND THERE WAS A
TIGHT ROPE WALKER. AND IT WAS A BIG TENT AND
THERE WERE FLAGS UP ON THE TENT. THE SUN
WAS BRIGHT THAT DAY.
— THE END —

20

At age four or five, children try to draw things they have experienced. This series of drawings shows a four-year-old's attempts to draw an elephant soon after seeing his first circus. He began with the most characteristic part of the elephant — the trunk. The child was dissatisfied with the results, but kept trying. Finally, he came pretty close to what he wanted to see. He then turned the drawing over, and drew a circus with an elephant, lion, juggler, and tightrope walker. This scene was so real for him that he asked his father to write down the story as he told about his picture.

A four-year-old girl did this self-portrait. A line around the edge shows an awareness of the whole paper. One hand with radiating fingers reaches out, balancing the composition perfectly. This was accomplished spontaneously after much previous experience, but without any adult guidance or conscious knowledge of design.

21

There is an international language of expression formed by children's art. These pictures from many parts of the world have the same basic visual vocabulary.

22

Bali

Switzerland

India

Indonesia

Ceylon

United States

Typical motifs recur in children's art throughout the world, but their uses and variations are infinite. With bold colors this child gave us a sun, a tree, and much more.

We all were children once and as children many of us were discouraged by negative experiences with so-called art. These discouragements were felt before we reached an age when we could draw complex pictures from our personal experience.

It is important that the boy who did this drawing was working with a subject that he knew well. It is also important that he had gained the self-confidence to draw what he knew.

23 A Child's Painting of a Tree
See color plate 1

24 Painting by a
Ten-year-old Child

25 TLAZOLTÉOTL.
Aztec Goddess of
Childbirth.
c.1500. Aplite with
garnets. Height 8⅛".

DISCOVERY AND EXPRESSION

Artists seldom if ever try simply to reproduce the appearance of the visual world. As Picasso has said, "Nature and art, being two different things, cannot be the same thing."[19] The artist's purpose is not merely to imitate nature, but to do what nature does, that is, to create "life" — to invent something that "works" — to express an inner reality more enduring than the shifting impressions of everyday life.

A work of art is a unique event fashioned out of the personal experience of the individual who creates it. This is true even when the style of art is strictly controlled by forces of the society within which the artist works, as in ancient Egypt.

To understand what art is and how it grows from and contributes to experience, it is revealing to examine a series of works with the same subject by different artists who are using different media and who hold very different attitudes. The works in this series have the subject of mother and child in common. This particular combination of figures has basic significance and interest, since each of us has had a mother and has been a child. The works have been selected to show how varied images of the same subject can each be a valid expression.

It would seem that the most important event related to the mother and child theme is birth itself, yet our culture has long avoided depicting it.

The Aztec sculptor who carved this image of birth gave powerful form to essential aspects of the process of giving birth as it was practiced by that culture. But this work is not a representation of a particular woman bearing a child. The artist has simplified the image, exaggerating some parts and underplaying or omitting others. By so doing he has created a symbol of great impact, as was his purpose.

Color plate 1   A Child's Painting of a Tree. Gouache. 9¾ x 14 5/16".

Color plate 2   Jan Vermeer. THE ARTIST IN HIS STUDIO. c. 1665. Oil on canvas. 31⅜ x 26".

The African Ashanti carving is part of a drum stand. The original work includes two animals supporting a large drum and a father as well as this nursing mother. The piece is a direct, geometrically clear depic-

tion of the subject. It has a great deal of honest charm. We might call it unsophisticated because its refined form is based on a design tradition that we are just beginning to understand.

26 Detail of AFRICAN SCULPTURE. Ashanti Tribe, Ghana, c. 19th century. Height 31". Photograph by Eliott Elisofon.

Primitive peoples are sometimes compared with children, but work based on long traditions should not be confused with the naive simplicity of children's art.

This mother and child is the work of a nine- or ten-year-old girl. There is no tradition here, only a universal language of boldly expressive form. Although the subject is Mary and Christ, the shy girl who painted it was working from deep inner experience. This is her mother and she is the child. She identified both with the tiny secure child and the large protective mother. The bold free lines and curving shapes contribute to the power of this painting. Feel the emotion expressed in the eyes of the mother.

The painted Byzantine Madonna and Child is at least as abstract as the Ashanti figure or the child's Madonna, and perhaps more removed from natural appearances. As a depiction of mother and child, it feels much more remote than the preceding painting by a child. The Byzantine style, still followed by artists working in the orthodox religious tradition, is a successful compromise between the desire to avoid worshiping graven images and the need to educate the illiterate through pictures. The highly stylized figures of Mary and Christ emerge from a throne symbolizing the Roman Colosseum where the early Christians met death for their beliefs. The entire image appears flat and richly decorative, emphasizing spiritual rather than physical concerns. The cloth covering the figures has been indicated by linear patterns, with scarcely a hint of three-dimensional form. This is certainly the image of no ordinary mother and child. Christ appears as a wise little man, supported on the lap of a heavenly, supernatural mother.

27

29 Fra Filippo Lippi
MADONNA AND CHILD
c. 1440–1445. Tempera on wood.
31⅜ x 20⅛".

28 ENTHRONED MADONNA AND CHILD
1200. Byzantine School.
Tempera on wood. 32⅛ x 19⅜".

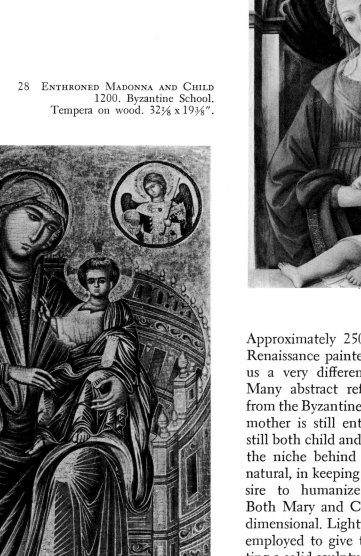

Approximately 250 years later, the Italian Renaissance painter Fra Filippo Lippi gave us a very different Madonna and Child. Many abstract refinements handed down from the Byzantine tradition are visible. The mother is still enthroned and her child is still both child and man. Yet the figures and the niche behind them now appear more natural, in keeping with the Renaissance desire to humanize medieval Christianity. Both Mary and Christ appear quite three-dimensional. Light and shade are effectively employed to give the figures and their setting a solid sculptural quality. Lippi was not one of the first Italian painters to make his figures look natural in this way, but he was one of the first to do it this well. Behind the appearance of naturalism, Lippi has given the painting quiet monumentality by basing the composition on simple geometric shapes.

30   Andrea Mantegna. THE MADONNA AND CHILD. c. 1445. Tempera.

Within only a few years Mantegna painted a picture of the Madonna that must have been a real surprise to his contemporaries. Here is a quite natural image of a real mother and child. If it were not for the title, we would have no clue that this tender scene is meant to be the Madonna and Child. The sacred image has now become fully humanized and secularized. We see the Madonna as a humble, accessible woman no longer enthroned. Christ is a sleeping infant with no clue given of his future. Only Mary's introspective gaze suggests that there is more to come. The painting is a universal statement of the mother-child relationship, apart from its intended Christian subject matter.

Picasso's drawing has much in common with the tempera painting by Mantegna. The drawing is a study for a painting of a circus family. Picasso tries several times to capture exactly the right gesture in the hands of the mother as she holds the baby. The relationship between the figures is emphasized by the child's upreaching arm and touching hand and by the mother's bent head and hanging hair bringing us back around to the child. Picasso is not opposed to modifying anatomy in order to strengthen his idea.

Compare the elegant calm of this mother and child with the brutal anguish of the mother holding her dead child on the far left in Picasso's painting GUERNICA and you will see the breadth of this man's visual expression. Each work carries its message well.

31   Pablo Picasso
Detail of GUERNICA
1937. Oil on canvas. *See illustration 242.*

32   Pablo Picasso
A MOTHER HOLDING A CHILD AND
FOUR STUDIES OF HER RIGHT HAND.
1904. Crayon. 13½ x 10½".

Elliott Erwitt's photograph may lead us to believe that here we are seeing the real thing — an actual mother and child. But it is not the real thing. It is a photograph taken by an artist who called upon all of his skill and intuition to capture this image from the flow of visual material around him. A mechanical device much more complex than the brush has made it possible to create a fully natural image defined by light, convincing us that we are there experiencing this intimate event.

We can see from the quality of the photograph that Erwitt had empathy with his subject. In art this is the rule rather than the exception. The creation of a work of art demands close contact with one's materials. Subject matter, media, and the language of visual form are the materials of the artist. A great deal can be learned by studying an artist's feeling for these interacting factors.

33 Elliott Erwitt. MOTHER AND CHILD. 1956.

34 Michelangelo Buonarroti
DEPOSITION FROM THE CROSS
Left unfinished, 1555. Marble.
Height 7′ 5″.

One of Michelangelo's last works was his DEPOSITION FROM THE CROSS. Although it was left unfinished, its expressive power is undiminished, and perhaps is enhanced, by this fact.

The body of Christ has been taken down from the cross. It is supported here by Mary, Joseph, and an angel. There is nothing in this piece of the comfortable support given Christ's limp body in Michelangelo's early PIETA (see page 100). The axis of Christ's figure is a sagging vertical barely supported by the smaller figures on either side. The group seems bound into unity by the hooded figure of Joseph appearing behind Christ. Not only is this figure the supporting father in a figurative sense, but it also reflects the image of the actual father of the work — the face is believed to be Michelangelo's.

With this sculpture a series of self-portraits begins. Only a few of them are self-portraits in which the artist puts primary emphasis on recording his own face. All of these works show clearly each man's involvement with the relationships between himself, his work, and the world at large.

35   Diego Rodrigues de Silva Velázquez. THE MAIDS OF HONOR. 1656. 18 x 15¾″.

Velázquez painted himself at work on the large canvas originally called THE ROYAL FAMILY, now known as THE MAIDS OF HONOR or LAS MENINAS. The Infanta Marguerita, the blond daughter of the king, is the center of interest. Velázquez emphasized her by making her figure the clearest, lightest shape and by placing her near the foreground close to the center. Around her Valázquez has created the appearance of his large studio, in which a complex group of figures interact with the princess and with the viewer. By masterfully controlling the light, color, and placement in space of everything in the room, Velázquez has led us through a very intricate composition. He has placed himself discretely in semishadow. Showing himself brush in hand, his image acts as a kind of signature to the work.

The picture is an enigmatic comment on painting. All the proper people are represented here for a court portrait, yet the work is much more than a portrait of a royal princess. The complicated interaction between ourselves and the subject could keep us in-terested indefinitely. As the king and queen viewed this work they saw themselves as painted reflections in the mirror on the far wall. As we view it today, we see it as if we were in the mirror ourselves. All this is put on the canvas with a masterful touch and we are witnesses.

Rembrandt dressed himself up and faced his mirror and his viewers directly — but not as a painter. Rembrandt, like his later countryman van Gogh, painted a great many self-portraits. Most of the time he almost seemed to look upon himself as a stranger, but with the same penetrating insight and depth of feeling that he brought to all his human subjects. These were no narcissistic presentations, but portraits of a man who studied himself carefully, realizing his own emotions and capturing them in paint. This knowledge enabled him to paint over sixty-three great portraits revealing the character of each sitter.

36 Rembrandt van Rijn
SELF-PORTRAIT
1658. Oil on canvas. 33¼ x 26".

Another painting that reveals profound insight is Jan Vermeer's THE ARTIST IN HIS STUDIO. Vermeer also painted himself at work, but here there is no royal portrait in progress. Our eyes move immediately past the heavy curtain pulled up to our left to the strong black and white contrast on the back of Vermeer's shirt. We find ourselves looking with him at his painting on the easel and beyond that to the model. The model (perhaps his wife) is posing as an allegorical figure who may represent fame. She is only mildly interesting; she seems like a prop and acts as a neutral pivotal point. Taken all together, however, the scene is fascinating. The painting is a complete self-portrait, although we cannot see Vermeer's face. He is showing us himself in his studio. But much more important than the physical circumstances is the way in which they are presented. His way. Although it looks as though we came upon this situation by chance, it is not so. Every relationship in this painting was carefully selected by Vermeer. As in the work of Velázquez, light and placement play very important roles. For Vermeer, light was a major element defining exactly the character of each thing he observed. The whole image is revealed by light as if created by light.

38 Pieter Brueghel
THE PAINTER AND THE CONNOISSEUR
c. 1568. Pen and bistre. 10 x 8⅜".

We are looking over the artist's shoulder again in Brueghel's drawing THE PAINTER AND THE CONNOISSEUR. Or are we? Maybe we do not wish to be identified with the connoisseur. He looks like a phony, clutching his money pouch and saying something inane, as he peers through his spectacles at Brueghel's work in progress. Of course, since Brueghel did the drawing, not the connoisseur, he gives us the whole story from the artist's point of view. The drawing has been done in such a way that if we identify with anyone here, it is Brueghel.

37 Jan Vermeer
THE ARTIST IN HIS STUDIO
c. 1665. Oil on canvas. 31⅜ x 26".
See color plate 2

39 Carlo Dolci
SELF-PORTRAIT
1674. Chalk. 7⅛ x 5½".

Carlo Dolci drew himself at work as Brueghel did. The two painters were quite different kinds of people, at least as we see
them here. Yet they had in common something shared by most if not all people working in the visual arts: they were craftsmen;
they worked with their hands. Perhaps that
is why Dolci painted a double self-portrait
in which he holds his drawing to show himself as both craftsman and thinker, thus clar-
ifying the dual character that artists must
possess.

40 Carlo Dolci
DOUBLE SELF-PORTRAIT
1674. Oil on canvas.

The relationship between an artist and his particular subject often reveals the character of that artist's attitude toward his environment and to life. Such is the theme of the following three works.

In 1917, Egon Schiele painted a portrait of his wife, himself, and their child, who had not yet been born. Schiele looks at us as a father who seems very moved by the anticipated completion of his family. He takes a position in the composition similar to that taken by Michelangelo in his DEPOSITION FROM THE CROSS (see page 31). By positioning his own image behind the mother and child, Schiele acts as the beginning in a sequence of forms emerging one from the other. His lanky arms and legs almost enclose his wife. Her position creates a simpler shape, from which the child emerges.

It is often said that a true work of art is alive. The work seems to have a life of its own because it has been put together in such a way that it goes beyond being merely a sum of its parts. As art, it acts as a container or carrier of meaning, and therefore has become more than an arrangement of materials.

There is another aspect of aliveness. Artists in various cultures have sometimes tried to make their works look as much like their subjects as possible. That is, they emphasized accurate visual representation over all other aspects of their subjects. By working in this way, an artist can achieve verisimilitude. When this practice is carried to its ultimate, especially in painting, it may fool the viewer into believing that he is seeing the actual thing. The French call this visual deception *trompe l'oeil*, literally meaning "fool the eye."

The Greek myth of Pygmalion tells of a sculptor who created a statue of a woman so beautiful that he fell in love with it. Aphrodite, goddess of love, responding to the artist's prayer, made the figure actually come

41 Egon Schiele
THE FAMILY
1917. Oil on canvas. 59 x 63".

to life, and they lived happily ever after. The lady is obviously on a pedestal as we see her here in a painting of the event by the academic French painter Gérôme. This image would lead one to conclude that woman was created by or from man for his pleasure. Anyone with a knowledge of mythology and history might realize that our culture is still suffering from such fantasies.

Eakins helps us back to reality. The lady comes down off the pedestal and thus takes her rightful place in the real world.

Thomas Eakins painted his friend, the sculptor William Rush, helping his model as she steps down from the stand on which she has been posing. Although the artist depicted is not Eakins, it is clear that he identified so strongly with his friend that it may as well be he.

42 Jean Léon Gérôme. PYGMALION AND GALATEA. c. 1860. Oil on canvas. 35 x 27″.

Eakins shows us that the artist is a man of considerable physical strength and yet is a gentle man. Rush has his mallet firmly in one hand and his model gently in the other.

The model is certainly no "raving beauty." She does not have the acceptable ideal figure. Yet she descends from the old stump as if she were a queen being helped from her royal carriage.

The model is the main subject here. Eakins has demonstrated an attitude that he asks us to share. It is an attitude of great respect and admiration for what is real as opposed to the artificialities of what has become a stereotyped ideal. What Eakins asks us to confront is the beauty of the ordinary human figure and perhaps, by extension, the importance of really seeing all so-called ordinary things.

43 Thomas Eakins. WILLIAM RUSH AND HIS MODEL. 1907–1908. Oil on canvas. 35¼ x 47¼″.

If we look at more than one work of a given artist, we soon begin to realize the point of view that is the basis of his personal style. Of course this can change and often does. As point of view changes, style changes.

Each one of us has a particular point of view that we have developed from past experience. This point of view or attitude determines how we experience the world around us, and also what we experience.

In every work of art, the artist creates form out of his own experience. In doing this he is saying, "Here I am. I exist. This is what is important to me. This is how I see life." In this sense every work of art is a self-portrait. In another sense even a representational self-portrait is not merely a self-image, but is also an attempt to give a personal experience universal significance. As art contributes to the expanding consciousness of the artist and his audience, it creates man.

The works of the following three artists demonstrate this. Although they lived during approximately the same time, they come from different countries and hold very different attitudes. They are each primarily interested in human beings, and, therefore, the human figure is their most frequent subject.

In 1908, Henri Matisse wrote the following statement about his work:

The purpose of a painter must not be conceived as separate from his pictorial means, and these pictorial means must be the more complete (I do not mean complicated) the deeper is his thought. I am unable to distinguish between the feeling I have for life and my way of expressing it.[20]

Matisse wrote these words a few years before he painted NASTURTIUMS AND THE DANCE. The work illustrates his point. The subject is a corner of his studio. He shows a chair, a sculpture stand topped by a vase of flowers, and against the wall a section of his large painting called THE DANCE. Here

44   Henri Matisse
NASTURTIUMS AND THE DANCE
1912. Oil on canvas. 75¾ x 45".
See color plate 3

Matisse expresses what the French call *la joie de vivre* or "the joy of life." Every line, shape, and color radiates with it. And this is true of practically all of his work.

The human figure had a particular importance for Matisse. He said:

What interests me most is neither still life nor landscape but the human figure. It is through it that I best succeed in expressing the nearly religious feeling that I have towards life.[21]

Matisse was a great master of the first half of our century. Although during his lifetime (1869–1954) there was plenty of human suffering in the world, he chose to emphasize other things.

In the article published Christmas Day 1908 quoted above, Matisse states his purpose as a painter:

What I dream of is an art of balance, of purity and serenity, devoid of troubling or depressing subject matter, an art which might be for every mental worker, be he businessman or writer, like an appeasing influence, like a mental soother, something like a good armchair in which to rest from physical fatigue.[22]

45 Henri Matisse
ARTIST AND MODEL REFLECTED IN A MIRROR
1937. Pen and ink. 24⅛ x 16⅛".

In 1937, he created something nice for the tired businessman (as he had been doing for years). In this drawing, Matisse himself appears in the mirror with the model's reflection. The model is very free and sensuous as Matisse has created her on paper. He pictures himself in coat and tie as if he were a businessman. His image acts as an effective point of contrast with the model, and appears, as in other works that we have seen, to remind us that this bunch of lines exists because of him. There is no chance that we might confuse this with an anonymous reflection of reality.

The third and fourth works by the master were cut from paper when Matisse was an invalid two years before his death. His feeling for life comes across as strongly as ever. These late works of Matisse are some of his most powerfully decorative and alive. Underlying Matisse's work is a profound and particular kind of expression. He would not let his works rest until they had achieved a balance of repose and personal intensity.

46 Henri Matisse
BLUE NUDE III
AND BLUE NUDE IV.
1952. Gouache cutout.
105 x 85 cm., 109 x 74 cm.

Käthe Kollwitz gives us a completely different kind of attitude. Her etching called THE PRISONERS is an image of suffering and struggle. With great skill she carefully depicted her own feelings related to a class war that occurred in Germany in the sixteenth century. Here the struggle is not a fact of history but a living event, part of the continuous struggle with which she identified. We see something of the artist's own features on many of the faces in this bound block of humanity.

The lithograph DEATH SEIZING A WOMAN was published in 1934. The original drawing for it was done in 1924. It is one of a large number of prints and drawings on related subjects. This print's great impact has been achieved by paring down the idea to its essentials. The mother holding her child in a powerful grip stares ahead in great fear as the symbolic figure of death presses down on her from behind. The dramatic lines focus attention on the terrified expression on the mother's face.

47   Käthe Kollwitz. THE PRISONERS. 1908. Etching and soft-ground. 12⅞ x 16⅝".

48 Käthe Kollwitz
DEATH SEIZING A WOMAN
1924. Lithograph. 25 x 21″.

The self-portrait done in 1934 is as clear and powerful as the other two prints. Color would only detract from these bold, graphic statements.

Käthe Kollwitz lived in Germany during a period that knew great difficulty and pain. She lost a son in the First World War and died herself toward the end of the Second. But her personal grief was secondary to her deep concern for humanity.

Although she knew considerable fame during her life, she did not let it detract from her simplicity. "She was the greatest woman artist the world has known so far, a great mother with a still greater heart for all the oppressed and humiliated, a woman 'of sorrow and acquainted with grief.' "[23]

49 Käthe Kollwitz
SELF-PORTRAIT
1934. Lithograph. 8 1/16 x 7 3/16″.

The photographer Werner Bischof had a
very broad contact with life. It is clear from
his photographs that he also had great compassion for all he saw of human life. His
photograph of a starving mother and her
child, taken in India in 1951, is one of the
most powerful photographs ever taken. By
coming close to his subject at a low angle,
he was able to bring together the pleading
hand and face of the mother. The gaze
of the child brings the composition back
around to us.

50 Werner Bischof
HUNGER IN INDIA
1951

51   Werner Bischof
SHINTO PRIESTS IN TEMPLE GARDEN
Meiji Temple, Tokyo, 1951

In the same year, Bischof photographed Shinto priests walking through falling snow in a temple garden. By carefully selecting his distance from the figures, he gives us their relationship to the trees, thus recording a classic image of a basic Asian attitude toward man in nature.

The final photograph by Bischof in this sequence is of a lone flute player in Peru. The lilting steps of the boy with his flute are captured with great lyric charm. A fine feeling for form, especially for light, as well as a deep human understanding, made him able to say NO! and YES! with conviction.

By developing his own responses to life, the artist is able to give of himself so deeply that it is no longer just himself he is giving. His experience becomes universal and therefore valuable and accessible to all.

52   Werner Bischof
LONE FLUTE PLAYER
Peru, 1954

What do we respond to in a work of art?

VISUAL COMMUNICATION

Verbal language consists of agreed upon meanings connected to certain sounds that are learned through continuous repetition. Verbal language is highly abstract; it is not representational. Word symbols, in most cases, have no connection to the things to which they refer other than learned association. Therefore, when repetition stops verbal language is soon forgotten.

The world brought to us by our senses has meaning for us apart from formal language. When we speak of a "language of sound" or a "language of vision" we are referring to the elements and groupings of audible or visual phenomena to which humans react in generally similar ways. There are common human responses to much sensory experience. However, there are no visual or auditory languages based on specific agreed upon meanings apart from verbal languages. With the help of words we can analyze and therefore better understand the ways in which artists work with the elements of visual form in order to communicate certain meanings.

The basis of the visual arts is visual form. Artists and their audiences are conscious of their own responses to visual things. They are visually literate in that sense. Although we live at a time when there is great emphasis on visual things, many of us are still visually illiterate. The first step toward becoming visually literate is to open up enough to realize what our senses are telling us. Enjoying the visual arts requires the ability to see, yet, as we have observed, few of us are given the chance to develop this ability.

Students taking an art course for the first time often ask, "What should I be looking for?" Although the question is usually sincere, it reveals a basic misconception, which can block further experience. The question implies that there is something hidden in a work of art that stands apart from the work itself; something that can be told like a story or put into a complete verbal description, so that what seems vague and confusing in the visual realm is fully clarified by translation into words. This is not so. If a work of art has value it is complete in itself. It may imply many things beyond itself, but these things are often peripheral, nonessential factors. Any verbal explanation of a work is no more complete than a verbal explanation of a person. It may be very revealing, but it is always merely an interpretation after the fact. The fact is the work itself.

Art is a form of communication. The artist interacts with his audience by way of the form he gives to his work. The artist is the source or sender. The work is the medium carrying the message. People must be receivers if the communication is to be complete — the language of visual form must come through.

44

Visual forms, like audible sounds, evoke responses in us whether they represent subjects or not. Many people are concerned more with subject than with form. Subject seems easier to identify with and therefore less demanding. But subject is a minor element in most of the arts. Without significant form subject is irrelevant.

An aim of this book is to help you arrive at the point where you do not need subject matter or verbal interpretation to recognize your own responses to visual form.

We humans are more than a collection of nameable parts. Each one of us is much more than all nameable things about us — our names, our physical appearance, and our accumulated knowledge and experience are all considerably less important than the total configuration, which is *you*, which is *me*. We are alive, unique, and valuable beings because of the total working relationship between all of our aspects. This is similar to the total working relationship that is established in a form worth being called a work of art.

There is much in common in being able to perceive and being able to create significant relationships. We experience the world in terms of relationships. Artists try to heighten the significance of these relationships. The elements of form within a work of art interact to create the relationships that give the work its effectiveness. In this way each of the visual elements becomes an aspect of a single form, which has a "life" of its own.

Clearly it takes action to put a work of art together. It is not so clear that appreciation is an act.

Most people mistakenly think that when they hear a piece of music, that they're not doing anything, but that something is being done to them. Now this is not true, and we must arrange our music and our art so that people realize that they themselves are doing it, and not something is being done to them.

John Cage[1]

Some works of art are lies designed to help us realize the truth. A painting of ocean waves crashing on a beach is not actually ocean waves, but is various colors of paint arranged in a way that represents the appearance of waves. When we look at this painting it is *as if* we see waves and a beach. Malevich presents his yellow quadrilateral *as is*. His painting is yellow pigment on a flat surface in the shape of a quadrilateral.

FORM AND CONTENT

We guide our actions by reading the form and content of the people, things, and events that make up our environment. Form in its broadest meaning refers to the sum total of all perceivable characteristics of any given thing or situation. Content is the cause, the meaning, the life within the outer form. Content determines the form and is expressed by it. The two are inseparable. All form has some content and any content must have form.

When we see faces of people we do not know, we automatically draw conclusions about them from the way they look. If we have seen them before they will probably look familiar. This is an example of our amazing ability to memorize certain visual configurations that are important to us.

53 Kasimir Malevich. YELLOW QUADRILATERAL ON WHITE. 1916–1917. Oil on canvas. 43¾ x 27¾".
See color plate 4

54   Charles Harbutt. Spectators. 1959.

As we live, we compile a vast file of information on faces in our memories. From this we make judgments about the character of the people we see. Sometimes our judgments are wrong. But we cannot and should not stop making them for that reason. Rightly or wrongly, we feel that the form of a face gives us a clue to the content of that person.

Faces are loaded with meaning for us. Many other observations are not significant in the same way. Each face, like each seeable form, exists to express itself — to be seen for itself. And each form is part of the continuity of visible and invisible phenomena that make up our environment.

Clouds, torsos, shells, peppers, trees, rock, smoke-stacks are but interdependent, interrelated parts of a whole, which is life. — Life rhythms felt in no matter what, become symbols of the whole.
                              Edward Weston, April 24, 1930[2]

Is Edward Weston's photograph of a green pepper meaningful to us because we like peppers so much? I think not. Weston has been able to create meaningful form on a surface with the help of a pepper. It is his sense of form that tells us how deeply he has experienced this pepper.

By exercising critical selection every step of the way, Weston finally achieved his goal of "significant presentation of the thing it-self."[3] Weston felt strongly that he wanted to present, rather than interpret, the many natural objects he was working with at the time. He wanted to record his feeling for life as he saw it in the "sheer aesthetic form"[4] of his subjects. In doing so he revealed with clarity and intensity what was there all along.

August 8, 1930

I could wait no longer to print them — my new peppers, so I put aside several orders, and yesterday afternoon had an exciting time with seven new negatives.

First I printed my favorite, the one made last Saturday, August 2, just as the light was failing — quickly made, but with a week's previous effort back of my immediate, unhesitating decision. A week? — yes, on this certain pepper — but twenty years of effort, starting with a youth on a farm in Michigan, armed with a No. 2 Bull's Eye Kodak, 3½ x 3½, have gone into the making of this pepper, which I consider a peak of achievement.

It is classic, completely satisfying, — a pepper — but more than a pepper. . . .[5]

55   Edward Weston. Pepper #30. 1930.

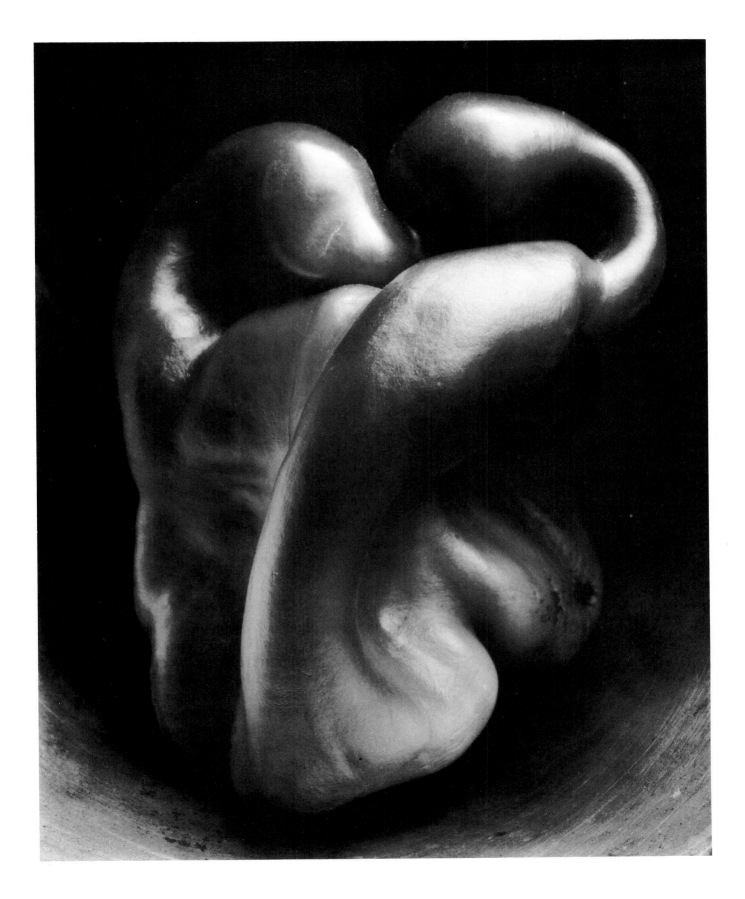

The temple carvings shown here were made by two anonymous sculptors, one Hindu, the other Christian.

The scene from Kandarya Mahadevā Temple in India seems to tell the worshiper that heaven or union with God is full of a kind of joy that is symbolically expressed by the physical pleasure depicted here. The natural beauty of the human figure is heightened by the symbolic exaggeration of maleness and femaleness. Fullness seems to come from within the rounded forms, heightening the sense of physical presence.

The saints and royal personages from the west portal of Chartres Cathedral are symbolic portraits of real individuals. They bid us to heaven by a very different route. Their tall, thin figures call our attention to spiritual concerns by a denial of the physical body. The human figure is scarcely suggested by the elegant vertical forms. A faint smile on the woman's face suggests inner peace.

57   SCENE FROM KANDARYA TEMPLE, Mahadeva, India. c. 1000.

56   SAINTS AND ROYAL PERSONAGES. Facade of West Portal, Notre Dame de Chartres, Chartres, France, c. 1145–1170.

These sculpted figures echo the cylindrical columns behind them, making a fine blend between architecture and sculpture. The figures from Chartres stand before their columns almost completely detached. They represent the first European attempt at sculpture-in-the-round since Roman times. Their gentle human heads show an early medieval move toward naturalism.

In spite of the great differences in form and content between the Hindu and Christian sculptures, their basic purposes are similar. They relate to an idea expressed in 1200 A.D. by Abbot Suger, the man responsible for starting the Gothic style of architecture in France. Suger believed that we could only come to understand God through the effect of beautiful things on our senses. He said, "The dull mind rises to truth through that which is material."[6]

58   Giovanni Bernini
The Ecstasy of
Saint Teresa.
1645–1652. Marble. Life-size.

Four centuries later, European religious sculpture had developed into something quite different. The Italian sculptor and architect Gian Lorenzo Bernini carved from marble this life-sized figure of Saint Teresa. It is an amazing work. It represents one of Saint Teresa's visions as she recorded it. In this vision, she saw an angel who seemed to pierce her heart with a flaming arrow of gold, giving her great pain as well as pleasure and leaving her "all on fire with a great love of God."[7] Bernini makes the situation visionary, yet as vivid as possible, by choosing to portray the moment of greatest feeling. The turbulent drapery heightens the expression of ecstasy on Saint Teresa's face, suggesting strong spiritual energy within.

Both Saint Teresa and Bernini were part of the Counterreformation, a movement within the Roman Catholic Church that tried to offset the effect of the Protestant Reformation of the sixteenth century. The dramatic realism of baroque painting and sculpture was part of the Catholic effort to revitalize the church. Bernini's Ecstasy of Saint Teresa is a major example. In it, Bernini symbolizes spiritual ecstasy by showing physical ecstasy. In this sense this work has something in common with the Indian sacred sculpture.

In the seventeenth century, two imperial villas were constructed on opposite sides of the world. Both were surrounded by extensive gardens. One of these was the French Palace of Versailles.

The supreme authority of the French Sun King, Louis XIV, was symbolized by the architecture and gardens of this impressive palace. The authority of the architecture is projected outward for several miles across the landscape in vast formal gardens to the west of the palace. Long, straight avenues eventually lead out from the main parade ground in front of the palace. The longest of these connects Versailles with Paris and runs along the axis bisecting the entire plan. Strong symmetry is quite apparent here. King Louis XIV organized nature in this way as a grand gesture of his power.

Versailles has one of the largest formal gardens ever conceived. Its terraces, reflective pools, and clipped hedges were planned to provide an appropriate setting for the king's public appearances and a playground for the gentlemen and ladies of the court, who, with the king, enjoyed great festivals in these outdoor rooms.

59 AERIAL VIEW OF VERSAILLES, FRANCE. 1624–1708.

The other imperial villa is Katsura, the Japanese palace near Kyoto. It was built under the direction of Prince Toshihito and his son Prince Toshitada. It occupies sixteen acres near the Katsura River. The river's waters were diverted into the garden to form ponds. Land, water, rocks, and plants are interwoven masterfully with one another and with the buildings in an irregular flow of man-made and natural things. The walls of the palace support no weight. They are sliding screens, which can be opened to allow interior and exterior space to blend.

When Katsura was constructed, the imperial family did not have much political power. The palace acted as a kind of retreat, in contrast to the imposing authoritarian character of Versailles.

By avoiding symmetry and maintaining simplicity, the builders of Katsura were able to give form to their attitude toward nature. Unlike Versailles, the palace complex was planned with no grand entrances either to the grounds or to the buildings. The palace is approached along "natural" garden paths. As one proceeds along these paths unexpected views open up. One of these is the view across a pond to the tea house. The view has been carefully planned to look unplanned. The tea house has much in common with the traditional Japanese farm house. Natural materials and humble design provide a perfect setting for the building where the *chanoyei* or tea ceremony is performed. The ceremony embodies the same attitudes of simplicity, naturalness, and humility that permeate the entire palace grounds. The dominant feeling of the place is one of timeless serenity. Katsura is a major work in a long Japanese tradition of respect for those factors that bring man and nature together in beneficial harmony.

60a Aerial View of Katsura. 17th century.

60b Gardens and Teahouse at Katsura

VISUAL ELEMENTS

Visual experience is one flow of complex interrelationships. However, in order to discuss visual form, it will be necessary to recognize the potential of the various elements and their interactions. The number of elements and the terms used to identify them vary considerably among artists and teachers. In presenting the elements separately, it is easy to assume that they can be separated. We can speak of them separately, but actually they are largely inseparable.

The words designating visual elements named here are merely tools for discussing form: light, color, mass, space, time, motion, shape, texture, and line. They represent an attempt to translate visual form into verbal symbols. This discussion will touch only on a few aspects of each work shown. It is impossible to equal visual form with words. Even a thousand words don't make a picture.

A serious attempt to describe even the most simple piece of machinery, such, let us say, as a kitchen can-opener with several moving parts, results in a morass of words that only a highly trained patent lawyer can cope with, and yet the shape (form) of that can-opener is simplicity itself as compared with the shape of such a thing as a human hand or face.[8]

As we begin to analyze works of art, you may feel that the process is killing the thing itself. Dissection of a "living" thing usually kills it. The frog cut open in biology class will never hop again. Since works of art are not biologically alive, they have a good chance of going back together again visually — hopefully freshly perceived and enjoyed more than before they were taken apart. Much of what is learned during analysis of one work can be applied to others.

It is also important to remember that throughout this book *reproductions* of works of art represent actual works, yet they are discussed as if they were the originals.

There is usually a great difference between an actual work and a copy or reproduction of that work. Sometimes the difference is as great as the difference between a person and a photograph of that person. Sometimes a reproduction looks better than the original. A good color slide of a painting projected on a screen in a totally dark room will usually have more color brilliance than the original painting. No reproduction can be 100 percent the same as the original work. Photographic reproductions of three-dimensional works, such as pieces of sculpture or buildings, become mere shadows of the originals when they are reduced to two dimensions. Since actual motion cannot be reproduced in a book, the presentation of kinetic sculpture and film must be superficial. Almost all works suffer when they are reproduced photographically because they lose the quality of the material from which they were made.

LIGHT

Light is a form of radiant energy. It is the vision-producing part of the electromagnetic spectrum. "Shadow is the obstruction of light." (Leonardo da Vinci.)[9] The source, color, intensity, and character of light determine the way things appear. As light

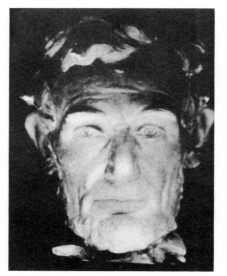

61a

61b

changes, things that are illuminated appear to change, often dramatically.

This fact is shown by two photographs of the head of the sculpture of Lincoln. When the monumental figure was first installed in the Lincoln Memorial in Washington, D.C., the sculptor, Daniel Chester French, was disturbed by the lighting. The entire character of his figure was changed from the way he had conceived it because the dominant light falling on the figure came at a low angle through the open doorway of the memorial. Finally this was corrected by placing artificial lights in the ceiling above the figure that were stronger than the natural light coming through the doorway.

Light alone had completely changed the character of Lincoln's sculpted face and, therefore, the viewer's whole concept of the man.

Value refers to the amount of light reflected from a surface. The value range goes from white to black. There is no such thing as perfect white or total black in visual terms. The whitest white would be so bright that it would damage your eyes. Pure white is total light as in the sun, in which there is all color. The blackest black has no light and therefore no visibility.

Light reveals a three-dimensional surface in the Lincoln sculpture. On a flat surface it is necessary to deal with illusions of light to make things appear to have volume. Subtle relationships between light and dark areas determine how things look.

The value scale shows that we perceive *relationships*, not isolated forms. The grey circles are identical, yet they appear quite different depending on their relationship to the value of the background.

63 Pierre-Paul Prud'hon
STUDY OF A FEMALE NUDE
c. 1814. Black and white
chalk on blue-gray paper. 28 x 22 cm.

Prud'hon gives the illusion of roundness to his figure by using black and white chalk on a middle-value blue-gray paper. Because the paper is a value halfway between white and black, he is able to let it act as a connective value between the highlights and shadows. If you follow the form of this figure you will see how it appears first as a light against a darker background (as in the right shoulder) and then as a dark against a lighter area (as in the under part of the breast on the same side). What happens here has the same principle as the value scale, but much more subtle. The background stays the same, appearing first dark, then light.

Look around you and you will see that all objects become visible in this way. Sometimes, as in the area between the shoulder and the breast on this figure, the edge of an object will disappear when its value at that point becomes the same as the value behind it, and the two surfaces merge into one. Usually we do not see this because our minds fill in the blanks from experience. We *know* the form is continuous, so we see it as continuous. A photographer, particularly, must see light directly, without preconceptions, if his work is going to have quality.

Light has been a crucial element in art since prehistoric times. Paleolithic cave paintings were painted and viewed by flickering torchlight. The changing sun's rays illuminate the stained glass walls of Gothic cathedrals, filling their interiors with colored light. Today we can produce and control light in new ways, but the changing lights of sun and fire have lost none of their fascination.

Man-made light is now being used as a medium. In 1905 Thomas Wilfred, one of the pioneers in light art, began experimenting with the relationship between moving colored light and music, and created one of the first light organs. In his later automated constructions, images of changing light move across a translucent screen in a continuous sequence. Wilfred's term for light art is "lumia." See page 243.

Light shows presented with rock and other forms of contemporary music became popular in the mid-1960s.

About 1967 a few artists began experimenting with laser light. The laser beam consists of a straight, narrow band of light, organized in direction and totally pure in hue. Because of its coherent nature the laser beam remains narrow indefinitely. A variety of pure light sculpture pieces have been produced with this new medium.

Laser light has also provided a new form of photography called holography. With ho-

lography it is possible to reconstruct a fully three-dimensional light image or hologram. There is no camera or lens involved. The hologram is a recording of lightwave interference patterns. As seen in the accompanying diagram, a reference beam from the laser is reflected and scattered by the object, then reassembled on a holographic plate, along with a portion of the still coherent reference beam that has bypassed the subject. After the light patterns have converged on the holographic plate the plate is developed by standard photographic techniques, freezing a complete "memory" of the subject. When illuminated by laser light this holographic plate releases a three-dimensional image of the original subject.

We are beginning to pay more attention to the kind of interior and exterior environmental light that we live with daily. Color, direction, quantity, and intensity of light have major effects on our moods. California architect Vincent Palmer has experimented with the effect on people of changes in the hue and intensity of interior light. He has found that he can modify the behavior of his guests by changing the light around them. Light quality changes the volume and intensity of their conversation and even the length of their visit.

Light is a key factor in photography, cinematography, television, stage design, architecture, and interior design. As our awareness of light's potential had increased, light artists have become more in demand. At first, lighting designers were primarily technicians or engineers. Now, that is not enough. The light artist uses his material with the subtlety that the painter can bring to paint.

64   THE HOLOGRAPHIC PROCESS

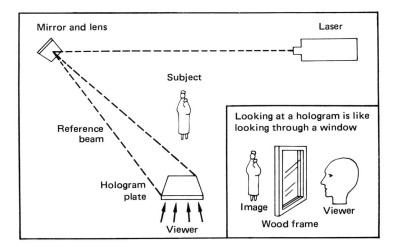

Highlight
Light
Shadow
Core of shadow
Reflected light
Cast shadow

65 SPHERE ILLUSTRATING
LIGHT AND DARK SYSTEM

The figure showing light falling on a sphere illustrates how a curved surface is defined by light and shade. Gradations of light and dark that give the effect of roundness are called chiaroscuro. This word means light and dark, from the Italian *chiaro* (light) and *oscuro* (dark), and relates to the English words "clear" and "obscure."

Compositions in which forms are determined by the effect of highlights and shadows rather than by sharp outlines are based on chiaroscuro. This technique makes it possible to create the illusion that the objects depicted on a flat surface are three-dimensional and freestanding.

Strong value contrast emphasizes the dramatic content of Zurbarán's ST. SERAPION. In simple compositional terms, the major visual element is a light rectangle against a dark background. Light and dark qualities are powerful elements in any design.

Minimal value contrast is seen in Monet's painting of MORNING HAZE. He gives us only the faintest suggestion of landscape. There is no stark drama here, only shimmering light.

66 Francisco de Zurbarán
SAINT SERAPION
1628. Oil on canvas. 47½ x 40¾".

Color plate 3
Henri Matisse
STURTIUMS AND THE
DANCE. 1912. Oil on
canvas. 75¾ x 45".

Color plate 4
Kasimir Malevich
YELLOW QUADRILAT-
ERAL ON WHITE.
1916–1917. Oil on
canvas. 43¾ x 27¾".

Color plate 5
Pierre Bonnard
DINING ROOM IN TH
COUNTRY. 1913. Oil
on linen. 64¾ x 81".

67   Claude Monet. MORNING HAZE. c. 1892. Oil on canvas. 29⅛ x 36⅝″.

COLOR

Color is one of the most exciting elements of form. It affects our emotions directly, modifying our thoughts, moods, actions, and even our health. Some painters of the past found color so dominating that they avoided pure colors to enable viewers to see the essence of the subject without being distracted. Fifty years ago color was used very little in everyday life in the United States. The French impressionist painters and their followers led the way to the free use of color we enjoy today.

Aristotle named only three colors in the rainbow: red, yellow, and green. The world also was then thought to be composed of four elements: earth, air, fire, and water. The Hindus, Greeks, Chinese, and certain American Indian tribes are known to have assigned colors to the elements symbolically. Even Leonardo da Vinci wrote, "We shall set down white for the representative of light, without which no color can be seen; yellow for earth; green for water; blue for air; red for fire; and black for total darkness."[10]

Such symbolic color associations were disputed following the Renaissance when the spiritual and physical were separated. In recent years artists as well as scientists have begun to study human responses to color: the visual, psychological, biological, cultural, historical, and metaphysical. Today there is a growing acceptance of the metaphysical, due, in part, to the work of psychologists and psychiatrists.

The psychic healer Edgar Cayce experienced a metaphysical response to color — particularly regarding colors related to "auras." An aura is thought to indicate the outer limits of a person's life energy force. It can be seen most strongly by a sensitive eye in the form of colored light emanating from the entire body. It is particularly visible around the head and shoulders. The long tradition of halos in both Western and Eastern art lends credence to the universal existence of auras for those who cannot see them. Spiritual or religious leaders would be expected to have strong auras. From his experience with auras Cayce generalized about his response to certain colors. The following are a few examples:

Red: force, vigor, energy, nervousness, egotism, the color of life
Yellow: health, well-being, friendliness
Blue: the color of the spirit, artistic, selfless, melancholy
Green: the color of healing, helpful, strong, friendly[11]

Our favorite colors may be those that complement our aura. Without realizing why, we may change our favorite color or colors as our aura changes.

Evidently the human ability to see color continues to expand. Some scholars believe we have only recently developed the ability to see hues with the shortest wavelengths, such as blue, indigo, and violet.

When we look at a color we may disagree about what we see or, more specifically, how we name what we see. Each color and variation of that color has its own character. Yet we see a color only in relationship to other colors. Even the color of a single surface is affected by the color of the light illuminating that surface. Each of us responds in his own way to color. To many people yellow seems to be a happy, free color, while others experience the same yellow as soft and quiet. The quality can change, however, depending on the kind of yellow, its association with other colors, and the mood of the person seeing it. The painter Kandinsky felt that bright yellow can be shrill and hard to live with. He pointed out that "the sour-tasting lemon and the shrill-singing canary are both yellow."[12] This was his response, and it may or may not be shared by others.

Before going on to more specific aspects of color, look at Bonnard's painting, DINING ROOM IN THE COUNTRY.

Bonnard was a great colorist. He took a somewhat ordinary domestic scene and intensified its effect on us by concentrating on the magical qualities of light and color on a summer day. He gave us a full experience of the mood of that day. The color is not what could have been recorded with a camera.

Bonnard's color is the result of a personal search. He worked with limited color during the 1890s. About 1900 he began to use more color in what can be described as a personal version of impressionism. As his color sense matured, his paintings became full of rich harmonies of hot and cool colors played off against each other. In these paintings his surfaces seem to shimmer with a light of their own.

The appearance of color in our surroundings is determined by a combination of light qualities, surface qualities, and our own experiences and attitudes. Actual objective color of a given thing is called local color. We seldom see true local color because our awareness of color is conditioned by preconceptions. The idea that the sky is blue, for example, can get in the way of our direct perception of a violet or yellow-orange sky. Words identify concepts and in turn play their part in determining color perception. In the Eskimo language there are at least seventeen words for white. By necessity the Eskimo perception of white is very refined.

68 Pierre Bonnard
DINING ROOM IN THE COUNTRY
1913. Oil on linen. 64¾ x 81".
See color plate 5

Local color is also modified by its association with surrounding colors and by the degree and quality of light. As light decreases individual colors become less distinct. In bright light colors reflect on one another causing numerous changes in the appearance of local color.

All pigment color depends on light. The visible portion of the electromagnetic field is called light. The light of the sun contains the full spectrum of color in balanced amounts.

The human eye responds to the visible portion of the electromagnetic field.

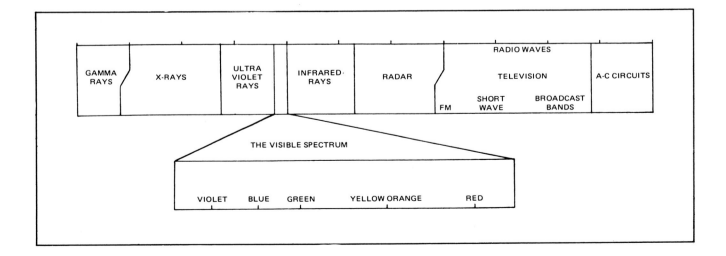

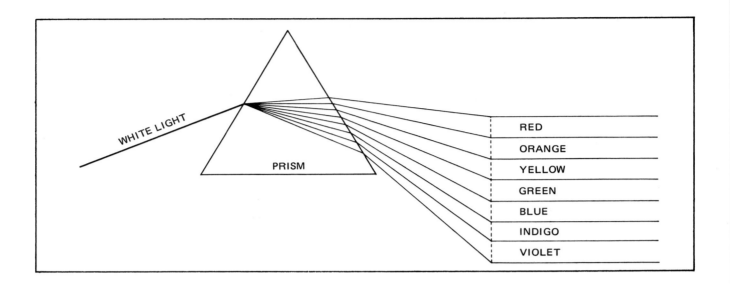

When white light is separated into its visible components by a prism, the hues of the spectrum appear as in a rainbow.

Hue designates a color in its pure form according to its specific wavelength. Spectrum-intensity red is spoken of as the hue red, as distinguished from the hue orange, its neighboring hue on the spectrum.

When colored light is combined it can eventually add up to white light. This is *additive* color mixture. Each hue that is added to a colored light mixture brings the mixture closer to pure white light. When the three light primaries are combined the result is white light. Light primaries are red, blue, and green. Red and green light when mixed make yellow light.

Our common experience of color is provided by reflective surfaces, not by pure prismatic light. The emphasis here is on color in terms of reflective surfaces and the changes in colored surfaces caused by pigments and their mixtures with light.

A red surface absorbs most of the spectrum except red, which it reflects. A green surface absorbs most of the spectrum except green, which it reflects, and so on with all the hues.

If the complements red and green are mixed together in equal amounts in pigment form as paint or dye the result is grey, because almosts all of the light of the spectrum is absorbed with little reflected. Red pigment absorbs green and green absorbs red. A red apple will look almost black under green light because most of the light is absorbed and very little is reflected.

Mixing color with pigment is quite different from mixing color with light. The more that pigments are mixed together the duller they appear, because they absorb more and more light as their absorptive qualities combine. This is *subtractive* color mixture.

• Primaries: red, blue, and yellow. The three pigment hues that cannot be produced by a mixture of pigments are called pigment primaries. Although pigment primaries are generally considered to be red, blue, and yellow, each major color system now in use is based on a slightly different set of primaries. See 1 on the color wheel, color plate 6.

• Secondaries: orange, violet and green. The mixture of two primaries produces a secondary hue. Secondaries are midway between the two primaries of which they are composed. See 2 on the color wheel.

• Tertiaries: red-orange, red-violet, blue-violet, blue-green, yellow-green, and yellow-orange. Their names indicate their components. Tertiaries stand between the primaries and the secondaries of which they are composed. See 3 on the color wheel.

There are many different color theories used by scientists and artists. These theories are workable, but none of them are complete.

The color wheel shown here is a contemporary version of the concept first discovered by Sir Isaac Newton. After Newton became aware of the spectrum, he found that both ends could be combined into the hue red-violet, thus making the wheel concept possible.

The three basic dimensions of color are demonstrated in the chart on color plate 6: hue, value, and saturation (or intensity). As discussed, hue refers to the particular wavelength of color to which we give a name. The term is important when distinguishing this aspect of color from the other two. Chromatic colors are colors with the property of hue in them.

Value (see pages 53–54) can be the range from white through the greys to black, independent of chromatic color, or within hues and mixtures of hues.

Saturation is purity. Pure hues are the most intense form of a given hue or color; it is the hue at its highest saturation. If white, black, gray, or another hue is added to a pure hue, saturation diminishes and intensity drops.

The blue-green side of the wheel is called cool and the red-orange side, warm. The difference between warm and cool colors is not normally perceptible to the touch, but colors are warm or cool by association. A room painted a warm color becomes warmed psychologically. Color affects our feelings about size as well as temperature. Cool colors usually appear to recede and warm colors

appear to advance.

Black and white may be thought of as colors, but they are not hues. A complete black is the absence of light and therefore the absence of color. White, on the other hand, as light or a reflective surface, is the presence of the whole spectrum or all color. White, black, and their combination grey are achromatic or neutral colors. Mixtures of pure hues opposite one another on the color wheel neutralize the hues, making various greys or browns depending on the components and the proportions of their mixture.

Color groupings that provide certain kinds of harmonies are called color schemes. The most common of these are:

• Monochromatic: variations on one hue only. A pure hue combined with colors made by mixing the hue with varying amounts of white (tints) and varying amounts of black (shades) adds up to a monochromatic scheme based on that hue. For example, a group of red (pure hue) with pink (tint of red) and maroon (shade of red) would be called monochromatic.

• Analogous: hues next to one another on the color wheel, such as yellow-green, green, and blue-green, each containing the hue green.

• Complementary: two hues directly opposite one another on the color wheel. Complementary hues, when mixed, form neutral grey, but strongly contrast, often appearing to vibrate, when placed side by side in fully saturated form. The complement of one primary is obtained by mixing the other two primaries. The complement of yellow is violet, obtained by mixing red and blue.

• Polychromatic: several hues and their variations. When a painter chooses his palette he visualizes color schemes in terms of his familiarity with certain available pigment colors. Most artists work intuitively when determining a color scheme.

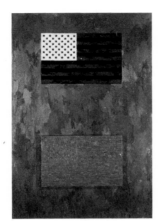

70   Jasper Johns
FLAGS
1965. Oil on canvas with raised canvas.
72 x 48". *See color plate 8.*

An afterimage appears to the eye when prolonged exposure to a visual form causes excitation and subsequent fatigue of the retina.

Color afterimages are caused by partial color blindness temporarily induced in the normal eye by desensitizing one or two of its three red, green, and blue color receptors. For example, staring at a red spot for thirty seconds under a bright white light will tire the red receptors in that segment of the retina on which the red spot is focused and make them less sensitive to red light, or partially red-blind. Thus, when the red spot is removed a blue-green spot appears on a white surface because the tired red receptors react weakly to the red light reflected by that area of the surface, while the blue and green receptors respond strongly to the reflected blue and green light. On a neutral surface, therefore, the hue of the afterimage is complementary to the hue of the image or stimulus.

A more complex example of this phenomenon can be experienced by staring for about thirty seconds at the white dot in the center of the flag at the top of Jasper Johns' painting of a flag, then looking down at the black dot in the grey flag below. What do you see?

The appearance of a given hue changes radically according to its relationship with its surroundings. In INJURED BY GREEN Anuszkiewicz painted a uniform pattern of dots in two sizes. Behind these the red-orange ground seems to change, but it does not. Intensity builds from the outer edges of the painting toward the center where we are "injured" by an area of yellow-green dots, which seems to pulse because it is almost identical to the background in value, yet almost opposite or complementary in hue. The blue tint of the dots in the outer border is slightly lighter in value than the background. The blue-green dots in the four triangular areas are slightly darker in value. If Anuszkiewicz had used straight blue-green, the complement of red-orange, rather than yellow-green in the center, he would not have achieved the startling subtle power that the painting now has, because value is as important as hue and saturation in the total effect of this op painting.

My work is of an experimental nature and has centered on an investigation into the effects of complementary colors of full intensity when juxtaposed and the optical changes that occur as a result.

Anuszkiewicz[13]

71   Richard Anuskiewicz
INJURED BY GREEN
1963. Acrylic on board. 36 x 36".
See color plate 9

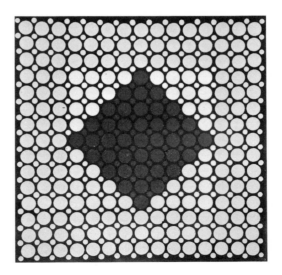

MASS

A two-dimensional area is a shape; a three-dimensional area is a mass. Mass is a major element in sculpture. In painting it is merely implied. Like other visual elements, mass is an aspect of total form, not a separate entity.

The head of Venus in this detail of Botticelli's BIRTH OF VENUS shows how a master uses a whole range of visual elements in order to create an image of great elegance. The rhythmic grouping of lines for the hair is particularly effective. Venus' head, neck, and shoulders are simplified shapes. Some shading indicates the three-dimensional qualities of the figure. But it would be difficult to imagine reaching behind this figure

72 Sandro Botticelli
Detail of BIRTH OF VENUS
c. 1490. Oil on canvas.
See color plate 7 and illustration 173

because Botticelli has emphasized the outlines or edge lines and underplayed the shading. Venus appears as a half-round rather than a fully three-dimensional mass. This is not a problem; it is simply a way of working. Everything in the painting works together in a shallow, decorative space.

Picasso's drawing of the head of a young man shows a use of lines that seem to wrap around in space, *implying* a solid or three-dimensional mass. The edge is underplayed to imply that the form is continuous in space. The drawing gives the appearance of mass because line acts to define surface directions and to build up areas of light and shade. Picasso's control over the direction and grouping of his lines makes it seem as if we were seeing a fully rounded head. Yet the vigor of Picasso's lines shows clearly that the work is a drawing on a flat surface before it is anything else.

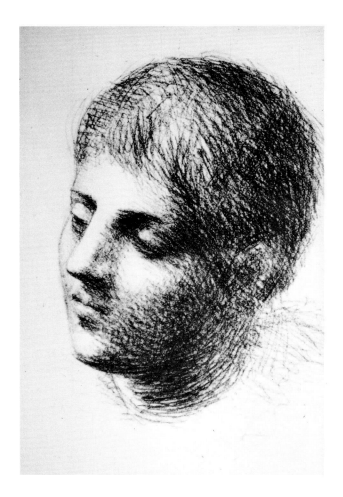

73 Pablo Picasso
YOUNG MAN'S HEAD
1923. Charcoal and graphite. 24¾ x 19".

The easiest way to start seeing the expressive possibilities of mass is to study a few contrasting pieces of sculpture.

Great control was exercised over Egyptian artists during the long period in which this ancient culture lasted. One of the dominant characteristics of their architecture and sculpture was its massiveness. They sought this quality and perfected it because it fit their desire to make things look everlasting. Egyptian art is largely funerary. The common function of their sculpture was to act as a symbolic container for the soul of some important person, helping him to live forever.

The figure of QENNEFER is carved from black granite — a type of rock known for its strength and endurance. He is shown in a sitting pose with his knees drawn up and his arms folded. All this is implied with minimal suggestion. The piece is a strong symbol of permanence.

Figures by the contemporary sculptor Alberto Giacometti evoke no such feelings of permanence. MAN POINTING is a notable example of his work. The tall, thin figure appears eroded by time — barely existing. The amount of solid material utilized to construct the figure is minimal. The content seems to imply the tentative or impermanent nature of man caught between birth and death and eaten away by the void that surrounds him.

Existential philosophy developed in our century around a new consciousness of the ever-present threat of death and the importance of coming to terms with *now* as the only facet of existence that we can know. One of the key thinkers in existentialism was Jean Paul Sartre. He found Giacometti's work a major expression of this attitude. On a metal armature Giacometti built up then chipped away the plaster of his original pieces before they were cast in bronze. The artist saw the process as an almost hopeless struggle to create something that satisfied himself. His struggle was rooted in an awareness of the human predicament in modern times.

Ancient Egyptian and contemporary European and American cultures could hardly be more different in their commonly held attitudes toward the nature of life. This can be seen by the way mass is used in these two pieces of sculpture.

74 QENNEFER, STEWARD OF THE PALACE
c. 1450 B.C. Black granite. Height 2′ 9″.

75 Alberto Giacometti
MAN POINTING
1947. Bronze. Height 70½″.

One of the characteristics of today's world is the variety arising from many antitraditional values. Unlike Egyptian culture, there are relatively few controls on society and, therefore, on artists. Thus, almost every conceivable kind of individual style can be seen today.

Henry Moore carved a reclining figure that is massive in a quite different way from Egyptian solidity and seems to have nothing in common with Giacometti's work. Moore's figure is like the windworn stone and bone forms that impressed him from his youth. Moore made his figure compact in its mass and at the same time opened up holes in the figure that allow space to flow around and through the stone. This gives the figure a timeworn quality. An active relationship exists between solid and void, positive form and negative space.

In Brancusi's BIRD IN SPACE mass is drawn out in a dramatic spatial thrust. Brancusi started working on this concept about a decade after the Wright Brothers began the history of man's rapid movement in space and long before the world was filled with streamlined aircraft, cars, and pens.

77   Constantin Brancusi
BIRD IN SPACE
1928. Bronze, unique cast. Height 54″.

76   Henry Moore
RECUMBENT FIGURE
1938. Green hornton stone. Height 54″.
See color plate 10

SPACE

The visual arts are referred to as spatial arts because visual elements are organized in space. Music is called a temporal art because in music elements are organized in time. Space is the indefinable, great, general receptacle of things. It is continuous and infinite and ever present. It cannot exist by itself because it is part of everything. I once naively asked a Japanese Buddhist priest and master calligrapher how he felt about space, and he answered, "What space? Parking space?"

The most physically apparent organization of space is found in architecture. We all spend much of our time within buildings, some of which can be thought of as architecture and many of which as just constructions. In some buildings space is defined by mass so that it contributes greatly to the quality of life within it. In many others the opposite is true.

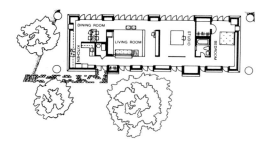

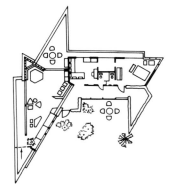

78   Rommert W. Huygens. HOME IN WAYLAND, MASSACHUSETTS.

79   Peter Jefferson. COTTAGE IN THE BAHAMAS.

One of the first considerations about any building is the relationship it will have to the site and its climate. The houses shown here were built to relate well to their location. The house in Massachusetts looks and is comfortably enclosed against harsh winters. The house in the Bahamas is open in its form and reaches out to the friendly moderation of the weather. In each case mass and space work together and with the surroundings, providing a setting for enjoyable living.

The huge interior spaces created by the Gothic builders are some of the most impressive in the history of architecture. Space enclosed by mass is called volume. Here volume becomes the dominant expressive element in the structure. The vast vertical space dwarfs human scale, intensifying the difference between the infinite nature of God (or Heaven) and the finite quality of man. Gothic interior space also provided the perfect acoustical setting for music. Voices filled the cathedrals with tones of different pitch, sounding together in new harmonies.

Art and engineering are one in these great structures. This is ritual architecture — architecture in which the emphasis in the design is on celebrating an idea rather than simply enclosing a function.

80   ARCADES AND VAULTS OF NAVE AT REIMS CATHEDRAL, Reims, France. 1225–1299.

On the edge of the city of Kyoto in Japan,
there is a small garden within a garden that
is part of Ryōan-ji Temple. This garden is
famous for its quality. Yet it is not what we
usually think of as a garden. There are no
plants. Abundant vegetation is all around,
but this vegetation is separated from the
garden by a low wall. On the surface
Ryōan-ji Garden is just a flat rectangular
area of raked gravel punctuated by a few
stones. In other words, it is mostly empty
space — a void. It was completed in 1473
by Soami, who worked according to the
ideals of Zen Buddhism. The garden was
conceived as a place for quiet meditation.
It still functions to promote quiet inner reflection when emptied of tourists and loud
guides. It is a nothingness garden, a great
exterior space designed for spiritual enlightenment.

81   RYŌAN-JI GARDEN. Kyoto, Japan, 1473.

82 Mu Ch'i
SIX PERSIMMONS
c. 1269. Ink on paper. 14¼ x 17⁵⁄₁₆".

The common surfaces for drawings, prints, photographs, and paintings are flat or two-dimensional. Yet almost any mark or shape on a flat surface begins to give the illusion of depth or the third dimension.

For centuries, Asian painters have handled relatively flat or shallow pictorial space in very sophisticated ways. The great Chinese master Mu Ch'i painted six persimmons in such a way that the painting has been well-loved for 700 years. The persimmons appear against a pale background that works both as flat surface and as infinite space. The painted shapes of the fruit punctuate the open space of the ground, reminding us of the well-placed rocks in the garden at Ryōan-ji.

Imagine what would happen to this painting if some of the empty space at the top were cut off. Space is far more than just what is left over after the important things have been laid down.

Some depth is indicated here. When shapes overlap, we immediately assume from experience that one is in front of the other. This is probably the most basic way of achieving the effect of depth on a flat surface.

A second method is with placement. When elements are placed low on the picture plane, they appear to be closer. This is how we see most things in actual space. As things move closer to us, they usually move farther below our eye level.

The word "perspective" is now frequently used to refer to any method of organizing the appearance of three-dimensional forms in two-dimensional or pictorial space. It is correct to speak of the perspective of Persian miniatures, Japanese prints, Chinese Sung painting, or Egyptian painting, although none of these styles uses a system that is in any way similar to Italian Renaissance perspective. It is also possible to speak of illumination perspective when referring to the ways in which the appearance of light can be used to imply space.

Linear perspective was developed by fifteenth-century Italian architects and painters. It is a geometric system based on what one eye sees at one moment in time fixed at one place in space. The artists observed that parallel lines appear to converge toward a common point (the vanishing point) and that objects grow smaller as they recede into the distance. In geometry the vanishing point is called infinity.

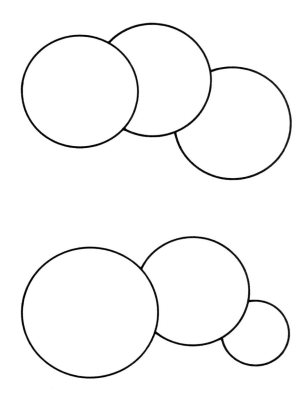

In the first diagram the spatial effect of overlap is shown. In the second this effect is reinforced by diminishing sizes, thus giving the sense of greater intervening distance.

Between medieval times and the Renaissance, Italian artists struggled with conflicting attitudes about space. Medieval pictorial space was symbolic and decorative, not intended to be logical or look real. Toward the end of the fourteenth and the beginning of the fifteenth centuries more and more artists followed Giotto's lead by attempting to construct the illusion of actual space on flat surfaces.

Looking closely at Puccinelli's painting of TOBIT BLESSING HIS SON, can you tell whether the angel is behind or in front of the son? It does not really matter, of course; angels do not have to live in logical space. Perhaps Puccinelli wanted to emphasize that fact.

83   Angelo Puccinelli
TOBIT BLESSING HIS SON
c. 1350–1399. Tempera on wood. 14⅞ x 17⅛".

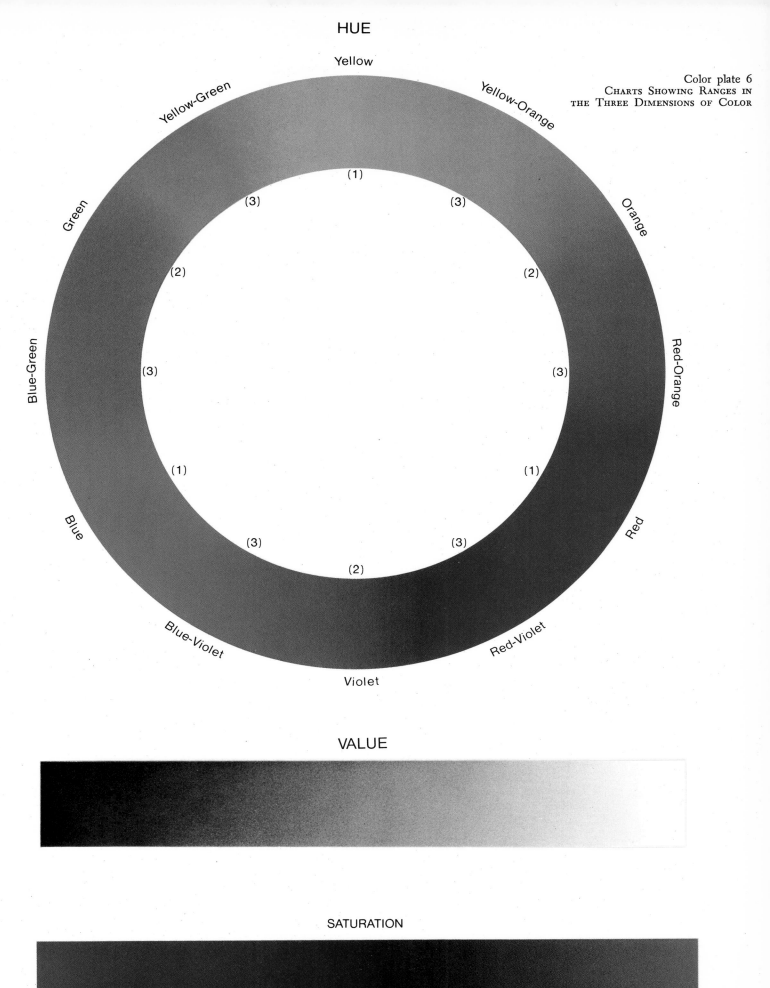

HUE

Yellow

Yellow-Green   Yellow-Orange

Green   Orange

(1)

(3)   (3)

(2)   (2)

Blue-Green   Red-Orange

(3)   (3)

(1)   (1)

Blue   Red

(3)   (3)

Blue-Violet   Red-Violet

(2)

Violet

VALUE

SATURATION

Color plate 7 Sandro Botticelli. Detail of BIRTH OF VENUS. c. 1490. Oil on canvas.

Color plate 8   Jasper Johns. FLAGS. 1965. Oil on canvas with raised canvas. 72 x 48".

Color plate 9 Richard Anuskiewicz. INJURED BY GREEN. 1963. Acrylic on board. 36 x 36″.

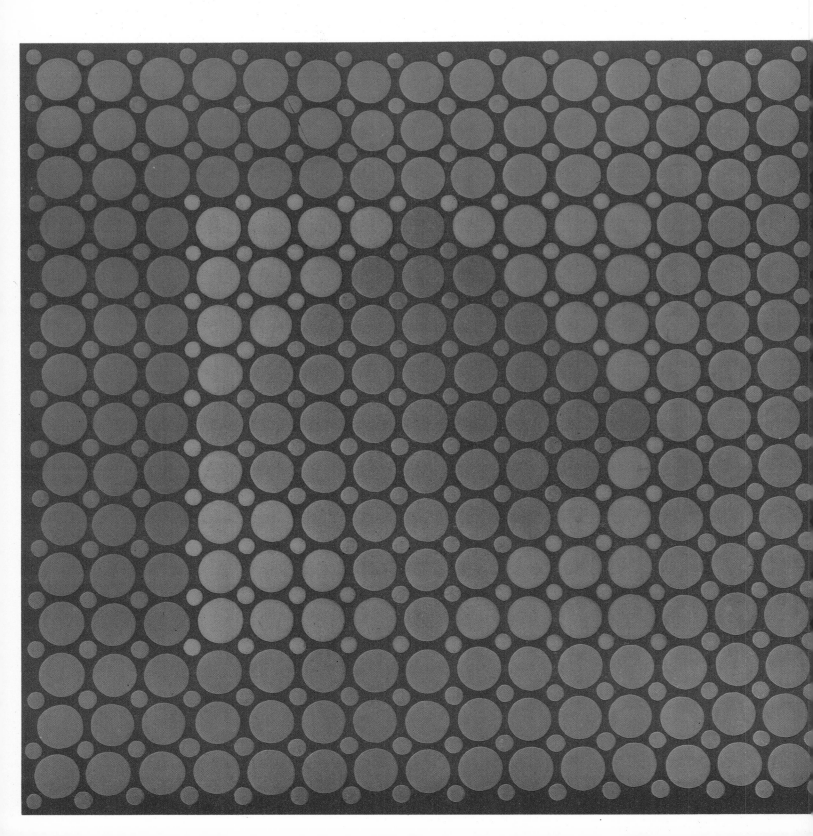

Men of the Italian Renaissance placed emphasis on the importance of the individual. Their spatial system related well to the new humanism of the fifteenth century because it visually implied a world determined by the individual. An easy way to understand linear perspective is to study the accompanying diagrams and apply these concepts to the many parallel lines moving away from you whenever you are in a man-made environment.

In a one-point perspective system all major receding lines are parallel. Two-point perspective means that there are two sets of parallel lines. There can be as many vanishing points in a given view as there are sets of parallel lines.

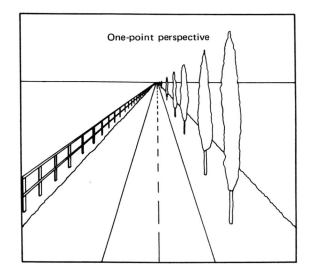

One-point perspective

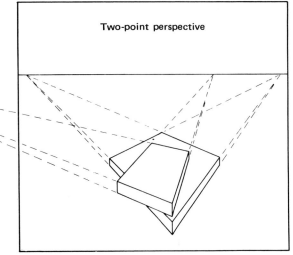

Two-point perspective

84 Jacopo Bellini
ANNUNCIATION
c. 1440. Drawing.

Jacopo Bellini did a preliminary drawing of the ANNUNCIATION to submit to the Church for approval before going on to do a painting. The subject is the Annunciation when an angel appeared to Mary to tell her that she was going to give birth to the Christ Child. The figures of the angel and Mary are almost lost in this very detailed drawing of imagined Renaissance architecture. Bellini was obviously much more concerned with the newly developed concept of linear perspective than he was with the traditional subject matter. Bellini put a great many converging "parallel" lines in his drawing. They all converge at one vanishing point on the horizon.

Again we see imagined architecture in the Renaissance style, providing a grand setting for the figures in Raphael's THE SCHOOL OF ATHENS. Raphael has achieved perfect balance here between interest in the group of figures and the pull into implied deep space created by linear perspective. The size of each figure is to scale according to his position in space, thus making the entire group seem very natural.

The great teachers of the School of Athens are Plato and Aristotle. We know that they are the most important figures in this painting because they are at the center of the series of arches and are framed by the one farthest away. Perhaps more important is the fact that they are placed on either side of the vanishing point, in a symmetrical composition based on one-point perspective. In other words, they are at the point of greatest spatial pull. Where we are pulled farthest back in space, they come forward creating a dynamic tension in implied space.

Lines superimposed over the painting reveal the basic one-point perspective system used by Raphael. A cube in the foreground is not lined up with the architecture and is therefore seen with two vanishing points or in two-point perspective.

85   Raphael Sanzio
THE SCHOOL OF ATHENS
1509. Fresco. Approx. 26 x 18'.

86   M. C. Escher. HAND WITH REFLECTING GLOBE. 1935. Lithograph. 32 x 21.5 cm.

M. C. Escher's lithograph HAND WITH RE-FLECTING GLOBE uses linear perspective inventively. By reflecting his own gaze, Escher emphasizes the origin of a linear perspective view. The mirrored surface of Escher's globe distorts normal perspective, giving a much more complete view of his room than could normally be seen from a single position, without eye movement. Four walls, the floor, and the ceiling are compressed into a single image. The lines defining these planes curve with the sphere's surface. The absolute center is the point between the artist's eyes. Whichever way he turns he is still the center. The ego is the core of his perception.

There is another kind of perspective which I call Aerial Perspective [now called atmospheric perspective] because by the atmosphere we are able to distinguish the variations in distance of different buildings, which appear placed on a single line. . . . You know that in an atmosphere of equal density the remotest objects seen through it, as mountains, in consequence of the great quantity of atmosphere between your eye and them — appear blue and almost of the same hue as the atmosphere itself when the sun is in the East.

Leonardo da Vinci[14]

Conditions of light and air change the appearance of objects as the distance between the observer and the object increases. This effect is called atmospheric perspective. It has been used in different ways by ancient Roman fresco painters, by European artists beginning in the fourteenth and fifteenth centuries, and by Chinese and Japanese painters, mostly during the period of the European Middle Ages.

The basis for atmospheric perspective is the fact that as objects get farther away from us they appear to be less distinct, cooler, or bluer in color, and more moderate in color saturation and in value contrast.

In THE HERDSMAN Claude Lorrain used atmospheric perspective effectively. The ground plane appears to recede from the base of the picture, which opens out on an implied deep space continuous to our own space. Interest is held in the foreground by the figure of the herdsman and his flock. The sun and its light come toward us from the distance, stopping us from going through the painting to infinity.

87   Claude Lorrain. THE HERDSMAN. c. 1655–1660. Oil on canvas. 47¾ x 63⅛".

88 Jacob Isaac van Ruisdael
WHEATFIELDS
c. 1670. Oil on canvas. 39⅜ x 51¼".

89 Paul Cézanne
THE TURNING ROAD
1879–1882. Oil on canvas. 23½ x 28½".
See color plate 11

The Dutch painter Jacob van Ruisdael offered us a visual invitation to take an imaginary walk into his painting WHEATFIELDS. The great spaciousness of the clouded sky sets off the seemingly endless flow of the land. Space is a major element here. Everything in the picture punctuates its vastness.

In THE TURNING ROAD another kind of pictorial space is constructed. We are not led into this painting along the curving road. Our vantage point is high above the road's surface. Cézanne intentionally tipped up the road plane, making it a major shape in the composition. Other planes in the painting have also been changed in order to strengthen the dynamics of the picture plane. Color acts to determine the implied spatial position of the various planes. A photograph taken of the subject exactly as Cézanne saw it would be of little interest.

Cézanne has us looking *at*, not into or through, the landscape painting. His achieved goal was to bring personal feeling and direct observation to the study of nature, to reconcile in his own way the three-dimensional reality of nature with the character of the flat picture surface on which he worked.

90 Georges Braque
HOUSES AT L'ESTAQUE
1908. Oil on canvas. 73 x 59 cm.

Cézanne's approach led the way to a total reexamination of picture space, after 400 years of the picture-as-a-window tradition. About 1907 Georges Braque and Pablo Picasso began developing a new kind of spatial configuration in their paintings. The new style completely abandoned the logical linear progression into implied depth that one finds in paintings in the Renaissance style.

The style was called cubism. HOUSES AT L'ESTAQUE is an early cubist painting done by Braque in 1908. It presents a kind of space to which we are now becoming accustomed. This is a twentieth-century landscape painting in which geometric shapes define a rush of forms that pile up rhythmically in shallow space. Buildings and trees seem interlocked in a spatial system that pushes and pulls across the entire picture surface.

From this point on, artists paid more and more attention to events that they could make happen *across* the picture surface rather than *into* it. Logical, step-by-step progression into pictorial space was abandoned in cubism. Painters used multiple vantage points to show more of a subject at one moment than was possible from a single, fixed position in space.

In the beginning of the twentieth century, painters began to work on two spatial problems: how to come back to the strength of the picture plane and how to express the totally new concepts of space. Changes in

science paralleled changes of time and space in art. Major discoveries, such as Einstein's theory of relativity, the splitting of the atom, and the airplane, gave man new ways of seeing. These concepts created the first major revolution in spatial concepts since the Renaissance invention of linear perspective. Philosophy, theology, technology, and art together brought us into a new era.

European systems for implying space are not necessarily the most important. We could also discuss the spatial systems of other cultures. If we consider art history as a whole, most of the paintings in the world have been designed in terms of shallow space, ambiguous space, or flat surfaces, and therefore have much more in common with the spatial concepts of international contemporary art than with the Renaissance concepts.

The Persian painter who created the miniature painting SOLOMON AND THE QUEEN OF SHEBA was interested in clearly showing all the important aspects of his subject without confusing things with illusions of deep space. I am sure spatial verisimilitude never occurred to him. Each thing is presented from the angle that shows it best. The result is an intricate organization of flat planes knit together in shallow space. The painting has its own spatial logic consistent with the Persian style. Persian perspective emphasizes narrative clarity and richness of surface design.

TIME

Time is the period between events or during which something exists, happens, or acts. We recognize that both clock time and psychological time are significant yet often opposing concepts of time.

92   Sassetta and assistant
THE MEETING OF SAINT ANTHONY AND SAINT PAUL
c. 1440. Tempera on wood. 18¾ x 13⅝".

91   SOLOMON AND THE QUEEN OF SHEBA
c. 1556–1565. Persian miniature painting. 13½ x 9⅛".
See color plate 12

To express actual time visually it is necessary to utilize space and motion. Implied time can be expressed by association.

Cinematography is a visual art in which actual and implied time are the most important elements. It is good that now when time seems so crucial to us we have an artistic medium with which to express our concerns. The concept of time in cinema is discussed in detail under Cinematography, pages 292–297.

Time in a painting can be seen instantly and wholly, whereas the physical experience of time in film is sequential.

Sassetta implied the duration of time in THE MEETING OF SAINT ANTHONY AND SAINT PAUL. Since the space is continuous we feel time must be also. There is a logical and parallel progression of both. Saint Anthony begins his journey far back in time and space at the city barely visible behind the trees. He comes into view first as he approaches the wilderness. Next we see him as he encounters the centaur. Finally he emerges into the clearing in the foreground where he meets Saint Paul. The road is painted to imply a continuous path of action.

 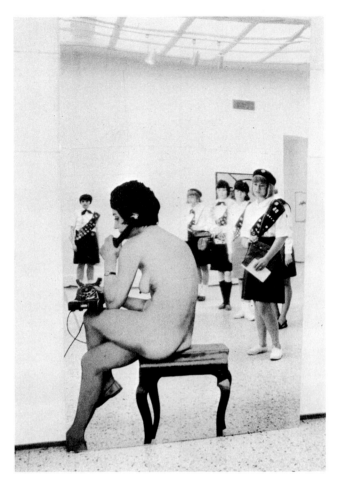

93   Michelangelo Pistoletto
Nude Woman Telephoning
1965. Paint on highly polished steel. Life-size.

In Nude Woman Telephoning Pistoletto has contrived to capture events in actual time on a flat surface. He created the figure with paint on paper. Then the painting was glued to a highly reflective, stainless steel surface, which mirrors the surroundings.

The only way to get the effect in a reproduction is to show the work at two moments in time as seen in two different galleries. The woman goes on telephoning whether she is alone or with the Girl Scouts. If we were there viewing the work, we would see a variety of different groupings in time and would be able to see actual motion — perhaps our own.

MOTION

Motion is action created by real or implied change of position.

Sassetta implied that Saint Anthony moved in time and space. In film, rapid sequences of still pictures are shown at a rate of twenty-four per second, thus creating (because of the persistence of vision) the illusion of actual motion.

Motion, particularly in drawing and painting, can also become inseparably linked with the action of lines and the repetition of shapes and/or rhythmic actions. In sculpture moved by wind, water, or motors, motion is an actual and important visual element.

94   Robert Breer. FLOATS. 1966. Motorized styrofoam.

95   Marc Chagall
I AND MY VILLAGE
1911. Oil on canvas.
75⅝ x 59⅝".

Imagine walking along a country road when suddenly you come upon a herd of small white blocks moving slowly along, each under its own power. The sculptor and film-maker Robert Breer made these apparitions out of shaped blocks of styrofoam. Under each one he placed a battery-operated motor and four wheels. Sculpture that moves in actual space and time is called kinetic or motion sculpture. See the work of Tinguely, page 236.

Anuszkiewicz' painting INJURED BY GREEN was designed to produce involuntary eye movement. See color plate 9 and discussion on page 62. Emphasis on optical sensations such as this is the common factor in op (short for optical) paintings. Both actual and implied motion have become increasingly important in the visual arts in recent years.

SHAPE

Shape refers to that aspect of form seen as a flat area, as in a silhouette. Marc Chagall's painting I AND MY VILLAGE is composed of simple geometric shapes. Chagall has abstracted the forms of the things he portrays. The major shapes implied in the composition are triangles and circles. The diagram of the design makes this clear.

There are two families of shapes: geometric and organic. But there is no hard dividing line between the two groups. For example, it can be said that Chagall simplifies natural, irregular, or organic shapes in order to strengthen their symbolic interaction. It can also be said that he softens the geometric regularity of the shapes in his compositions in order to create a more natural flow between the various parts.

The prevalent shapes in nature are organic or irregular. The most prevalent shapes in the man-made world are geometric.

Most artists have a personal style, which includes a preference for certain configurations of visual form. Gauguin evidently became attached to the unique shape that he used for the tree trunk in his painting WORDS OF THE DEVIL, because he used it also in FATATA TE MITI. The shape of the girl about to enter the water in FATATA TE MITI was cut into a block of wood and reversed in his woodcut AUTI TE PAPE. The shape of the woman sitting in his painting AHA OE FEII was also used in the woodcut.

A composition can be strengthened by combining normally separate objects into composite shapes, as Gauguin has done with the two female figures in AHA OE FEII.

96   Paul Gauguin
WORDS OF THE DEVIL
1892. Oil on canvas. 37 x 27".

97   Paul Gauguin
FATATA TE MITI
1892. Oil on canvas. 26¾ x 36".

98   Paul Gauguin. AUTI TE PAPE (WOMEN AT THE RIVER).
1891–1893. Woodcut printed in color with the aid of stencils. 8⅛ x 14″.

99   Paul Gauguin. AHA OE FEII (WHAT, ARE YOU JEALOUS?) 1892. Oil on canvas. 26 x 35″.

100   Edvard Munch
KISS BY THE WINDOW
1892. Oil on canvas. 72.3 x 90.7 cm.

101   Edvard Munch
THE KISS
1895. Dry point and aquatint. 343 x 278 mm.

During the same decade that Gauguin was
doing much of his best work in Tahiti, the
Norwegian painter Edvard Munch produced, among other things, three works
with the common subject of a couple in an
embrace kissing one another. The first is
a painting, finished in 1892. The couple
stands to the side of a window, their figures
joined in a composite shape balanced by the
tree outside.

The second work is a drawing done three
years later. Here the couple stands un-
clothed before the window. Munch has
boldly emphasized the outlines of the figures and has made them into one relatively
simple shape. By removing the line that
would normally indicate the division between their faces, he has emphasized their
unity.

The third work is a woodcut done five years after the painting in which he first put down his idea. He used two blocks of wood, printing one uncut, wiped with just enough ink to bring out the grain and printed as a background for his final version of THE KISS. He has here simplified his basic concept to its essence. Simplicity of this kind is very difficult to achieve. Munch did not come to this result all at once; he let it evolve from one work to the next. When he did the first painting he may never have intended to return to the idea. Of the three versions, the woodcut is the best known because it so effectively symbolizes the basic content desired.

102 Edvard Munch
THE KISS
1897–1898. Woodcut. 467 x 465 mm.

103   Hans Holbein
Sir Thomas More
1527. Oil on wood. 29½ x 23¾".

TEXTURE

Texture is surface quality revealed through the sense of touch. Wayne Miller's photograph of a baby being breast fed shows the beginnings of our experience of texture (see page 17). Tactile experience is important to babies. It is much later that we learn to "feel" texture with our eyes.

Texture can be actual or implied. Actual texture can be experienced through the tactile sense without the aid of vision. Implied texture, as in a photograph or painting, must be seen to be felt.

Holbein implies a variety of textures with paint in his portrait of Sir Thomas More. If we were blind we could not feel the softness of the fur or the velvet because the actual texture of the painting is smooth. Holbein has observed the variety of textures with great care. Notice how carefully he has portrayed the texture of the face alone.

Rembrandt applied his oil paint in thick strokes, creating both actual and implied tactile qualities. There is only a hint here of the textural difference between skin and hair, but there is a great deal of feeling demonstrated for the tactile possibilities of paint. The head of Saint Matthew is constructed with oil paint to create illusionary light and shade. Many contemporary painters use even thicker paint to develop exciting textural surfaces. When paint the consistency of thick paste is applied directly to a surface, it is called *impasto*. In MEADOW SPLENDOR (page 273) Hans Hofmann builds up a thick impasto, creating actual texture.

104   Rembrandt van Rijn. HEAD OF SAINT MATTHEW. c. 1661. Oil on wood. 9⅞ x 7¾″.

105   Meret Oppenheimer
OBJECT. 1936. Fur-covered cup, 4⅜″ diameter; saucer, 9⅜″ diameter; spoon, 8″ long.

The notorious fur-lined tea cup was put together in 1935 by Meret Oppenheimer. The refined tactile experience associated with a tea cup is reversed here. We are faced with an intentionally revolting object. The actual texture of fur is pleasant, and so is the texture of a tea cup. But the combination makes the tongue crawl. The work was designed to evoke a strong response. Social and psychological implications are abundant, and intended.

LINE

Line is the path left by a moving point. It is a path of action, the character of which is determined by the quality of the motion that created it. A line may vary in length, width, density, and direction, with each variation having its own character.

Line is a basic element in defining visual form. Line, like the other visual elements, represents a human concept employed in order to symbolize what is seen, felt, or imagined. Lines are marks with length on a two-dimensional surface, or they are the perceived edges of things in two- or three-dimensional space. Lines can appear smooth and flowing or nervous and erratic. They can be angry or happy, harsh or gentle.

Steinberg shows what happens to a highly irregular line when it is transformed as a result of undergoing a certain experience.

Color plate 10 Henry Moore. Recumbent Figure. 1938. Green hornton stone. Height 54".

Color plate 11
Paul Cézanne
The Turning
Road.
1879–1882.
Oil on canvas.
23½ x 28½".

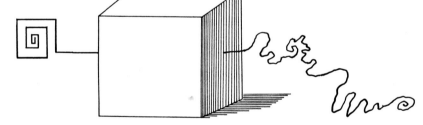

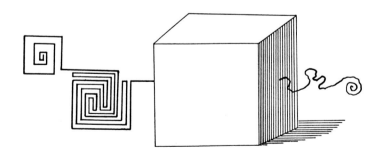

106 Saul Steinberg

From the element of line comes writing, drawing, and painting. These art forms have been interrelated for a long time. The earliest form of written language was pictography or picture writing. Until recently, drawn, painted, and written lines were often created with flexible brushes and pens, which produced lines of varying thickness.

In China and Japan writing and painting are closely interrelated. Writing is often found on paintings. The quality of line created by the heart, hand, and brush working in unison expresses the depth of character and feeling of the person writing or painting. Calligraphy, or writing, has been an important art form in Asia for countless generations.

Lettering was a highly developed art in Europe before the invention of the printing press. In fact, to "take pen in hand" was an important expressive act until the invention of the ball-point pen.

107   Gibon Sengai
THE CRAB
c. 1800. Ink on paper.

108   FRENCH GOSPEL LECTIONARY. 13th century.

The crab, not moving back and forth between good and evil as humans do, only moves sideways.

The crab makes his world
the harbor of Naniwa.
And goes sideways
through the reeds of good and evil.[15]

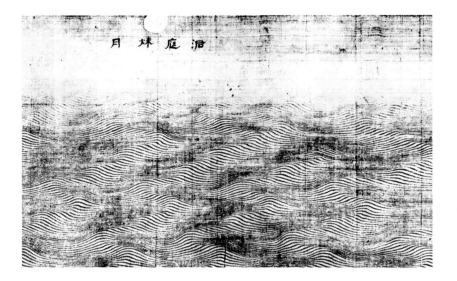

109   Unknown Chinese artist
A WAVE UNDER THE MOON
12th century. Ink on silk, detail of a scroll.

Lines on a flat surface can act as independent elements, define shapes, imply volumes, or suggest solid mass. Lines can be grouped to make patterns or portray shadows.

An unknown Chinese artist of the twelfth century painted A WAVE UNDER THE MOON. The small moon sets off a large area of rhythmically vibrating lines. The work is very close in feeling to that of some contemporary painters.

110   Bill D. Francis. PEACOCK FEATHER.
1969. See color plate 13.

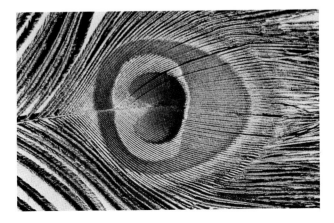

Implied lines are important elements in the composition of many works. One person pictured as looking at another implies a line of contact between them. Although the line is not actually drawn, its force can be a major factor in the composition. In Chagall's painting I AND MY VILLAGE (see page 81), this type of implied eye-to-eye contact line is emphasized by the implied line created with dashes.

All shapes having greater length than width are felt to have a core line or axis following the center of the form along its dominant dimension. In I AND MY VILLAGE objects like the cow's ears and the human figures have these axis lines acting as directions or paths of force in the picture. Notice how the ear at upper left picks up the diagonal line beginning below the cross at lower right.

Nature consists of forms having perfect co-ordination of all elements. The eye of a peacock feather is consistent in its design. Color, shape, line, and rhythm work together in a single harmonious unity. The segments of the feather work with each other and with the form of the bird to which it belongs. And the peacock acts as a colorful accent within the natural environment of which it is a part.

DESIGN

The process of ordering visual elements is called design. In general usage, to design means to prepare the preliminary sketches or plans for a work to be executed, or to conceive and develop such ideas in one's mind. In a deeper sense, design is basic to all of the arts as the structuring of elements into a consistent whole.

Design in nature and in art grows from within by inner necessity. In nature, survival depends on the interrelationship of a form with its function. The human body, like other forms of life, is consistent within itself. The design of the body is determined by its function, yet the design is more than mere utility. The body's function is expressed in the complex variety of its parts and in the interrelationships that bring those parts harmoniously together.

The origin of man's need to design stems from his desire for harmony. We seek harmony in all we perceive and do. Harmony is a refined form of order. The order is not necessarily apparent, but is always inherent — order determined by the essential character of what is organized. Order and chaos for their own sakes are contrary to human sensibilities. Individually we define what is chaos and what is order.

Each day our actions include many unconscious design decisions related to such things as where we live, what we wear, and how we eat. Design makes our environment comprehensible.

An artist develops his sense of design as part of a personal way of seeing, not as something tacked on after other things are considered. Each work of art derives its unity from a single unifying concept operating within it. This does not mean that every work must have an intellectual idea behind it. The unifying concept is often a strong, motivating feeling within the artist.

The sensitive interrelationships of elements in a work of art make possible the moods, feelings, and associations aroused in the viewer. We may not be consciously aware of them, but several factors are involved in aesthetic experience. For example, the overall proportions and scale of a work of art, affect the viewer immediately. Artists who paint on surfaces more than seven feet in their shortest dimension make use of the natural impact of things that are larger than human scale. See Al Held's Greek Garden on page 241.

When the size of any work is modified to be reproduced in a book, its character changes. No art work is reproduced exactly to size in this book. Almost all of the originals are larger. The scale of the Greek coin on page 299 was increased. By looking at reproductions, we can only imagine the impact the originals have. Size is an integral part of a work of art. Our senses register size as part of our overall responses — a small-sized work may have monumental impact; a large statue or painting may appear intricate or delicate. Our feelings about works of art change as their relationships to human scale change.

Everything that we perceive is relative. A tall man next to a short woman exaggerates the tallness and shortness of each. In the diagram the inner circle in both groups is the same measurable size.

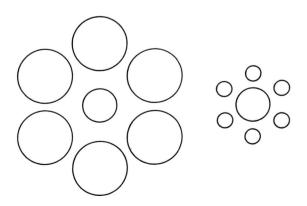

111 Kasimir Malevich
SUPREMATIST COMPOSITION: WHITE ON WHITE
c. 1918. Oil on canvas. 31¼ x 31¼".

We perceive in terms of relationships. Our perception is meaningful to us because of our mental ability to create our own sense of wholeness. First a configuration appears, then the separate elements. The extraordinary phenomenon of perception is more than the combination of separate elements of sensation.

If two or more shapes are combined we tend to see them as a whole, as in Malevich's SUPREMATIST COMPOSITION: WHITE ON WHITE. Our ability to see things as a whole allows us to form a complete mental picture of something presented to our eyes only as a fragment. Overlapping shapes appear to be passing in front of or behind other shapes. See the diagrams of overlapping circles on page 72.

Similar shapes or colors are immediately associated with each other, even though they may be far apart on a picture plane. The eye of the viewer moves about, relating similar elements. The simplicity of Malevich's minimal painting allows us to experience the tight relationship of one white square to another. This is design distilled to its essence.

In the following pages design is presented primarily in terms of the organization of relationships on a picture plane. Three-dimensional design problems are different in kind as well as in complexity. The intention is simply to demonstrate some of the most fundamental principles of basic design. These principles can be applied to all design problems.

Our physical reactions to gravitational forces are applied to what we see. Shapes within a form appear to fall, be pulled, float, move, be free, or be confined. Jokes are often made about hanging abstract paintings upside down. It makes quite a difference, because as soon as something is turned its whole relationship to our world of up and down changes. In several books reproductions of Malevich's painting WHITE ON WHITE have been turned in different directions by mistake. Notice how the forces in the painting change as it is seen from two points of view. Malevich selected the second position.

112 Hans Holbein
ANNE OF CLEVES
1539. Oil on wood panel.

Holbein's portrait of ANNE OF CLEVES is a
symmetrical composition of tightly inter-
locking shapes. Balance is obtained by the
symmetrical placement of the shapes, organized along a central vertical axis, creating
a feeling of formal dignity.

Verticals and horizontals symbolize human experience. A vertical appears as standing and a horizontal as lying down. A horizontal line has a feeling of rest and inaction and provides a ground plane for a vertical. A vertical line is one of poise. The two together provide a deep sense of composure. Both horizontal and vertical lines are static.

Within this century several artists have limited the kind and number of elements in their work in order to concentrate on the expressive possibilities of one element. Barnett Newman has worked primarily with vertical bands for more than a decade. In the work reproduced here two vertical lines balance one another asymmetrically against a changing textural ground.

113   Barnett Newman
DRAWING
1959

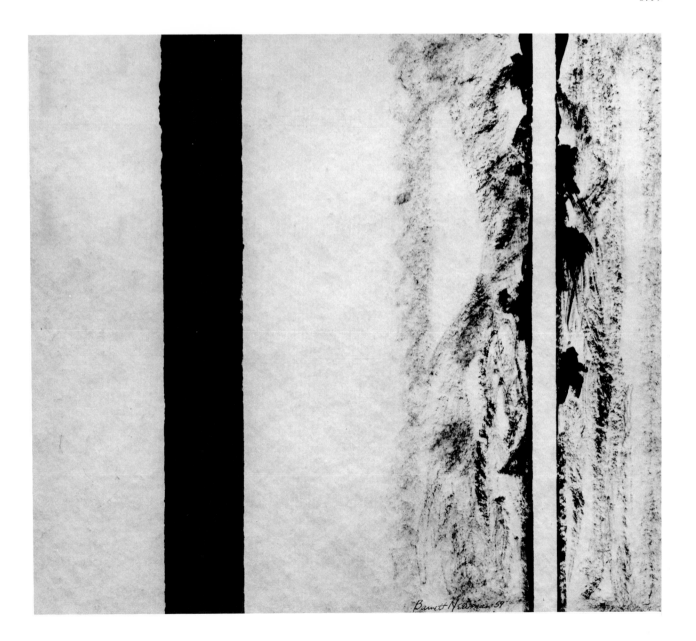

In Shopping on a Sunday Morning, Rue Mouffetard, Cartier-Bresson released his shutter just at the moment when everything went together to emphasize the jaunty swagger of the boy. The major axis of the composition runs asymmetrically through the boy's figure and is a slight diagonal. If that line were vertical the photograph would not have its visual impact. Diagonal lines or axes cause a sense of tension in the viewer because they disrupt our sense of vertical balance. A gravitational pull provides the sensation of motion.

114   Henri Cartier-Bresson
Shopping on a Sunday Morning, Rue Mouffetard. Paris, 1958.

Goya was a great master who was sensitive to the dynamics of the picture plane. His remarkable etching, BULL FIGHT, is a good example of suspended action poised at a great moment of tension. Most of the interesting subject matter is concentrated in the left two-thirds of the rectangle. We are drawn to the point of emphasis by the intersecting horizontal and vertical lines behind the lower hand of the man on the pole. This linear movement seems to hold the picture together, in spite of the dramatic sense of movement given by the diagonal force lines of the bull and the man.

115 Francisco Goya
BULL FIGHT
1810–1815. Etching. 12¼ x 8⅛".

116 José Clemento Orozco
ZAPATISTAS
1931. Oil on canvas. 45 x 55".

A progressive visual rhythm is set up across
the picture plane in Orozco's ZAPATISTAS.
The line of related figures acts as a sequènce
of diagonals grouped in a rhythmic pattern.

Rhythm is used to provide continuity in the
visual arts, as in music. It can provide flow,
equanimity, and dramatic emphasis. Visual
rhythm, like audible rhythm, operates when
there is an ordered recurrence of shapes.
Variations build on the major beat.

117 Pieter de Hooch
INTERIOR OF A DUTCH HOUSE
1658. Oil on canvas. 29 x 25".

In INTERIOR OF A DUTCH HOUSE by Pieter
de Hooch, there is a regular recurrence of
rectangles. A definite rhythm is set up by
the pattern of the floor and the windows.
The rectangular theme repeats the horizontal and vertical directions that begin with
the edges of the picture plane.

118 Raphael Sanzio
MADONNA OF THE CHAIR
c. 1514. Oil on wood. 2' 4" round.

For contrast, notice how the basic shapes of
Raphael's MADONNA OF THE CHAIR echo in
curving rhythms the circular picture plane.
The flowing curves running through this
composition are stabilized by the single
straight axis of the vertical chair post.

Every work must be received on its own terms. Therefore, it is misleading to make comparisons between works in which the artists' intentions are substantially different. It is fair and revealing, however, to compare works with the same subject and similar intention.

The Italian word *Pietà* refers to any picture or sculpture depicting the Virgin mourning over the dead body of Christ. The subject was developed in the late Middle Ages to show the end of Christ's life, as the figure of Mary with the infant Christ on her lap shows the beginning.

Making a composition in which a baby appears on its mother's lap is much easier than showing a fully grown man in such a position. Imagine being a sculptor who was commissioned by the Church to depict this subject.

Michelangelo made the figures seem quite natural. The body of Christ is comfortably held on Mary's lap. Mary appears young,

which emphasizes the idea of her virginity. But how can a young woman hold a fully grown man across her lap?

In the version done by an unknown sculptor the proportions of each figure are true to life, yet they seem unnatural. Christ's body appears to hang uncomfortably out in space without support.

Michelangelo concealed Mary's immensity in proportion to Christ with massive folds of drapery. Her vertical figure spreads out to accommodate the almost horizontal curve of Christ's limp body. Imagine what Mary would look like if she stood up. Michelangelo made Mary's body into that of a giantess. Yet we are so taken with the natural-appearing relationship between the figures that the distortion does not disturb us.

The sculpture is organized within a cone or pyramid, making its form self-sufficient and solid. The complex detail on its surface is controlled by the dominant stability and calm expressed by the basic mass.

119 Unknown Italian artist. PIETÀ.
c. 1430. Polychromed terra cotta.

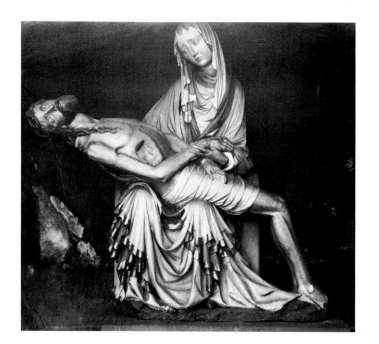

120 Michelangelo Buonarroti
PIETÀ
1501. Marble. Height 6′ 8½″.

Artists achieve quality in their work by applying critical evaluation to their own efforts.

Matisse showed his public the result of a long search, rather than the search itself. This makes many of his paintings look easy — as if they were done with little effort.

People often stand in front of his work and say things like, "My kid could have done it."

Because Matisse wished to please and relax the viewer, he worked very hard to make his compositions look as if they were done effortlessly.

a

b

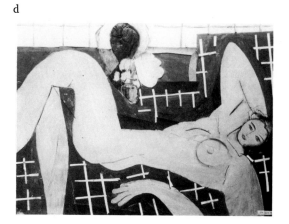

c

d

e

f

122 Henri Matisse
PINK NUDE
September 15, 1935. Oil on canvas. 26 x 36½".

-Six stages in the progress of PINK NUDE are shown here, followed by the final version. These six stages represent only some of the repaintings of this work. Matisse attached pieces of colored paper to the surface of the picture to determine how the possible changes would look before repainting began. Typically, Matisse would repaint the entire composition of the versions he liked, instead of trying to correct the relationships that displeased him. In each stage Matisse selected and strengthened those aspects of the image that contributed most to the overall concept. Finally, when he felt that everything in the composition worked together, he stopped.

121 Henri Matisse
Six States of PINK NUDE
Oil on canvas

a   State 1, May 3, 1935
b   State 6, May 23, 1935
c   State 9, May 29, 1935
d   State 11, June 20, 1935
e   State 13, September 4, 1935
f   State 23, September 15, 1935

Then a moment comes when every part has found its definite relationship and from then on it would be impossible for me to add a stroke to my picture without having to paint it all over again.

Henri Matisse[16]

is reduced in size to give the appearance of looking up at her across the footlights.

Lautrec's sense of line, color, and shape, and his strong feeling for his subject, work together here to form a painting of great vitality.

This third version of the subject is a color lithograph, which advertised Jane Avril's talents on the streets of Paris in the 1890s. Lautrec simplified Jane's image and added the suggestion of a bass player in the right foreground. This forms one of the dramatic compositions for which he is so famous.

123 Henri de Toulouse-Lautrec
JANE AVRIL
c. 1893

124 Henri de Toulouse-Lautrec
JANE AVRIL
1893. Oil on cardboard. 38 x 27″.

Toulouse-Lautrec sought to capture the vivacious charm of the great Parisian night club star Jane Avril. A photograph, probably taken by Lautrec as a study, shows her smiling face, but becomes absurd below the chin. The photographic equipment employed could not record her figure in action. Since a fairly long exposure was necessary, Jane had to hold what would normally be a spontaneous gesture. The photograph is ridiculous. The axis of her figure is vertical, making the image static. Her arms, holding her right leg, are lost beneath her garments. Her right leg appears tacked to her shoulder by mistake, like something that might have happened in a game of Pin-the-Leg-on-the-Lady.

There are no such problems in Lautrec's oil sketch of the subject. He masterfully organized every detail into a dynamic whole. We sense the axis now as a figure S beginning at the left foot. Notice what a difference it has made to change the angle formed by the lower ankle into two diagonals. The diagonal of the lower leg leads us to the point where the right leg is now clearly supported by the curve of the arm. The head

125   Henri de Toulouse-Lautrec. JANE AVRIL. 1893. Lithograph. 49⅝ x 36⅛".

Ideally, each person viewing a work of art will determine his own idea of its quality. This is difficult to achieve because each of us brings preconceptions to everything we see. We have heard that Leonardo da Vinci's painting called Mona Lisa is a great work of art. If this is foremost in our minds when we see the Mona Lisa, our own evaluation of quality becomes limited. But, can true quality be determined in this way?

Quality is relative. Concepts of what is valuable change from person to person, from age to age, and from culture to culture. Vermeer received some recognition in his own time. But he was largely forgotten in the eighteenth century and rediscovered in the nineteenth century. In the twentieth century Vermeer has received international acclaim. See color plate 2.

If a work of art contributes to your experience, it has quality for you. Works of art that are considered great are those that have contributed to the experience of many people over a long period of time. Art's quality cannot be judged on the basis of how well it imitates the appearance of the world around us. Art is selection and interpretation, not imitation.

126 Leonardo da Vinci. Mona Lisa. c. 1503–1506. Oil on wood. 30¼ x 21".

What was art like in the past?

A WORLD VIEW

To me there is no past or future in art. If a work of art cannot live always in the present it must not be considered at all. The art of the Greeks, of the Egyptians, of the great painters who lived in other times, is not an art of the past; perhaps it is more alive today than it ever was. Art does not evolve by itself, the ideas of people change and with them their mode of expression.

Pablo Picasso[1]

We are not separated from the majority of men by a boundary, but simply by another mode of vision.

Hermann Hesse[2]

Art history differs from other kinds of history because works of art from the past are still with us in the present. As long as a work of art exists as a physical object, it lives in the present, with the potential of revealing itself in new ways.

If art of the past is seen as an expression of the feelings and experiences of living people, it becomes much more accessible. The people of thirteenth-century France called their cathedrals *opus modernum* or "modern work." Each age has its "modern art." The art that we call modern today has roots from many cultures going far back in time.

This chapter is designed to give you a sense of the art of your own time and its relationship to the art of the past. It begins with selected works from a variety of world art traditions. That section is followed by works representing developments in Western art to the end of the nineteenth century. The chapter concludes with a glimpse of some of the many styles that have emerged in the twentieth century.

Peoples of all cultures tend to be locked into their own beliefs, including their own history. The habit of considering one's own people, language, and history as THE people, THE language, and THE history seems as common now as it ever was, even though the revolution in communications media is increasing tremendously the general awareness of other cultures. An awareness of art history helps to expand our capacity to see beyond a limited self-interest. Works of art embody the essence of their times and places and are themselves uniquely accessible "facts" of history. Through their works, artists both reflect and affect the age in which they live, even though inspiration for art comes as much from art as from life.

Our understanding of works of art is helped immeasurably by a knowledge of the cultures from which they came. This also works in reverse. Works of art and artifacts are frequently the only evidence that we have of a culture, and, therefore, what we know of the culture is influenced by our understanding of its art. We may also consider individual works of art as events in themselves, which may or may not become clearer to us when we know their general cultural background.

127 FACSIMILE OF CHUMASH INDIAN ROCK PAINTING. Santa Barbara, California area, c. 1500–1900.
Photograph by Campbell Grant.

There is no one line of development in art history. Within a given culture there are progressions toward the perfection of an idea, but these progressions are frequently isolated from one another by barriers of time and distance and by radical shifts in attitude.

A common vocabulary of basic visual symbols is found in all human cultures. They appear frequently in the work of young children. The two accompanying figures come from opposite sides of the world and were done about 6,000 years apart, yet they appear as if they were variations of a shared symbolic language of visual form. We are not troubled by classifications like East or West, ancient or modern, as we study these forms. They act as a point of departure to understanding similarity, sequence, and change in the history of art.

All art is abstract in the sense that it is not possible for an artist to reproduce an exact equivalent of what he sees. "A horse imitated by a painter," Shankuka observes, "does not appear to the spectator as being either real or false."[3]

What is generally called *abstract* art is art based on preexisting objects, in which the natural image of the subject is changed or distorted. It assumes that there is communicative value in visual form that exists independent of recognizable subject matter. As a verb, "to abstract" means to take from, to extract the essence of a thing or an idea.

A *representational* work is based on a depiction of the appearance of things, in which objects in the everyday world are presented again or re-presented. (Also called *naturalistic, realistic,* and *figurative.*)

A *nonrepresentational* work rejects the representation of appearances. It presents a visual configuration without reference to anything outside itself. (Also called *nonfigurative*, and *nonobjective*.)

Art terminology is not standardized, but for the purposes of this book these terms are most often used.

At various times in history the emphasis in visual art has been on abstract or representational or nonrepresentational. The Renaissance belief that art should represent the appearance of the everyday world is widely assumed to be the usual thing for art to do. Yet, if we take a world view of art history, the Renaissance concept is simply a provincial development and not a norm at all. It is a learned way of seeing.

Some of the earliest signs of the presence of man on earth were symbolic marks made on surfaces with fingers and tools. Many of these marks are unintelligible; they pile up one over the other. The activity of making marks must have been more important in prehistoric times than the creation of single images. Sometimes hands themselves were imprinted or traced on the surfaces of an-

cient caves. This was one of the many ways in which images were recognized and developed. Carving marks and recognizing images must have formed the basis on which art developed.

Art probably began when early man found pieces of wood, stone, bone, and other objects that were useful as tools. Some of these articles no doubt were highly treasured. If one was lost, stolen, broken, or worn beyond usefulness, another like it had to be found. This was next to impossible. At that point someone discovered that it was easier to make a copy of the original than to find a replacement. This was the beginning of man, the maker of things. It was also the beginning of representational art. The first "artist" made a copy or *re-presentation* of the desired object that was no longer available.

After developing this basic ability to make copies of natural objects, someone must have figured out that a copy could be refined to increase its usefulness. The artists or toolmakers over a period of many generations gradually refined the design of the artifact to the essence of the form best suited to its function. This was a process of extracting the idea of essential usefulness from the original natural form and exaggerating that usefulness. The result was an *abstraction* of the original form. We cannot say that a modern hammer is a representation of a natural object. It is an abstraction, the refined product of an idea with a long evolutionary history.

128 Detail of POLYCHROME WALL PAINTING
From house in Teleilat Gahssul,
Valley of the Jordan River, Jordan, c. 4000 B.C.

129 POMO STORAGE BASKET.   California, 19th century.   Coiled basketry.

No line needs to divide objects or paintings made for a primarily visual function from those in which visual appearance is just one of several functions. The major art form developed by the Indians of the California area was basket weaving. The Pomos achieved a high level of quality. Pomo baskets were made with such incredible tightness that they could hold water. In some baskets one can count sixty stitches to the inch. There was great variety in shape and decoration. Surface designs developed out of the weaving process. The storage basket reproduced here shows a characteristic stepped pattern spiraling outward across the surface. Many patterns have names, such as fish teeth, earthworm, or arrowhead. The natural colors and textures of bark, roots, grasses, and other fibers form the design. Sometimes dyes were used to provide a greater range of values.

130 POMO FEATHERED BASKET. California, c. 1945.
Diameter, 2⅞"; diameter of mouth, 2"; depth, 1¹⁄₁₆".
See color plate 14

Pomo craftsmen were particularly noted for their feather-covered baskets. These brightly colored baskets were highly treasured objects, given as gifts on special occasions. Their primary function was for visual enjoyment.

The walls of massive rocks at Tassili Plateau in the Sahara Desert of North Africa show numerous paintings, done about 4,000 B.C. They contain group scenes of people and animals in a flat, semiabstract style. This painting, like the others, is a colorful depiction of daily life, showing sophistication in group compositions and in depicting human and animal gestures.

131 FACSIMILE OF POLYCHROME CATTLE
Jabbaren, Tassili-n-Ajjer, Sahara Desert, c. 4000 B.C.
Detail of rock painting. *See color plate 16.*

132 IVORY MASK
Benin district, Nigeria
16th century. Height 9".

This mask from the district of Benin, Nigeria, West Africa, is a work of sophisticated beauty. It was carved in ivory, probably after 1500. The consistency of the tradition from which it comes is clear when we realize that modern versions of this type of mask are still worn at the oba's (king's) waist in ceremonies. The crown consists of a row of stylized images of Portuguese men.

The "civilized" Europeans were amazed when they saw these sculptures, because they could not imagine how such refined art could come from people they considered "naked savages" living in mud and straw huts. This attitude was partly due to the belief that tribal peoples were caught in a stage of human development low on the evolutionary scale. These feelings of superiority can be put in perspective by realizing that the art of the Gothic cathedrals was also created by the hands of people who lived in crude huts.

This photograph shows a shaman of the Cameroons region of West Africa wearing a lion mask. It gives some feeling for the original symbolic power of the mask. The shaman is convinced that he *is* a lion. This is not a pretense. He shares a psychic iden-

tity with the animal. Contemporary Western man has cut himself off from such associations, thus depriving himself of a basic link with the natural world. These psychic associations still persist in the unconscious, even though we ignore them.

133 SHAMAN WEARING LION MASK. Cameroons region, West Africa, c. 1950. Wood.

For many people art serves to fill the gap between what is known and what is felt. Art is magic. It has physical form, yet it contains spirit. "Man, with his symbol making propensity, unconsciously transforms objects or forms into symbols (thereby endowing them with great psychological importance) and expresses them in both his religion and his visual art." (Carl Jung.)[4]

In the art of some societies birds appear with human figures. Many times these bird symbols act as guides or messengers between the physical world of the living and the spiritual world of deceased ancestors.

In this particular work the bird seems to guide the man. The sculpture is a carved figure from Maravo Lagoon, New Georgia, in the Solomon Islands. It was attached to the prow of a canoe just above the water line. In this position the bird and man acted together as a protector spirit, possibly a symbolic lookout for shoals.

The carving is only six and one-half inches high, but looks much larger because of the boldness of its form. The exaggerated nose and jaw help to give the head its forward thrust. The wood is blackened and inlaid with mother-of-pearl, providing the white shapes for the eyes and the rhythmically curving linear ZZZ bands that help to unify the design.

Archeological excavations in China during this century show that the previously legendary Shang dynasty was at its peak from about 1500 to 1059 B.C. Scholars disagree on the dates of this literate culture and on the exact significance of its works of art. The works, however, are able to divulge their expressive power without agreement on their purposes, meanings, and dates of origin.

One of these works is the bronze container shown here. It is not a single, highly original work, but one of a type, probably used to hold heated wine for sacred rites. During the Shang dynasty fine bronze castings were produced. Most Shang vessels have a similar feeling of overall compactness. The surfaces are covered with sophisticated geometric ornamentation in which animalistic symbols crowd together. On this particular work the large squatting figure is encrusted with images. A deer acts as a handle for the lid. On the bottom of the container there is a coiled serpent. At the back, an elephant's trunk comes out of a tiger's mouth, providing a third support.

The sculpture from the Solomons and the Chinese bronze vessel express man's faith in the power of art to provide for safety in a mysterious and threatening world. The container depicts a bear or tiger spirit. Because the man's head is just below and almost within the ferocious jaw of the beast, it could seem that the man is about to be devoured. But this is not so. The man's hands are relaxed. He is holding onto the monster for protection. Perhaps the most fascinating aspect of this work is the contrasting relationship between the gentle wonder expressed on the man's face and the aggressive protective power of the animal.

134 CANOE PROW ORNAMENT
Maravo Lagoon, New Georgia, Solomon Islands,
collected 1929. Wood with mother-of-pearl.
Height 6½". Photograph by Axel Poignant.
See color plate 15

135 CHINESE SACRAL VESSEL. c. 1500–1059 B.C. Cast bronze. Height 14″.

136 STANDING BUDDHA
5th century. Red sandstone. Height 5'3".

The mystical energy and compassion of Christ is given symbolic force in the early twelfth-century relief carving over the central doorway of Saint Madeleine Cathedral at Vézelay, France. The linear folds of drapery covering the figure are different from those of the Buddha, even though the drapery style in both of these carvings can be traced back to Greco-Roman origins. The rendering of the drapery is highly abstract. The folds swirl and eddy in rhythmic patterns that are charged with vitality.

137 Detail of CHRIST OF THE PENTECOST
Saint Madeleine Cathedral, Vézelay, France
1125–1150. Stone. Height of tympanum, 35½".

Much of Asian art is Buddhist. Early Buddhism and Christianity did not favor the worship of images. Eventually, however, religious practice needed icons as support for contemplation. Buddhist sculpture varies considerably in style according to the culture that produced it. As Buddhism moved from India to Southeast Asia and across Central Asia to China, Korea, and Japan, it influenced, and in turn was influenced by, the religious and aesthetic traditions with which it came in contact.

The standing Indian Buddha shown here was carved in red sandstone in the fifth century A.D. The simplified mass of the figure seems to push out from within. Its rounded form is set off by a sequence of flowing curves that are repeated rhythmically down across the figure. The "string-type" drapery lines seem wet as they cling to and accentuate the round softness of the body beneath. In contrast to the intense energy implied by the linear folds of Christ's robes, these lines seem to evoke feelings of great inner peace achieved through calm communion with universal truth.

In Hindu belief Shiva is the Supreme Deity, encompassing all things. For this reason Shiva takes various forms in Hindu sculpture. Reproduced here is an image of Shiva as Nātarāja, Lord of the Dance, performing the cosmic dance within the orb of the sun. As he moves, the universe is reflected as light from his limbs.

The figure seems to embody motion, yet it does not move. Movement is implied in such a thorough way that it seems contained in every aspect of the piece. Each part is alive with the rhythms of a dance tradition that has been strong in India for several thousand years. The multiple arms add to this sense of movement.

In his book THE DANCE OF SHIVA, the great Indian art historian Ananda Coomaraswamy poetically relates the nature of Shiva's dance:

In the night of Brahma, Nature is Inert, and cannot dance till Shiva wills it: He rises from His rapture, and dancing sends through inert matter pulsing waves of awakening sound, and lo! matter also dances appearing as a glory round about Him. Dancing, He sustains its manifold phenomena. In the fulness of time, still dancing, he destroys all forms and names by fire and gives new rest. This is poetry; but none the less, science.[5]

138 SHIVA NĀTARĀJA
11th century. Bronze. 43⅞ x 40".

Works of art can reveal basic attitudes of a people toward their environment. The accompanying three works depict man as a relatively small creature.

The twentieth-century photographer Henri Cartier-Bresson emphasizes the tiny scale of man surrounded by the vast structures of New York City. His composition sets off two natural beings, man and cat, against the towering vertical slabs of a totally man-made environment. Here man is dwarfed by things of his own making.

The other two works are paintings. This one is the work of the Flemish painter Joachim Patinir, probably one of the first European artists to use landscape as the main subject. He helped to establish a tradition that lasted approximately 400 years.

139   Henri Cartier-Bresson
NEW YORK CITY
1947

140 Joachim Patinir. REST ON THE FLIGHT INTO EGYPT. 1515–1524. Oil on wood. 6¾ x 8⁵⁄₁₆".

Patinir also emphasized the scale of man, but in this case the setting presents man's small physical stature in relation to nature, symbolically expressing his relationship with God. In the foreground, rock formations tower above the Holy Family. In the middle ground, a village fits comfortably into the land. In the background, sky and water meet in infinity behind the distant hills. Patinir's interest in deep space and horizontal movement is apparent.

In the landscape by Wang Hui, painted in 1692, the scale of man is smaller than in either of the last two works. According to Chinese tradition, man is only a small part of the universe. Nature is seen as alternating positive and negative forces, which are vast and powerful. When man is humble he fits comfortably within these universal forces. He is one with nature. Rich textural patterns enliven the surfaces of earth forms, which writhe with dragonlike energy. The ancient Chinese were among the many who expressed the belief that this energy is found throughout nature.

Chinese landscape painting is a major facet of world art. Wang Hui's painting comes late in a Chinese art tradition that lasted more than 1,000 years.

Wang Hui was probably the most celebrated painter of his day. Even in his youth he was so gifted with a brush that he could paint and draw as he wished. He remained faithful to nature and to the Chinese tradition by following the brush conventions of earlier masters. Each stroke of the brush derives from calligraphy and works as a symbol for natural form. The artist created variations on traditional themes.

Wang Hui felt the responsibility of man as artist to be sensitive to the forces of nature so that his spirit becomes rich and strong. As he achieves this himself, his art in turn becomes full of life. In this way the artist's insight and vitality passes through the work to the viewer.

141 Wang Hui
DEEP IN THE MOUNTAINS
1692. India ink and pale color on paper.
43¾ x 19⅛".

We are living through a time when everything seems to change overnight. Most traditions from our various cultural heritages have been swallowed up. Many of us alive today were born into frantic change. It is very difficult for anyone conditioned by the concept of "new is better" to conceive of cultural traditions that remained relatively consistent for several thousand years.

Japanese aesthetic traditions have been much more stable than European ones, yet compared to the traditions of ancient Egypt, India, and China, Japanese art may appear as volatile as European art.

The abstract power of the image of Minamoto Yoritomo, done in the twelfth century, has much in common with the design quality found in Japanese woodcuts of the eighteenth century. Their shared style is thoroughly Japanese. In this painting Yoritomo is shown seated, dressed in the ceremonial robes of a senior court official. His light face accents the dominant angular shape of his garments. The black hairpiece rising from the back of his head repeats the shape and direction of his white fan.

142 Fujiwara Takanobu
PORTRAIT OF MINAMOTO YORITOMO
1142–1205. India ink and color on silk.
55½ x 44¼".

Color plate 12 SOLOMON AND THE QUEEN OF SHEBA. c. 1556–1565. Persian miniature painting. 13½ x 9⅛".

Color plate 14 Pomo Feathered Basket. California, c. 1945. Diameter, 2⅞"; diameter of mouth, 2"; depth 1½6".

Color plate 16
FACSIMILE OF
POLYCHROME CATTLE.
Jabbaren, Tassili-n-
jjer, Sahara Desert,
c. 4000 B.C.

Color plate 17
LEFTHAND WALL,
GREAT HALL OF
BULLS.
Lascaux Caves,
Dordogne, France,
15,000–10,000 B.C.
Polychrome rock
paintings.

Color plate 18
Claude Monet
IMPRESSION: SUNR
1872. Oil on canv
19½ x 25½".

Color plate 19
Auguste Renoir
LE MOULIN DE LA
GALETTE.
1876. Oil on canva
51½ x 69".

143 Unkei. Detail of MUCHAKU. c. 1208. Wood. Height 75″.

Japanese artists have long respected the flat character of a two-dimensional picture surface. In traditional Japanese art there has never been a lasting break from this value. Although there have been many changes of style in Japanese art, until recently artists have rarely accepted seriously the Western Renaissance concept of a picture as an illusion of natural space.

In the three dimensions of sculpture, representational form is less of an illusion. When the refinements of court life in the Fujiwara period (897–1185 A.D.) gave way to the aggressive soldiers of the Kamakura period (1185–1333 A.D.), a new style of art emerged that emphasized greater strength and realism. One of the greatest artists of the time was the sculptor Unkei. His portraits are made of thin pieces of wood that have been joined, carved, and painted. They are some of the first portraits known in Asia in which careful depiction of a man's personality appears in natural detail.

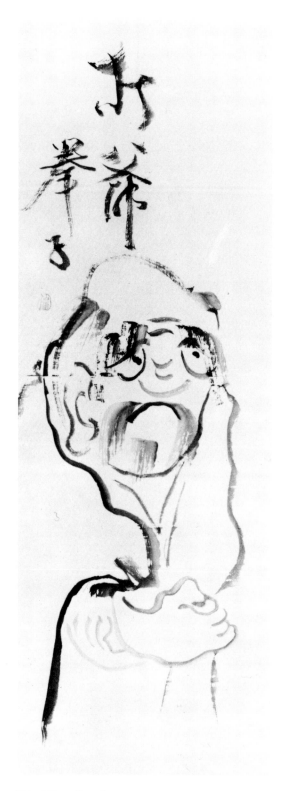

The Zen Buddhist monk Sengai is known for his rugged visual epigrams of Zen thought. Each hit of the brush against the paper produced a stroke that has power and significance. In THE FIST THAT STRIKES THE MASTER, he illustrates the story of a great Chinese Zen priest, Rinzai, who found enlightenment and struck his teacher with his fist. His images are graphic in every sense of the word.

Japanese prints were an important influence on European and American painters toward the end of the nineteenth century. Utamaro's image of a woman looking at herself in a mirror is composed of bold shapes and flowing lines. The woodcut is several times removed from ordinary appearances. The center of interest is the reflected face of the woman, set off by the strong, simple curve representing the mirror's edge. The depiction of everyday life and the sense of design in prints like this one inspired Western painters, such as Manet (see pages 166–167), to break with the sagging neoclassical Renaissance tradition.

144 Gibon Sengai
THE FIST THAT STRIKES THE MASTER
c. 1800. Ink on paper.

145 Kitagawa Utamaro
ONE OF THE SEVEN WOMEN SEEN IN A MIRROR
c. 1790. Color woodcut.

146 MARKET HALL AT MEREVILLE, FRANCE
15th century

147 INTERIOR OF A MANEABA
Drumond Island, Gilbert Islands, 19th century

A primary aspect of the art of architecture is the making of human shelter. In medieval Europe, secular and sacred buildings shared a common structural heritage. Complex Gothic cathedrals such as Chartres represent a branch from the same architectural tree that produced houses, barns, and halls such as the Market Hall at Mereville, France.

In market halls people gathered to buy, sell, and socialize. The large roof and open sides provided shelter without inhibiting traffic. The structure works as both roof and partial wall. This is even more true of the *maneaba* or "great meeting house" of the Gilbert Islands. All community life, including ceremonies, recreation, and the maintenance of law and order, took place in this great space.

148   Oscar Niemeyer
CONGRESS AND ADMINISTRATION BUILDINGS
Brasilia, Brazil, 1959

149   THE GREAT STUPA
Sanchi, India, c. 10 B.C.–15 A.D.

Architecture can be defined as the art of making sculptural enclosures that serve both to shelter and to delight. The basic geometric solids of Oscar Niemeyer's government buildings in Brazil work in this manner. They are contemporary, yet in the expressive clarity of their sculptural form, they relate in feeling to ancient ritual architecture, such as the Great Stupa at Sanchi in central India. Both structures dominate flat landscapes.

Traditional Indian Buddhist architecture emphasizes domelike sculptural form, often with little or no enclosed space. The *stupa* evolved from a small burial mound. Its large, completely solid mass symbolizes the cosmos. The Brazilian political structures reflect the twentieth-century emphasis on geometric simplicity in architecture.

WESTERN ART

Western art history is like the corner of a piece of fabric with many threads coming in and out, each becoming part of an ongoing tapestry of human experience, now fusing with Eastern sources in a worldwide experience.

There is a pattern in Western art history that can be followed back to prehistoric times. This pattern shows stylistic changes following one another in cycles. These recurrences are like the movement traced by a point on the edge of a wheel. Each time they appear the wheel of time has moved on to a new location, making the circumstance and hence the style different although similar.

We now believe that human beings have been on earth for about a million years. There is no evidence that man behaved differently from other animals for the first 600,000 years or so. The purposeful shaping of stone tools marks the beginning of a phase in human development that we call the Paleolithic Age. Toward the end of that period, about 20,000 B.C., the earliest known works of art appear. Although these works are the first art known to us, their high quality indicates that they must have been preceded by thousands of years of development.

The large herds of big game then roaming Europe were evidently the major source of food. Early man had to hunt in order to survive. The hunter and the artist were the same individual. On the undulating surfaces of cave walls the hunter-artist discovered animallike and humanlike rock formations, which he emphasized by drawing, painting, or carving.

The images reproduced here were created on the wall of a deep inner cave chamber at Lascaux in southern France. Animals large and small were painted in a representational style. The images are based on keen observation gained through considerable direct contact with animals. Whoever made these paintings must have had extraordinary visual memory, because spontaneous poses are depicted as if caught by a high-speed camera. Earth colors were blown and daubed on the walls, mixed with animal oils as a medium. Some of the bulls at Lascaux are as much as eighteen feet in length.

Paleolithic man must have gained confidence by being able to create images of the creatures that were so crucial to his life. By doing this, man himself went from creature to creator.

a

b

150 (a) Forequarters of Bull, Painted Gallery. (b) Lefthand Wall, Great Hall of Bulls. Lascaux Caves, Dordogne, France, c. 15,000–10,000 B.C. Polychrome rock paintings. *See color plate 17.*

Many hand-sized carvings have been found at prehistoric sites in Europe. Such sculpture has the same expressive naturalism as pre-

151 HEAD OF NEIGHING PREHISTORIC HORSE
Le Mas d'Azil, Ariège, France
c. 30,000–10,000 B.C. Bone relief

historic drawings and paintings. The head of a neighing horse, possibly carved from an animal's antler, shows that its maker was able to combine skill with careful observation and considerable feeling. Often the artist saw the final form revealed in the natural form of his material.

Current understanding of prehistory suggests that violent climatic changes from about 10,000 to 8,000 B.C. caused wildlife to diminish. Scarcity of game forced hunters to rely on other food sources. Cultivation of crops had been tried before in various parts of the world, but never to the extent that it developed in the fertile lands of the Near East about 8,000 B.C. There, small groups of people successfully planted crops and domesticated animals. This shift from nomadic hunting to agricultural communities stabilized human groups. Man learned to utilize seasonal rhythms. Food had to be stored in order to provide a year-round supply. It is not surprising that the major articles made by these people were clay storage pots.

The vigorous naturalism of Paleolithic art died out. New emphasis was placed on geometric decoration for articles of daily use. These decorations included highly abstract images of animals and men. Some of the symbols referred to weather gods and other forces of nature.

The painted and glazed earthenware pot shown here was found at Ziwiye, in what is now Iran. Its abstract decoration is based on plant and animal forms. A wreath of lotus petals surrounds the shoulder of the vessel. Below this a band of bull and plant images are outlined against the background of blue. Compare this stylized bull with the animals of Lascaux and the Tassili frescoes.

152 PAINTED AND GLAZED EARTHENWARE VASE
Ziwiye, Iran, 8th–7th century B.C.
Height 43.5 cm., diameter of mouth, 11 cm.

153 MAN PLAYING A SYRINX
Cyclades Islands, Greece, 2600–2000 B.C.
Marble. Height 10½″.

We know little about the life and traditions of the Bronze Age people who inhabited the Cyclades, a group of islands near Greece in the Aegean Sea, from about 2600 B.C. to 1100 B.C. The only evidence of this culture includes numerous nude marble figures found in simple stone tombs. These carved figures range in size from a few inches in height to life size. Most of them are female. Both male and female figures were refined to a sophisticated geometric abstraction of human form. The one shown here depicts a man playing panpipes. The strong frontality in this work is typical of Cycladic sculpture.

Geometric abstraction is also apparent in the Egyptian sculpture of Mycerinus and his queen, done about 2500 B.C. The sculptor paid considerable attention to human anatomy, yet he stayed within the traditionally prescribed geometric style, thus making his figures representational, as well as expressing strength, clarity, and lasting stability.

The couple is locked together in a frontal pose that had been established for such royal portraits. The base reveals the shape of the slate block from which the figures were carved. The presence of the original block is still felt in the overall attitude of the figures.

154 King Mycerinus and Queen. c. 2525 B.C. Painted slate. Height 4'8".

During the archaic period of Greek civilization (from late seventh to late fifth century
B.C.) Greek art revealed the assimilation of
major influences coming from Egypt and the
Near East. Numerous life-sized nude male
and clothed female figures were carved during this era.

Nudity seldom occurred in Egyptian sculpture. In the Greek culture idealized nudity
related to the concept of the supreme
athlete and appeared early in male sculpture,
possibly to commemorate Olympic victors.

Both male and female types show Eastern
influence. The representation of the male
figure, called *kouros* (youth), follows a rigid
frontal position that is a direct adaptation
of the stance of Egyptian figures. Both the
Egyptian sculpture of Mycerinus and this
kouros are standing with arms held straight
at the side, fingers drawn up, and left leg
forward.

In spite of the similarity of stance, the
character of Egyptian sculpture is quite different from the Greek work. The Egyptians
were preoccupied with life after death, while
the Greeks were primarily concerned with
perfecting physical life and the human body.
The kouros figure is not attached to the
back slab of the original block as are the
Egyptian figures. The kouros is free standing. The so-called archaic smile on the face
of the Greek figure accentuates an overall
aliveness not found in Egyptian sculpture.

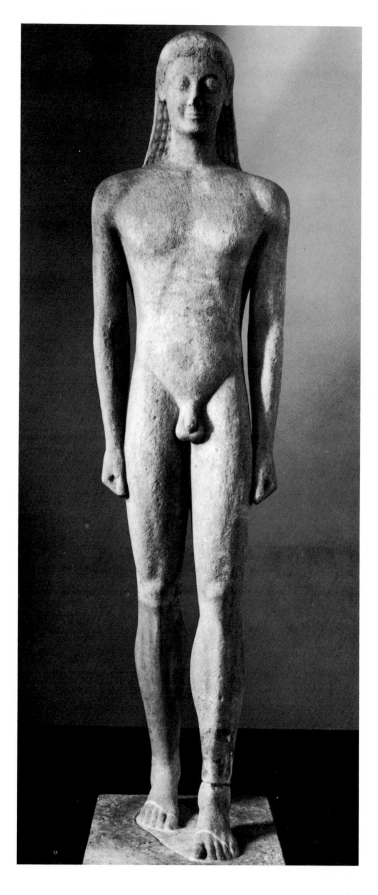

155 STANDING YOUTH
Melos, Greece, c. 540 B.C. Marble.

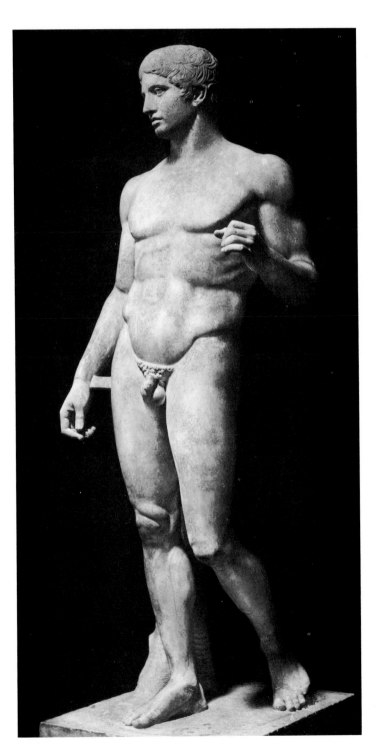

Within 100 years after the date of the kouros figure, Greek sculpture became increasingly active and soft with more natural proportions.

The bronze Spear Bearer by Polyclitus was carved about 450 to 440 B.C. This marble Roman copy demonstrates the full awareness of anatomy and ideal proportions that the sculptor brought to his work. It is an example of the completely developed classical Greek style.

The Spear Bearer does not stand at attention with the left leg forward as the Egyptian and early Greek figures did, but tilted so that the hips and shoulders are no longer parallel. This flexible pose created a more relaxed human stance. The major divisions of the body are set off from one another in a form of balance that is known by the Italian word contrapposto, meaning "counter pose."

Contrapposto was described by the seventeenth-century sculptor Gian Lorenzo Bernini when he pointed out that a person standing in a natural position will seldom rest his weight on more than one leg unless he is very old. Bernini said that the artist must be careful to reproduce this posture by making the shoulder of the side on which the leg bears the body's weight lower than the other. He found that good Greek and Roman statues all conformed to this rule.[6]

The statue is balanced asymmetrically so that the central, vertical axis forms a series of graceful curves, whereas the axis of the kouros is completely rigid. Geometric abstraction is present in the figure of the spear bearer, but it structures the work from within rather than from without, as in the earlier Greek and Egyptian works.

156 Polyclitus
Spear Bearer
c. 450–400 B.C. Copy in marble. Height 6′6″.

157a   Ictinus and Callicrates. ACROPOLIS. View from southwest. Athens, Greece, 447–432 B.C.

The city-state of Athens was the center of ancient Greek civilization when that culture was at its height. Above the city on a large outcropping of rock called the Acropolis, the Athenians built one of the world's most admired structures. Today, even in its ruined state, the Parthenon continues to express the high ideals of the people who created it.

This temple, one of several sacred buildings on the Acropolis, was designed and built as a gift to Athena Parthenos, protectress of the Athenian navy, goddess of wisdom, arts, industries, and prudent warfare. It expressed the gratitude of the Athenians for naval and commercial success.

The Parthenon exhibits the refined clarity, harmony, and simplicity that comes from the heart of the Greek tradition. The relationship of its parts is similar to the democratic structure of the Greek city-state and it reflects the Greek ideal of human proportion found in the sculpture of the same period. When Ictinus and Callicrates designed the building they were following a well-established tradition in temple design. The Greeks spent generations improving their basic architectural vocabulary. In the Parthenon the Greek temple form reached a state of perfection.

The outer form of the temple relates to exterior space. It was located so that it could be seen against the sky, the mountains, or the sea from vantage points around the city. It was the focal point for large outdoor religious festivals. Rites were performed on altars placed in front of the eastern entrance. The interior space was designed to house a forty-foot high statue of Athena. Laymen were permitted to view the magnificent figure through the eastern doorway. Only temple priests were allowed inside.

The architects took advantage of natural light in designing the building. The axis of the building was carefully calculated so that on Athena's birthday the rising sun coming through the huge east doorway would fully illuminate the gold-covered statue.

The Parthenon's proportions are based on a single mathematical formula and a consistent set of ratios. The ratio of the height to the widths of the east and west ends is 4 to 9. The ratio of the width to the length of the building is also 4 to 9. The diameter of the columns relates to the space between the columns at a ratio of 4 to 9, and so on. None of the major lines of the building are perfectly straight. The columns bulge almost imperceptibly above the center, giving them an elastic quality. Even steps and the tops of doorways rise slightly in perfect curves. Corner columns, seen against the light, are slightly larger in diameter to counteract the diminishing effect of light background. The axis lines of the columns lean in slightly at the top. If extended into space these lines would converge 5,856 feet above the building. The unexpected variations are not consciously seen, but they are strongly felt. They give the building its sense of perfection. Nothing could be added to or subtracted from the design without damaging the whole. The subtle deviations from straight horizontal and vertical lines may correct the optical illusions, but perhaps more importantly, they relate the structure to the site and give it a sense of natural vitality.

The Greeks originally built their temples with wood. Whole tree trunks served as columns. The use of marble, which is stronger than wood in compression, allowed the Greek templebuilders to increase the size of the superstructure.

In 1687 A.D., the Turks used the Parthenon as a powder magazine during a war with the Venetian Republic. In the fighting their supplies were blown up, causing great damage to the building. If it had not been for that tragic incident, the building might still look very much the way it did when it was completed.

Fairly recent analysis of Greek temples shows that exterior surfaces were painted with bright colors, such as pure blues and reds. Can you imagine what European and American cities would look like if all the Greek-style banks, schools, churches, and government buildings were painted according to this recent discovery?

In its working life [the Parthenon] . . . was not simply a cool and aloof exercise in refinement of form; it contained within its precise, geometrical framework a controlled explosion of polychromatic and sculptural energy and enshrined in its core a holy place of the deepest mystery.[7]

157b ACROPOLIS. View of PARTHENON from northwest.

159 PORTRAIT HEAD
c. 80 B.C. Bronze. Height 12¾".

158 Praxiteles
Detail of HERMES AND THE INFANT DIONYSIUS
c. 330–320 B.C. Marble. Height 7'1".

A detail of the head of Hermes from HERMES AND THE INFANT DIONYSIUS, finished about 330 B.C., shows the famous Greek ideal, the classical profile. It is essentially the same in its features as the head of the SPEAR BEARER, except for an added emphasis on idealized physical beauty and softness of form. This does not represent a man, but rather a godlike man as seen again and again in the features of Greek sculpture. The ideal man was for the Greeks the link between themselves and what they believed to be the basic order of the universe. "The Greek world is chiefly one of sunlight, though not the sun, but man, stands at its center."[8]

In the Hellenistic period (323–100 B.C.) following the decline of classical culture, Greek art became more dynamic and more representational. Most sculpture was free-standing or in groups. Everyday activities, historical subjects, and portraiture became more common than the earlier idealized forms.

This portrait head, part of a full-length statue of an unknown individual, is not an abstract god-hero, but the character of a fully mature human personality. The sculptor revealed his desire to depict the inner man.

The change in Greek tradition carried over
into Roman art. Romans were a practical
and materialistic people. Many pieces of
Greek sculpture were brought to Rome as
trophies of war. A copying process was devised by the inventive Romans to make
many reproductions of one sculpture. Greek
artists were enslaved and used to teach as
well as to create the more ornate and sensual
forms demanded by the private Roman citizen.

160 FEMALE PORTRAIT
54–117. Marble. Life-size.

Not all Roman art was imitative. Roman portraiture achieved a high degree of individuality rarely found in Greek sculpture. The representational style seems to have grown out of the Roman custom of making wax death masks to be placed in the family shrine. This practice was part of an exaggerated interest in factual documentation. Early in the first century B.C., these images were transferred to marble to make them more durable. Roman sculptors keenly observed and recorded those physical details and imperfections that gave character and individuality to each person's face. Today a bust of Beethoven on a piano or a photograph of the Founding Fathers in an office recalls this practice.

161 MALE PORTRAIT
c. 100. Marble. Life-size.

162 Giovanni Paolo Panini
THE INTERIOR OF THE PANTHEON
c. 1750. Oil on canvas. 50½ x 39".

163 PANTHEON
Rome, 118–125. Concrete and marble.

Simpicity of design, coupled with its immensity, make the Pantheon a memorable structure. The cement and brick building is essentially an upright cylinder, with one entrance framed by a Greek portico. This classical porch is reminiscent of the Parthenon. In contrast to the Parthenon, the Pantheon's most impressive aspect is its huge domed interior space.

The cylinder walls supporting the dome are fourteen feet thick. The dome is constructed of horizontal layers of brick set in thick cement. These layers are reinforced by a series of arches that converge in the dome's crown, leaving a central opening called an *oculus*. The oculus, thirty-three feet in diameter, illuminates the interior and provides contact with the heavens.

The Romans built roads and waterways over much of southern Europe. The aqueduct called le Pont du Gard at Nimes, France, shows how the Romans used the arch as a basic structural device to create functional forms of great beauty.

The first level serves as a bridge for foot traffic. Water is carried in a conduit at the top. The combined height of the three arcades is sixty feet.

164 Le Pont du Gard. Nimes, France, 15 A.D. Limestone. Height 161', length 902'.

By the time Emperor Constantine was converted to Christianity, Roman attitudes had changed considerably. The material grandeur of Rome was rapidly declining. As confidence in the material world fell, men turned inward to more spiritual values. The now recognized Christian religion had been slowly gaining in popularity. This great spiritual change is expressed in the colossal head of Constantine, carved in marble in about 312 A.D. It was once part of an immense seated figure. The abstract style of this sculpture developed from conflicting attitudes. In its great size it is definitely heroic, yet its large introspective eyes express an inner spiritual life that is not typically Roman. This is not a realistic portrait of Constantine. It is a symbolic physical manifestation of the transition from Greek and Roman civilization into the Christian era. This is Early Christian sculpture. It seems to have more in common with the abstract Byzantine images of Christ than with the representational portrait heads of Greece and Rome.

Much Early Christian art between 300 and 1200 A.D. was created in Constantinople, the Byzantine capital of the Eastern Roman Empire. There is no sharp dividing line between Early Christian art and Byzantine art. Other art centers were located at Rome, Antioch, and Alexandria. The art forms were affected by a controversy between the iconoclasts, who felt that images were idols, and the iconophiles who wanted religious figures. The Roman emperor issued an edict in 726 A.D., prohibiting the use of representational images. Many abstract symbols and floral patterns were incorporated into Christian imagery during the next 100 years. Byzantine Christian abstractions stemmed from associations with Eastern religions, in which flat patterns and nonrepresentational designs were employed.

Following the iconoclast period (726–843 A.D.), the abstract style was integrated with more emotional, figurative, and natural imagery. However, Eastern influence continued in the ordered placement of subject matter in Byzantine church decoration, with Christ in judgment occupying the dome.

165 CONSTANTINE
c. 312. Marble. Height 8'.

High in the center of the dome of the Monastery Church at Daphne, Greece, there is a mosaic depicting Christ as the *Pantocrator,* the Ruler of the Universe. This awesome spiritual work, created in the eleventh century, is one of the most powerful images of Christ. The huge scale of the figure emphasized its religious importance to the worshipers. Christ appears within a circle against a gold background. The artist has exaggerated the features of His face with bold, black outlines. The large eyes, nose, and mouth work together to form an expression of omnipotence. This flat, linear symbol of Christ as Divine Ruler was designed with such skill and feeling that it has become an image of lasting strength and appeal.

A row of windows circles the base of the dome, giving light to the church. The mosaic surfaces depend on the direction of light from the windows and from artificial sources such as candlelight. Each small tessera — glass, marble, shell, or ceramic — was placed on the adhesive surface, carefully tilted to catch the light. This produced a shimmering, luminous surface.

166 CHRIST. Detail of dome mosaic, Monastery Church, Daphne, Greece, c. 1100.

167a NOTRE DAME DE CHARTRES. View from southeast. Chartres, France, 1145–1513 (portals and lance windows, c. 1145; south tower, c. 1180; north spire, c. 1507–1513). Façade height, 157'; cathedral length, 427'; south tower height, 344'; north tower height, 377'.

In the Middle Ages, Roman influences diminished, and then returned with the new surge of building activity called Romanesque. The stone arch of Roman architecture influenced the development of these new forms. Stone vaults replaced fire-prone wooden roofs, thus giving the new structures a close resemblance to Roman interiors. There was a wide variety of regional styles, within which a common feeling of security was provided by the massive, fortresslike walls. Small window openings let in little light, causing the interiors to be dark and the walls to appear heavy.

During these feudal times, Romanesque monasteries and churches offered Christians refuge in a hostile world. Chartres Cathedral afforded such a place of refuge in its earliest structure. The west facade and right spire were built in the Romanesque period.

The new architecture of the mid-twelfth century had a unique sense of harmony based on a combination of the best features of Romanesque architecture, thus acting as a culmination of Romanesque and a beginning point for the Gothic style. In Gothic sacred architecture the flying buttress, pointed arch, and ribbed groin vault provided for greater interior height and larger window spaces. See diagrams. Extensive use of flying buttresses carried the tremendous weight of the vault laterally and downward to the ground. Stained glass windows filled the interior with rich, luminous color. The space of Gothic interiors gave a feeling of joyous spiritual elevation not found previously. Construction of the cathedrals grew out of medieval Christian theology. They are parallel constructions. The theology found its expression in architecture; the cathedral is visible theology.

167b NOTRE DAME DE CHARTRES. West front.

The Gothic design of the Chartres cathedral was begun in 1145 A.D. It was partially destroyed by fire and rebuilt in the High Gothic style between 1194 and 1220. See the plan.

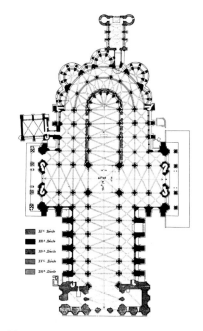

167d NOTRE DAME DE CHARTRES. Plan of cathedral, 1194.

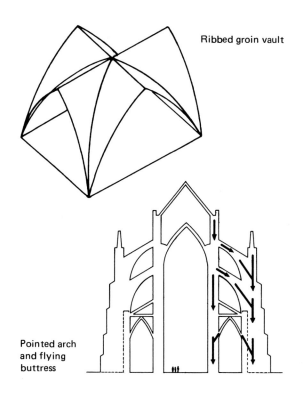

167c NOTRE DAME DE CHARTRES. Interior. Nave, approx. height 122′, width 53′, length 130′.

Ribbed groin vault

Pointed arch and flying buttress

The entire community worked on Notre Dame de Chartres (Our Lady of Chartres). Its form rises above the flat countryside on the site of a pre-Christian sacred spring. The people who began its construction never saw it in its present form. It continued to change and grow for more than 300 years. There is no quarrel here between art and engineering — in the Gothic cathedral they are one.

What would the architects of the Parthenon have thought of this complex and seemingly irrational structure? The plan of the building is based on the Latin Cross. It follows a clear, rational geometry, yet from the outside you cannot see this plan as you can see the logic of a Greek Temple. Chartres appears to reach beyond the earth and human scale. It is the symbolic Christian Kingdom of Heaven.

168   Giotto di Bondone. THE DESCENT FROM THE CROSS. c. 1305. Fresco. 78¾ x 78¾".

Another major shift in attitude occurred as the religious feeling, irrationality, and mysticism of the Gothic era were increasingly challenged by the triumphs of logical thought. The beginnings of this transition became apparent in the late thirteenth century.

The Italian Gothic painter Giotto led the way toward a more concrete vision of the world. He is considered the father of Western painting because he turned away from the relatively flat, stylized images of medieval painting to the three-dimensional natu-

ralism that reached full maturity in the Renaissance. Before Giotto, sculpture had been the dominant art form. The era of painting in Western art began with Giotto's solid sculptural figures. Giotto organized his painted figures in a shallow stage of implied space that seems continuous with the actual space we occupy. His compositions have an all-at-once quality, which was quite unique in his day. From his work came the tradition of making a painting like a window onto nature, which was not radically challenged until the development of cubism in the early twentieth century.

The revolutionary change in world view became fully visible in the fifteenth century. It was called the Renaissance by those who brought it into being. *Renaissance* means "rebirth" in French, and refers in this context to the great revival in art and ideas, which the men of fourteenth, fifteenth, and sixteenth century Europe based on the reaffirmation of man and man-centered pre-Christian thought, as found in the rediscovered cultures of ancient Greece and Rome. This humanism gave the people of the Renaissance an increased sense of personal worth and independence.

Florence, Italy was the center of the rebirth of humanism in the fifteenth century. Filippo Brunelleschi was among the first generation of Renaissance artists who found inspiration in the literature and art of ancient Greece and Rome. His careful study of Roman ruins enabled him to create a new kind of architectural style expressing the dignity of man rather than the omnipotence of God.

Brunelleschi's design for the Pazzi family chapel acted as a model for an architectural vocabulary that eventually spread to all of Europe. The essence of this building is a simple, rational clarity, achieved through a new emphasis on symmetry, regularity, and human scale.

The main interior space is rectangular, with the altar placed in a niche opposite the entry. A Roman dome caps the central space. Dark stone pilasters and mouldings divide the walls and vaults into geometrically distinct zones that call attention to the spatial clarity. The unfinished porch is reminiscent of a Roman triumphal arch. Its balanced horizontal and vertical forms are certainly different from the soaring vertical thrusts of Gothic cathedrals.

The Pazzi Chapel completely breaks with Gothic tradition. Brunelleschi brought rational clarity and the relationship of human scale back to architecture.

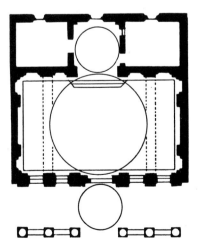

169 Filippo Brunelleschi
PAZZI CHAPEL. Florence, 1429–1430.

The symbolic use of the circle and the square goes back to prehistoric times. In the Renaissance the square symbolized the earth and the circle stood for the cosmos. Leonardo da Vinci's famous ILLUSTRATION OF THE PROPORTIONS OF THE HUMAN FIGURE (1485–1490) symbolizes the dual nature of man by showing how human proportions work with both of these geometric forms. From this drawing the geometry hidden within THE LAST SUPPER becomes apparent.

Vitruvius, a Roman architect of the first century B.C., provided a system of mathematical relationships for intelligibly representing the anatomical structure of the body. Following this system Leonardo drew a man circumscribed by both a circle and a square. "If you set your legs so far apart as to take a fourteenth part from your height," Leonardo wrote to explain his drawing, "and you open and raise your arms until you touch the line of the crown of the head with your middle fingers, you must know that the center of the circle formed by the extremities of the outstretched limbs will be the navel, and the space between the legs will form an equilateral triangle."[9] The human body can also be inscribed in a square, because "the span of a man's outstretched arms is equal to his height."[10] In this case the center moves from the navel to the sacrum at the base of the spine.

It is curious how one drawing can be a religious symbol, a scientific study, and a work of art.

The spirit of Renaissance humanism is revealed by comparing the Byzantine mosaic of Christ (see page 141) with Leonardo da Vinci's Christ in THE LAST SUPPER. The Byzantine Christ is far away in a dome; Leonardo's Christ is sitting across the table at eye level. The Byzantine mosaic is an abstract icon. Leonardo, however, wanted to paint a likeness of Christ in an earthly setting.

170 Leonardo da Vinci
ILLUSTRATION OF PROPORTIONS
OF THE HUMAN FIGURE.
c. 1485–1490. Pen and ink. 13½ x 9¾".

THE LAST SUPPER began to deteriorate soon after it was completed because Leonardo tried an oil-tempera medium that did not adhere permanently to the wall. We can only imagine its original visual quality.

Leonardo placed the Last Supper in an interior setting that reflects Renaissance architectural style. This setting supports the figures. The center of the composition is Christ. With His image, the natural world of everyday appearances becomes one with the supernatural world of divine harmony. The style of the work could be defined as representational on the surface, but as geometric abstraction within. In this way, the painting relates to classical Greek art, in which representational naturalism is organized according to rules of proportion, which are based on geometric harmonies.

Leonardo chose to depict a moment of great drama, just after Christ announces, "One among you will betray me." The apostles are deeply shaken by this remark, yet, in spite of their agitation, which earlier painters had not tried to depict, the overall feeling of the painting remains calm. The calm seems to emanate from the figure of Christ, but the background is largely responsible for this atmosphere. The interior space is based on a one-point linear perspective system, with the single vanishing point, infinity, exactly in the middle of the composition, behind the head of Christ. Leonardo placed Christ, not only in the center of the two-dimensional picture plane, but also in the center of the implied spatial depth. Christ's head is directly in front of the point of greatest spatial pull. Over Christ's head an architectural pediment suggests a halo, further setting Him off from the turbulent, overlapping shapes of the figures on either side.

The figures of the protesting apostles are organized in four groups of complex shapes. In his TREATISE ON PAINTING Leonardo wrote that the "figure is most praiseworthy which by its action best expresses the passions of the soul."[11] In contrast to the distraught figures surrounding Him, Christ is shown with arms outstretched in a gesture of submission that fits His statement, and makes His image appear as a stable, equilateral triangle.

171   Leonardo da Vinci. THE LAST SUPPER. c. 1495–1498. Fresco. 14′5″ x 28′¼″.

172   Leonardo da Vinci. DRAPERY STUDY. c. 1475. Black and white brush drawing on linen canvas. 26.6 x 23.4 cm.

A third work by Leonardo da Vinci points the way of things to come. Leonardo was a keen observer of the visual world. He suggested that students could sharpen their skill at representing the visible world by comparing their work with a mirror image.

When you want to see if your picture corresponds throughout with the objects you have drawn from nature, take a mirror and look in that at the reflection of the real things, and compare the reflected image with your picture, and consider whether the subject of the two images duly corresponds in both, particularly studying the mirror. . . . Thus, you see, a painting done on a flat surface displays objects which appear in relief, and the mirror — on its flat surface — does the same.[12]

Leonardo was one of the first to give a clear description of the *camera obscura* (dark room), an optical device that captures light images in much the same way as the human eye. This later developed into what we know today as the camera. It was a valuable tool for anyone trying to create representational images of the visual world. Leonardo described the principle:

Light entering a minute hole in the wall of a darkened room forms on the opposite wall an inverted image of whatever lies outside.[13]

The study of drapery shown here was done by Leonardo as a black and white value study, using the concept of chiaroscuro as he had developed it. The image represents the manner in which light has revealed the original subject. Leonardo drew what he saw with brush on canvas, rather than by projected light on film, as we might work today.

173   Sandro Botticelli. BIRTH OF VENUS. c. 1490. Oil on canvas. 5'8⅞" x 9'1⅞".

Except for the chapel by Brunelleschi, which comes from the early Renaissance, other Renaissance works are selected from the late fifteenth century. It was a time when leading artists were applying humanism to secular subject matter from their own and earlier traditions.

Botticelli painted the BIRTH OF VENUS, the Roman goddess of love, known to the Greeks as Aphrodite. According to one myth, the god Saturn fertilized the sea, and from its foam Venus was born. In this painting, she is gently blown to shore in a large shell, propelled by two zephyrs. A beautifully gowned symbol of an hour stands ready to wrap the goddess in a large, pink-flowered mantle.

By centering the figure, Botticelli placed her in a position of great importance, held for centuries by the Virgin Mary. Church patronage was still important, but many patrons, such as the Medicis and the Vespuccis, hired artists to sculpt and paint for their homes. The Medicis commissioned Botticelli to paint the BIRTH OF VENUS. These patrons were influential men of politics and commerce who were not interested solely in sacred subjects.

The viewer is more enchanted with the realness of Venus than by the myth about her. Botticelli understood anatomy, light, and polychromatic color. He also understood how to achieve great lyric beauty by keeping the background relatively flat and by distorting the figures to emphasize their grace. He utilized sharply drawn lines, which add life and movement to the painting. The vertically curved lines of Venus contrast markedly with the horizontal line of the horizon and the straight lines of the trees.

The artist expressed the Renaissance spirit in his humanistic treatment of "pagan" subject matter. The human body became the true subject, with fine attention to natural detail.

174b   Detail of DAVID

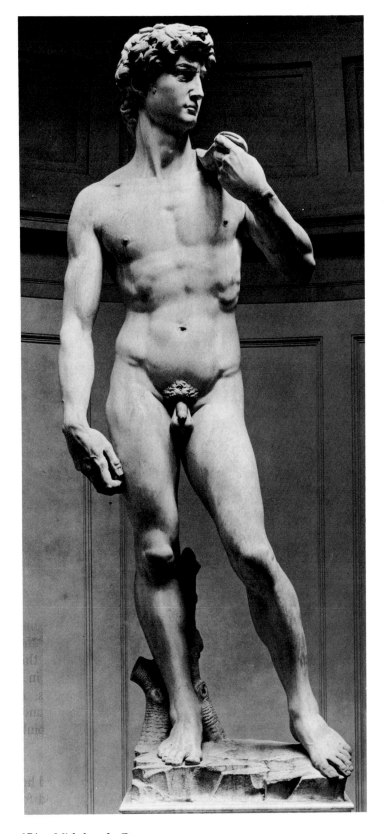

The Old Testament story of David and Goliath is more a myth or allegory than a sacred story. It has had strong appeal for centuries. Michelangelo carved the image of David from a single block of marble. The sculpture is about eighteen feet tall. We could expect these proportions for Goliath rather than David.

We identify with David. David represents man — man as he rediscovered himself in the Renaissance. Imagine looking up at this tremendous figure as you stand before it. Legend has it that when Michelangelo revealed the sculpture, the people of Florence were so pleased that they pulled it through the streets in a great procession that lasted for three days.

The influence of Greek sculpture is apparent, but this is not an idealized Greek figure. Up close, the face reveals an inner struggle, perhaps anxiety based on a new and painful self-awareness that followed close behind the new humanism. These feelings can be traced directly to the sculptor. How different this head is in feeling from Praxiteles' head of Hermes (see page 134).

174a   Michelangelo. DAVID.
1501–1504. Marble. Height 18'.

Michelangelo Merisi da Caravaggio tried to make his paintings as lifelike as possible. He brought to the stories of the Bible the vivid intensity that he experienced in his own life. He wanted his paintings to be accessible and self-explanatory to everyone. The clergy for whom he painted rejected his style. His dramatic realism was too much for people accustomed to aristocratic images demonstrating little more than insincere piety.

Caravaggio developed the use of illusionary light as an element capable of unifying and intensifying the subject. The illusion of strong light is characteristic of much of baroque art. It is no accident that Caravaggio chose to depict the conversion of Saint Paul: "And suddenly there shined round about him a light from heaven: and he fell to the earth."[14] Light from an unknown source creates a blinding flash, dramatizing the evangelist's enlightenment. The stabilizing inner geometry of Renaissance painting is replaced with a scene in which the major figure is foreshortened and pushed into the foreground, presenting such a close view that we feel we are there witnessing the event. Although the subject matter is sacred, the style is robust and reflects street life. The gestures and surfaces of the figures seem natural, in spite of the supernatural character of the event. Caravaggio gives a mystical feeling to ordinary things.

175 Michelangelo Merisi da Caravaggio
THE CONVERSION OF SAINT PAUL. 1600–1601.
Oil on canvas. 100⁹⁄₁₆ x 68¹⁵⁄₁₆".

Jan Vermeer, a Dutch seventeenth-century painter, had a great love for the way light reveals surfaces. Recent research shows that he used a table-model camera obscura in order to see this quality more accurately.

GIRL WITH A RED HAT is one of the painter's early works. It was painted on a small wooden panel about the same size as the frosted glass on which the image would appear in the camera obscura. Vermeer evidently taught himself to see with photographic accuracy by copying images from the ground glass. In GIRL WITH A RED HAT the focus has a narrow range. Only part of the girl's collar and the left edge of her cheek are in focus. Everything in front of and behind that narrow band becomes increasingly blurred. The carved lion's head on the arm of the chair in the foreground looks like shimmering light, just as it would appear in an out-of-focus photograph.

176 Jan Vermeer
GIRL WITH A RED HAT
c. 1660. Oil on wood. 9⅓ x 7⅛".

For Vermeer, the camera obscura was a point of departure, not a crutch. With it he was able to develop his perceptive powers and to give form to his excitement over optical reality as revealed by light. He did not stop at the imitation of surfaces. His own deep sense of design was behind each brush stroke. The personal sense of order that he gave to the composition of his subjects contributes to the lasting strength of his paintings.

The camera obscura shown in this drawing dates from the eighteenth century. It is a slightly more advanced model than the one Vermeer must have used.

The indirect camera viewpoint is an accepted way of seeing today. It is significant that two of Vermeer's earliest paintings, GIRL WITH A RED HAT and GIRL WITH A FLUTE, showing most clearly the influence of the camera obscura, remained unknown until this century. Earlier, their apparent camera effects would have disturbed most viewers. With normal direct perception, near objects do not seem so large and so near, nor distant objects

so small. Also unique are the way the camera frame slices off the subject and the intensity and accuracy with which Vermeer depicted light on colored and textured surfaces. These are qualities felt to be real and acceptable to modern eyes because of the conditioning of our perception by photography.

177 CAMERA OBSCURA. 1872.

Color plate 20
Vincent van Gogh
THE SOWER
1888. Oil on canvas.
17⅜ x 22⅛".

Color plate 21 Paul Gauguin. Two Nudes on a Tahitian Beach. 1892. Oil on canvas. 35¾ x 25½".

If form is thought of as the total of a work's perceivable characteristics, then the environment in which a given work was intended to be seen must be considered, since it modifies the form of the work. As a friend of mine once said, "It's not just the wine, it's the person you're with, the light in the room, and the music playing in the background."

Opera came into being during the seventeenth century. It was a major musical art form of the baroque period. In opera the arts combined in elaborate dramas. An operatic quality is found in much Catholic baroque art. As part of the Counterreformation the Catholic Church spent large sums of money for art, intended to give new appeal to sacred subjects. In the Cornaro Chapel in Santa

178 Giovanni Bernini. CORNARO CHAPEL. Santa Maria della Vittoria, Rome, 1647–1652.

Maria della Vittoria in Rome, Bernini gave us a monument of baroque art that has many of the qualities of opera. Architecture, painting, and sculpture work together to set off the drama of the central figures above the altar. Bernini designed the entire setting for his carving of THE ECSTASY OF SAINT TERESA, the altar, and the building housing the altar. This elaborate theatrical setting established a background underscoring the celestial qualities of Saint Teresa's dream. At close range the main figures become less than visionary (see page 49). Above the saint and her heavenly messenger, actual sunlight filters through a hidden window, illuminating the work in such a way that it appears to dematerialize the figures.

In box seats on either side of the altar, sculptured figures of the Cornaro family witness the event, making symbolic contact between sacred and secular experience. Bernini intentionally broke the lines usually drawn between architecture, painting, and sculpture, as well as between illusion and actuality.

The heavy, theatrical realism of baroque art gave way to the rococo style in France early in the eighteenth century. Rococo paintings are light and airy. Some of the movement, light, and gesture of the baroque style is still present, but the total effect is much different. The arts moved out of the marble halls of Versailles into the fashionable town houses. It was a period known as the Enlightenment or the Age of Reason. Reason was a mental faculty that could be developed by those who chose to do so. It did not mean cold intellectuality. Reason encompassed common sense, good judgment, the development of taste, and the ability to question freely. It was during this time that the fruits of rationalism — scientific knowledge and the ideals of freedom — became available to the people. The artistic creations of this period are highly irrational — an apparent contradiction — yet they express the new sense of freedom. Their forms were inspired by the curves found in nature.

In THE BATHERS by Fragonard we see one of the finest rococo paintings. There is not a straight line in the entire composition. There are no hints of horizontal or vertical axes that might tie things down a bit. Everything flows in a pastel world. Compositions during this period were often as visually loose as the subjects were morally loose. It was part of the endless game-playing that centered in the French court.

That was all changed by the revolution of 1789. Many wealthy art patrons were beheaded, France's economy was upset, and tastes changed radically. One of the men who led the way to revolution was the painter Jacques-Louis David. When he painted his OATH OF HORATII David was intentionally

179 Jean-Honoré Fragonard
THE BATHERS
c. 1765. Oil on canvas. 25¼ x 31½".

classical in approach. He employed a rational, controlled style, and a subject which called a halt to what he saw as the frivolous nonsense of the rococo. He was a moralist.

The subject matter is a story of virtue and a readiness to die for liberty, in which the sons pledge to take the swords offered by their father to avenge the enemies of Rome. The heroic sense of duty to defend the homeland had great appeal to the French people. This painting acquired political meaning and was one of many factors that helped to precipitate the French Revolution.

David's classical style created an atmosphere of austerity in the painting. The lines are severe and angular, giving an impression of austerity. The three arches set on columns give strength to the composition and provide a proper setting for the Roman figures. The two center columns separate the three major parts of the subject. The stable verticals and horizontals are aligned with the edges of the picture plane. Dramatic use of light sharply emphasizes the figures against the deeply shadowed areas behind the arches.

Following the revolution, David was politically powerful enough to close the Royal Academy. However, through David's influence, his friend Fragonard was named a member of the Museum Commission. This appointment made it possible for Fragonard to preserve many works of rococo art.

180   Jacques-Louis David
OATH OF THE HORATII
1784. Oil on canvas. 10'10" x 14'.

Many of the freedoms won by the French Revolution were soon lost, either to dictators or counterrevolutionaries. The great Spanish painter Francisco Goya was a contemporary of David's. He was well aware of the revolution, and personally experienced some of its aftermath.

At first glance Goya's early work seems to follow the accepted rococo manner, in which warmth and optimism dominate. On closer inspection we discovered that Goya subtly revealed sinister stupidity lurking behind the façade of frivolity. In 1792 a serious illness

left Goya totally deaf. From that point on his work took on greater intensity.

From his youth Goya felt strongly about the liberal ideas of the Enlightenment. Throughout the later part of his life he was able to give form to these feelings, even though he held the position of painter to the degenerate Spanish royal family.

Because his sympathies were with the French Revolution, Goya welcomed Napoleon's invading army. He soon discovered that this army of occupation was destroying rather

181   Francisco Goya. THE THIRD OF MAY 1808. 1814. Oil on canvas. 8′9″ x 13′4″.

than defending the ideals he had associated with the revolution. Madrid was occupied by Napoleon's troops in 1808. On May 2, a riot occurred against the French in the Puerto del Sol. Officers fired from a nearby hill and the cavalry was ordered to cut down the crowds. The following night a firing squad was set up to shoot anyone who appeared in the streets. These events marked the beginning of a sequence of brutalities that were to be vividly and bitterly expressed by Goya in his powerful indictment of organized murder, THE THIRD OF MAY 1808, painted in February 1814.

The painting is large — eight feet, nine inches by thirteen feet, four inches — and yet it is so well conceived in every detail that it delivers its meaning in a single, visual flash. Throughout the long hours necessary to complete such a large work, Goya maintained the intensity of his original feelings. The essence of the scene is organized and given impact by bold patterns of light and dark. A wedge of middle value is formed by the edge of the hill and the edge of the lighted area on the ground. This wedge takes

our glance immediately to the soldiers. From their dark shapes we are led by the light and the lines of the rifle barrels to the man in white. The entire picture is focused on this man in the white shirt. As more people are forced into the light for execution, he raises his arms in a final gesture of defiance. The irregular shape of his shirt is illuminated by the hard, white cube of the soldier's lantern. Cold regularity marks the faceless firing squad, in contrast with the ragged group forming the target. Goya clearly showed what Kenneth Clark called "the predetermined brutality of men in uniform."[15]

Goya was appalled at the massacre. Although it is not known whether he saw this particular incident, he did see many similar brutalities. His visual sensitivity, magnified by deafness, made war experience all the more vivid, enabling him to give it lasting form. THE THIRD OF MAY 1808 is neither an heroic reconstruction of history, nor a glorified press photograph. It is history — clarified, intensified, and given lasting life through art.

THE THIRD OF MAY 1808 is a picture of a real event that has become universal in its significance. This universality becomes all the more apparent when Goya's work is compared to Paul Revere's record of the Boston Massacre. The subject of both pictures is the same, but what a difference! The engraving has historical interest to Americans because it was done by a famous patriot, and because of the symbolic significance of the event. The direct nature of its naive drawing adds quaintness to the scene. But Revere's work has little of the lasting impact of the Goya. Actually, Revere was an engraver. In the interest of delivering an important news picture to the public, he copied this design from an engraving of the same incident by Henry Pelham.

182 Paul Revere after Henry Pelham
THE BLOODY MASSACRE
1770. Metal engraving. 9⅞ x 8¾".

183   Louis Jacques Mandé Daguerre
LE BOULEVARD DU TEMPLE
Paris, 1839. Daguerreotype.

Photography emerged as a medium in its own right during the third decade of the nineteenth century. In 1826, Joseph Nicephore Niepce applied discoveries about light-sensitive compounds when he captured and held an image made with light on a sheet of pewter, thus producing the first photograph. Later he joined Louis Jacques Mandé Daguerre, a scenery designer, who perfected the system for fixing a light-created image on a flat surface. The images produced by Daguerre's photographic process came to be known as daguerreotypes or tintypes. Daguerre's camera, however, was only a slight improvement over the camera obscura, which projected light images but could not hold them.

At first, the technique could only be used to catch images of stationary objects. Exposure time went from about eight hours, at first, down to about half an hour. When Daguerre recorded this view of Paris in 1839, the streets appear deserted because only stationary objects made lasting light impressions on the plate. However, this is one of the first photographs of a human being; one man stayed still long enough to become part of the image. He was having his shoes shined. You can see him at the street corner in the lower left section of the photograph.

Now images of actual things could be recorded without the skillful hand of a painter. It was a great moment in history. Some artists felt that the new medium was a form of unfair competition that spelled the death of art. Certainly it was the beginning of a time when art again became accessible to all.

The French romantic painter Eugène Delacroix was one of the first to recognize the difference between camera vision and human vision. He understood the unique advantages of both. For him the camera and the photographic process developed by Daguerre were of great benefit to art and artists: ". . . let a man of genius make use of the daguerreotype as it is to be used, and he will raise himself to a height that we do not know."[16]

Delacroix drew and painted from daguerreotypes and paper prints. He would set up a painter's composition with a model, and then

184   Eugène Delacroix
PHOTOGRAPH FROM ALBUM. 1855.

with the help of the photographer Durieu, make a photograph. In an essay for students, he wrote:

A daguerreotype is a mirror of the object, certain details almost always overlooked in drawing from nature take on in it characteristic importance, and thus introduce the artist to complete knowledge of construction as light and shade are found in their true character.[17]

Thus, a photograph rather than a drawing became the basis for a painting.

Toward most inventions of his day, such as the steamboat, Delacroix felt man was driven by the devil. He expressed himself strongly and with a good deal of insight:

Here is another American invention that will let people go faster, always faster. When they have got travelers comfortably lodged in a cannon, so that the cannon can make them travel as fast as bullets . . . civilization will doubtless have taken a long step. . . . it will have conquered space but not boredom.[18]

185   Eugène Delacroix. ODALISQUE.
1857. Oil on canvas.

186 MERCHANTS' EXCHANGE. Philadelphia, 1832–1834.

From the sixteenth to the eighteenth centuries, many architects did little more than
adapt and rearrange ideas from earlier traditions. This practice is called eclecticism. By
the nineteenth century, historical styles had
been carefully catalogued so that the architect could borrow freely from one or all. In
church design the Byzantine, Romanesque,
or Gothic styles dominated. For public buildings, Renaissance, Greek, and Roman designs were preferred, and often mixed. This
approach lasted well into the twentieth
century.

187 SAINT CLOTILDE. Paris, 1846–1857.

The three buildings shown here were constructed between 1830 and 1860. Each one demonstrates the architect's excellent feeling for form already perfected. Greek, Romanesque, and Gothic styles are represented. The façade of the Merchants' Exchange is of Greek origin. The portico bears a striking resemblance to the east side of the Parthenon (see page 133). The entire structure of Saint Clotilde follows a basic Gothic plan similar to Chartres (see page 143). The church at Potsdam is built in the Romanesque style. The building is heavy and Roman arches allow only small openings for light. For another example, see the lower portion of the west front at Chartres (page 142).

In September 1850, construction began on Joseph Paxton's Crystal Palace, a large exposition hall designed for the Great Exhibition of the Works of Industry of All Nations. There is no eclecticism in this building. The Industrial Age had produced new methods, materials, machines, and designs, which Paxton used to advantage. The light, decorative quality of the glass and iron combination is created, not by applied ornamentation, but by the modular structure.

By getting back to structure and function, the success of Paxton's Crystal Palace helped clear the way for the creation of new architectural forms that would be relevant rather than eclectic. Paxton's innovations provided the background for the concept "form follows function," formulated by architect Louis H. Sullivan.[19] This became the basic architectural philosophy of the twentieth century.

188   FRIEDENSKIRCHE. Potsdam, 1845–1848.

189   Sir Joseph Paxton. CRYSTAL PALACE. Interior view. 1850–1851. Cast iron and glass. Width 408′, length 1,851′.

In 1854, Henry David Thoreau wrote WALDEN, in which he recorded the following thoughts:

What of architectural beauty I now see, I know has gradually grown from within outward, out of the necessities and character of the indweller, who is the only builder — out of some unconscious truthfulness and nobleness, without ever a thought for the appearance; and whatever additional beauty of this kind is destined to be produced will be preceded by a like unconscious beauty of life. The most interesting dwellings in this country, as the painter knows, are the most unpretending, humble log huts and cottages of the poor commonly; it is the life of the inhabitants whose shells they are, and not any peculiarity in their surfaces merely, which makes them *picturesque*; and equally interesting will be the citizen's suburban box, when his life shall be as simple and as agreeable to the imagination, and there is as little straining after effect in the style of his dwelling. A great proportion of architectural ornaments are literally hollow, and a September gale would strip them off, like borrowed plumes, without injury to the substantials.[20]

These words of advice from artist-teacher Thomas Couture summarize the prevailing attitude in academic circles during most of the nineteenth century:

Remember . . . one must always think of antiquity. Nature, my friend, is good as a tool for study, but it is of no interest. Style, you see, is the thing that matters.[21]

190   Thomas Couture. ROMANS OF THE DECADENCE. 1847. Oil on canvas. 15'1" x 25'4".

Couture's huge painting, called ROMANS OF THE DECADENCE, is of a romantic subject in a neoclassical setting, and so brings into one work the dominant conflicting styles of nineteenth-century French academic art. Academic art follows formulas laid down by an academy or school. In this case the academy was the officially recognized l'Ecole des Beaux Arts (the School of Fine Arts), that held power over what was considered acceptable art in France during most of the nineteenth century.

This painting represents the dying gasp of concepts that had been worked and reworked since the Renaissance. Couture was a great success in the salons because he fed the sexual needs produced by Victorian society. The canvas is about twenty-five feet long. As Victorian people looked at the giant painting, they could enjoy it fully because it was clearly a moralizing picture. The disapproving looks by the statues above the orgy provide stand-ins for the public.

Even photography, that medium so suited to staying in touch with reality, was pulled into service in the academic manner. With exceeding care, O. G. Rejlander combined negatives to achieve THE TWO PATHS OF LIFE. The moral content is blatantly apparent: Which path does one choose?

Rejlander entered the print in the Manchester Art Treasures Exhibition of 1857. It measured sixteen by thirty-one inches. Queen Victoria, who was an amateur photographer, purchased the work.[22]

Painters whom we now consider the key masters of nineteenth-century art were frequently outsiders — set apart from the acceptable art circles of the day. Men like Goya, and later Daumier, Courbet, Manet, Monet, Gauguin, and van Gogh gave birth to the idea of the artist as an isolated figure, starving in a garret studio.

191   O. G. Rejlander. THE TWO PATHS OF LIFE. 1857. Photograph. 16 x 31".

192   Jean-François Millet
THE GLEANERS
c. 1857. Oil on canvas. 32⅞ x 43¾".

Jean-François Millet was also an outsider, until shortly before he died. He rejected the decadent art of the city academies, choosing instead to depict the humble, hard-working country peasants that he knew as a child. He painted them with a gentle, romantic touch. THE GLEANERS shows three country women doing the backbreaking work of picking up precious bits of grain left over after the major harvest has been completed. Millet idealizes this activity. We are not made aware of the painful struggle for survival, but of the timeless rhythm of basic work.

At about the same time, Gustave Courbet painted his own life-sized version of humble workers, entitled THE STONE BREAKERS (now destroyed). Courbet rejected even more than Millet the past romantic and neoclassical formulas. We are asked to look directly at these figures as he has done. Courbet neither idealized the work of breaking stones nor dramatized the struggle for existence. He simply said, "Look at this." The style is stark realism.

Realism describes a visual style that focuses on representing an equivalent of the retinal image. This approach was used before the nineteenth century, notably in Roman, Flemish, and Dutch painting. However, in the 1850s Courbet reinstated this idea with new vigor by employing a direct technique and objective vision to represent images of contemporary life. By doing this, he broke with the artificial grandeur and exoticism of the popular and academically acceptable styles of his day and paved the way for a new way of seeing. Manet fused this realism with his own concepts and, in turn, sparked the enthusiasm for everyday reality so basic to impressionism. In America, Eakins (see page 37) developed his own powerful realism based on Manet, Courbet, and Veláz-quez (see page 32). As we have noted, photography made its own contribution to this reawakening of direct vision.

193   Gustave Courbet. The Stone Breakers. 1849. Oil on canvas. 5'5" x 7'10".

Portable, slow-drying oil colors became available in 1841 when Windsor and Newton first introduced the collapsible tin tube. This technical breakthrough made it possible for artists to paint outdoors without preliminary drawings or preconceived plans. Courbet was one of the first to work directly from nature, rather than from memory or sketches. This shift in practice opened up a whole new way of seeing. The artist was able to capture in full color his first clear impression without intervening processes to dull his vision.

By rejecting previous visual preconceptions, Courbet was able to look directly at the physical reality of the immediate everyday world. His subject fits his visual realism and his enjoyment in painting textures. His figures are neither historical nor allegorical; they are neither religious nor heroic. They are contemporary, but not even newsworthy. Strong feeling would only detract from the immediacy of the painting. When this work was hung in 1850 in Paris, it was attacked as unartistic, crude, and socialistic. For later expositions, Courbet set up his own exhibits, which laid the groundwork for independent, individually organized shows.

Of his own work Courbet said, "To know in order to create, that was my idea. To be able to represent the customs, the ideas, the appearance of my own era . . . to create living art; that is my aim."[23]

The revolution that occurred in painting in
the 1860s and 1870s has sometimes been
referred to as the Manet Revolution.
Edouard Manet was a student of Couture.
Compare Couture's Romans of the Decadence with Manet's Gare Saint-Lazare. It
is difficult to believe that the paintings were
done at about the same time. One asks us to
look backward, the other, forward. The difference between these works says more visually than could possibly be put into words.

194   Edouard Manet
Gare Saint-Lazare
1873. Oil on canvas. 36¾ x 45⅛".

Couture helped Manet to develop his skill in representing the visible world. But Manet rejected most of what his teacher stood for. Manet's study of the refined, flat shapes of Japanese prints helped him to develop paintings based on a new awareness of the picture plane. See page 280. In GARE SAINT-LAZARE the iron bars of the fence provide a vertical grid that keeps us near the painting's surface. Behind the black lines a cloud of white steam appears, acting as a light area that strongly contrasts with the bars, thus pushing forward against the girl looking back. The visual tension of this spatial sandwich is balanced by the figure of the mother, who looks directly at the viewer.

Manet minimized chiaroscuro and illusionary space, and maximized the visual power of value and shape. His direct brush work reflects Courbet's influence. In addition, Courbet's controversial subject matter, his mixture of reality, allegory, social comment, and portraiture, and his independent thinking, provided the encouragement that Manet needed to paint contemporary, commonplace events. It is difficult for us today to understand how shocked the viewers and critics were. Art was reserved for so-called uplifting subjects, not the contemporary, which was considered vulgar, ugly, improper, and even depressing. Émile Zola, novelist and art critic, tried to understand Manet's work and pleaded for fair judgment. In a series of newspaper articles, he wrote,

Our fathers laughed at M. Courbet and now we go into raptures over him. We laugh at M. Manet, and our sons will go into raptures over his canvases. . . . A place is waiting for M. Manet at the Louvre.[24]

If Courbet painted the present, Manet painted *in* the present.

Manet was an independent, who, by his interest in light, everyday visual experience, and the fresh use of visual form, led the way into impressionism. He was intimate friends with the young painters who composed the im-

pressionist group: Monet, Renoir, Degas, Pissaro, Sisley, Morisot, and Cézanne. These artists, in turn, all went their own ways. Late in his career, Manet was himself influenced by the younger impressionists.

Effects of light on color, atmosphere, and time of day were of primary interest to Claude Monet when he painted IMPRESSION: SUNRISE in 1872. Solid forms and strong value contrast disappeared from Monet's work as he captured the momentary experience of light in nature. Other painters, working in a similar way, joined him for an independent showing of thirty works, held in 1874. The public and the critics displayed mixed emotions. One art critic derisively called them "impressionists," due to the title of Monet's painting. Today we often refer to these painters as "old masters."

195 Claude Monet
IMPRESSION: SUNRISE
1872. Oil on canvas. 19½ x 25½".
See color plate 18

Monet was the leader of the impressionists. They called themselves "illuminists," and thought that anything could be beautiful if properly lighted. The group and its style were strongest between 1870 and 1880. After 1880 it was Monet who continued for more than thirty years to be true to impressionism's original ideals. Instead of painting from sketches, he painted out of doors. In order to capture the momentary visual experience, Monet would set up his easel so that the subject could be painted in a variety of atmospheric light conditions. Since he painted with touches of pure colors, an intensity was created that allowed the viewer, from a distance, to experience "optical mixing." From about 1890 until his death in 1926, Monet painted the waterlilies in the watergarden that he had built around his country home in Giverny, France. The lilies provided him with a neutral, ever-changing subject. It is not the waterlilies or the reflections in the water that make these paintings great. It is Monet. He used his observation of the reflective light and color on the surface of the pond as a basis for paintings of lyrical richness.

These paintings led to the large nonrepresentational paintings of the abstract expressionists in the mid-twentieth century, who created form that was built up with vigorous brush strokes and free applications of color.

196   Claude Monet
WATER-LILIES, GIVERNY
1906. Oil on canvas. 34¼ x 36¾".

When Auguste Renoir painted LE MOULIN DE LA GALETTE in the summer of 1876, the impressionists were at the peak of their activity. Renoir summarized impressionism in this painting. Renoir and a friend carried the canvas from Renoir's studio to an outdoor café, where he worked on the large canvas directly from the subject, a Sunday afternoon dance. The young men and women shown in the painting are conversing, sipping wine, dancing, and otherwise enjoying themselves at the open-air cabaret. The subject, the composition, and the technique are joined in a single moment in time. The people he painted are savoring the fleeting delights of the moment. The painting is a lasting conception of the good life, encouraging us today to live fully in the present.

197   Auguste Renoir
LE MOULIN DE LA GALETTE
1876. Oil on canvas. 51½ x 69". See color plate 19.

Color plate 22
Georges Seurat
SUNDAY AFTERNOON
ON THE ISLAND OF LA
GRANDE JATTE.
1884–1886.
Oil on canvas.
81 x 120⅜″.

Color plate 23
Paul Cézanne
MONT SAINTE-
VICTOIRE.
1904–1906.
Oil on canvas.
25⅝ x 31⅞″.

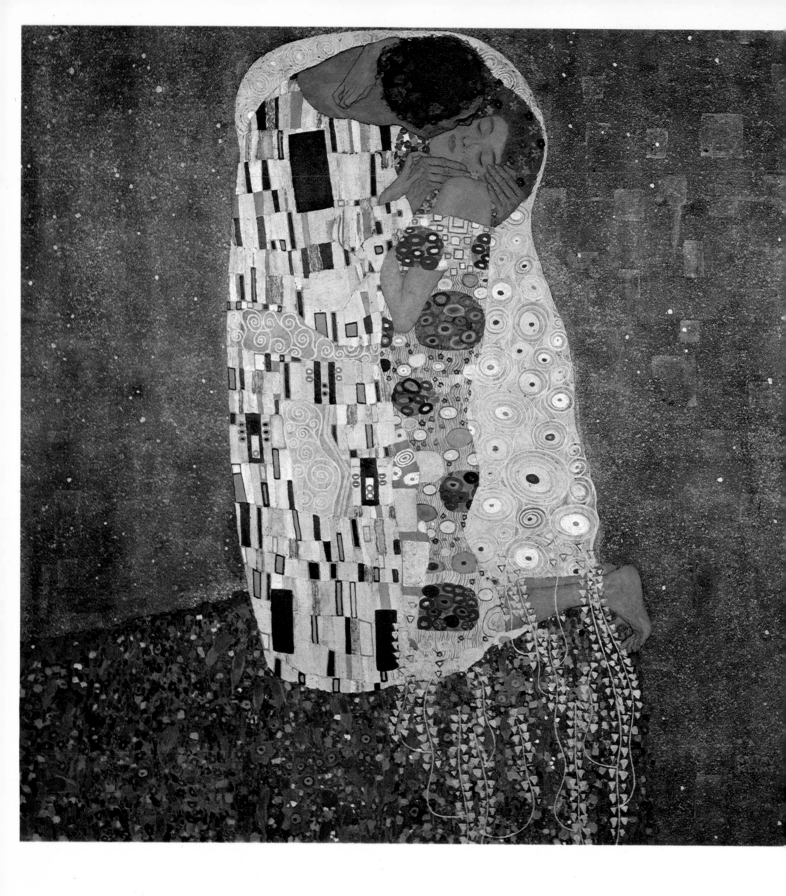

Color plate 24   Gustav Klimt. THE KISS. 1908. Oil on canvas. 71 x 71".

Edgar Degas was a member of the impressionist group in Paris, but he saw things in his own way and remained on the fringe of impressionism. He went further than the other impressionists in his presentation of the fleeting world. He used a camera as a studio tool and was much intrigued by the way in which the camera fragmented the things seen in actual, continuous space. In PLACE DE LA CONCORDE he painted a group portrait, but it is certainly more than a portrait. These people are not posed in any acceptable manner. We have happened to see them by chance along the street. Degas based his composition on the accidental quality of normal visual experience. He chose to paint marginal events, as though the meaning of any main event is expressed by the people on the sidelines and by the surrounding empty spaces.

The implied lines set up by the directions in which the dog, the girls, and the man are looking act as axes of force in the composition. Everyone is looking in a different direction! At the far left a man appears, cut off by the top and side edges of the picture plane, giving the impression of a candid photograph. If we study the composition carefully, we realize that the center of interest is in the empty area just in front of the dark doorway in the distant wall. The quality of Degas' vision and his sense of meaning in interrelationships help us to see the revealing impact of certain common visual occurrences that are usually ignored.

198 Edgar Degas
PLACE DE LA CONCORDE. c. 1873. Oil on canvas. 31¾ x 47⅜".

Painters like Manet, Monet, Renoir, and Degas were interested in seeing directly the spontaneous life happening around them. They rejected the artificial poses and tonal color prescribed by the academy. Because they rebelled, they made few sales in their early years. Critics blasted their work with degrading remarks. Today, they are the ones whose works give us lasting pleasure. The successful painters of the academic school are forgotten. Are the critics of today's art missing what is meaningful?

In America, the accomplished painter Thomas Eakins worked in collaboration with the action photographer Eadweard Muybridge to make studies of nude athletes in motion. Eakins designed a camera with revolving discs to produce stop-action stills, anticipating the principle of the motion-picture camera.

Eakins was a realist. His paintings showed that he looked at things with feeling, tempered by objectivity (see page 37), as did Courbet. His photograph of a man making a running jump is more interesting historically than as a work of art, yet it acts as a key step towards cinematic vision in which motion becomes a major element.

200   Eadweard Muybridge
GALLOPING HORSE
1878. *See illustration 354.*

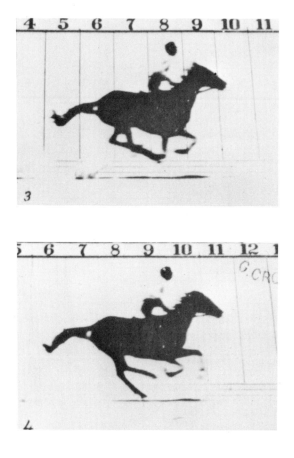

199   Thomas Eakins. NUDE ATHLETE IN MOTION. 1884–1885.

Eadweard Muybridge was the first photographer to make elaborate studies of animals and people in motion. His stop-action stills of a galloping horse made it possible to see how a horse actually moves. Muybridge's photographs proved that a horse's feet leave the ground in a rolling sequence rather than in pairs. A comparison between the photograph by Muybridge and a painting of racing horses by Géricault makes clear one of the many ways in which photography has given us new ways of seeing. Géricault had a great knowledge of horses and of painting, but he could not see how horses really moved. The photographic process had not been invented when he painted HORSE-RACING AT EPSOM.

201   Théodore Géricault. HORSE-RACING AT EPSOM. c. 1819. Oil on canvas. 34⅝ x 47¼".

Postimpressionism refers to the composite of styles that followed impressionism between 1880 and the turn of the century. Painters who had tried impressionism early in their careers came to feel that solidity of form and composition had been sacrificed for the sake of light and color. They sought a new balance. Postimpressionism is a confusing term because it refers to a complex of reactions about impressionism, rather than a single style. There were two dominant tendencies during the period, expressionism and formalism. An understanding of these tendencies can help us to understand the major personal styles of the time.

Four men stand out in retrospect: Gauguin, van Gogh, Seurat, and Cézanne. The main reason they stand out now is that they had a greater influence on what was to follow than other artists, who perhaps were equally creative. Gauguin and van Gogh brought emotional intensity and spontaneity to their work. They used bold color contrasts, shapes with abruptly changing contours, and, in van Gogh's case, swirling brush strokes. Gauguin often outlined areas of modulated color. Van Gogh distorted natural forms to add expressive power. They were the romantics, the expressionists.

Seurat and Cézanne were more interested in structure and rational clarity. They were the classicists or formalists. Both organized visual form in order to achieve a new formal clarity. They brought together the reality of nature with the reality of the picture plane.

Since all art is ordered in some way and all art is expressive, these distinctions are relative. They indicate preferences underlying the *personal* styles of these men.

The difference between the basic attitudes represented in impressionism and expressionism becomes clear when Monet's impression of sunflowers is compared with van Gogh's. In relative terms, Monet records the visual effect of the subject, concentrating more on what he sees than on what he feels. Van Gogh paints what he *feels* about what he has seen. This revealing of a personal emotional response formed the basis of expressionism.

202   Claude Monet
SUNFLOWERS
1888. Oil on canvas. 39¾ x 32".

203   Vincent van Gogh
SUNFLOWERS
1888. Oil on canvas. 37⅜ x 28¾".

We have already mentioned the influence of Japanese prints on European and American painting in the late nineteenth century.

Van Gogh shows us how and what he learned from the Japanese artist Hiroshige. His copy of Plum Trees in Blossom is quite accurate. In his painting of The Sower, van Gogh demonstrates his newly acquired sense of bold, simple shapes and flat color areas. The wide band of a tree trunk cuts diagonally across the composition as a major shape, its strength balancing the sun and its energy coming toward us with the movement of the sower.

It is not necessary for an artist to work with a conscious knowledge of all the visual elements and how they interact. These interactions can be intellectually formulated most thoroughly after the creative work is completed. A strong desire to share personal experience motivated van Gogh. After tremendous struggle with materials and techniques, he finally reached the point at which he was able to put his intensity on paper and canvas. "The artist does not draw what he sees but what he must make others see. Only when he no longer knows what he is doing does the painter do good things."[25]

204   Vincent van Gogh
The Sower
1888. Oil on canvas. 17⅜ x 22⅛". See color plate 20.

205   Vincent van Gogh after Hiroshige
Plum Trees in Blossom
1888. Oil on canvas. 55 x 46 cm.

The forefathers of twentieth-century expressionism were Toulouse-Lautrec, van Gogh, and Gauguin, followed by Munch. Van Gogh and Gauguin learned the methods of impressionism. They learned about color and about the vitality of broken brushwork. Soon, both men were using color with excitement, not to record soft impressions of light, but to employ color as a means of emotional expression.

Comments by both artists reveal their attitudes toward visual form. From van Gogh:

206 Paul Gauguin
Two Nudes on a Tahitian Beach
1892. Oil on canvas. 35¾ x 25½". See color plate 21.

Instead of trying to reproduce exactly what I have before my eyes, I use color more arbitrarily so as to express myself forcibly . . . I am always in hope of making a discovery there to express the love of two lovers by a marriage of two complementary colors, their mingling and their opposition, the mysterious vibrations of kindred tones. To express the thought of a brow by the radiance of a light tone against a sombre background.[26]

And Gauguin:

A word of advice: don't paint too much direct from nature. Art is an abstraction! Study nature, then brood on it and think more of the creation which will result, which is the only way to ascend towards God — to create like our Divine Master.[27]

In painting one must search rather for suggestion than for description, as is done in music.[28] [T]hink of the highly important musical role which colour will henceforth play in modern painting.[29]

Speaking of colors:

They are intended absolutely! They are necessary and everything in my work is calculated, premeditated. It is music, if you like! I obtain by an arrangement of lines and colours, with the pretext of some sort of subject taken from life or from nature, symphonies, harmonies which represent nothing absolutely real in the vulgar sense of the word, which express directly no idea, but which provoke thoughts, without the help of ideas or images, simply through the mysterious relationships which exist between our brains and these arrangements of lines and colours.[30]

Gauguin's painting, Two Nudes on a Tahitian Beach, has a shallow spatial feeling, in spite of the fact that the subject suggests a background of infinite space. Like van Gogh, Gauguin was interested in what happened across the picture surface. Implied deep space could only detract from his design. Also like van Gogh, he made the color quite vivid, only suggesting the actual color of the subject. The subject, as he said, was only a pretext for symphonies of line and color.

Seurat's large painting SUNDAY AFTERNOON ON THE ISLAND OF LA GRANDE JATTE has the subject matter, the broken brushwork, and the light and color qualities of impressionism. But this painting is not of a fleeting glimpse; it is a structural design worked out with great precision. Seurat set out to systematize the broken color of impressionism and to create a more rigid organization with clearly edged, simplified forms. A large number of drawn, photographed, and painted studies of the subject preceded the final work. With them, Seurat studied carefully the horizontal and vertical relationships, the character of each shape, the pattern of light and shade, and the color. His system of painting is called "pointillism."

With pointillism Seurat tried to develop and apply a scientific painting method that would make the intuitive approach obsolete. He developed his method by studying the principles of color optics being discovered at the time. He applied his paint in tiny dots of pure color to achieve optical mixture. This method had a direct influence on modern color printing, in which tiny yellow, red (magenta), blue (cyan), and black dots give the appearance of full color. Seurat's friend, Paul Signac, defined it as a "method of securing the utmost luminosity, color and harmony by the use of all the colors of the spectrum and all degrees of those colors without any mixing."[31] Seurat considered the science of his system to be responsible for his achievement: "They see poetry in what I have done. No, I apply my method, and that is all there is to it."[32]

The final painting shows the total control that Seurat sought through the application of his method. The frozen formality of the figures seems surprising, considering the casual nature of the subject matter. Can you imagine how Renoir would have handled this? But it is precisely its calm, formal grandeur that gives the painting its lasting appeal.

207 Georges Seurat. SUNDAY AFTERNOON ON THE ISLAND OF LA GRANDE JATTE. 1884–1886. Oil on canvas. 81 x 120⅜". *See color plate 22.*

Of the many great painters working in France during the last twenty years of the nineteenth century, it is said that Cézanne had the most lasting effect on the course of painting. Because of this he is referred to as the "Father of Modern Art."·

Cézanne, like Seurat, was more interested in the structural or formal aspects of painting than in its ability to render emotions. He shared the impressionists' practice of working directly from nature. But in his later work he wished to achieve a lasting formal image. "My aim," he said, "was to make Impressionism into something solid and enduring like the art of the museums."[33] He worked for a new synthesis between nature and a thorough study of past masterworks, particularly the paintings by Poussin. As Cézanne said, "I want to do Poussin over again from nature."[34]

208 Nicholas Poussin
SAINT JOHN ON PATMOS
1645–1650. Oil on canvas. 40 x 52½".

209 Paul Cézanne
MONT SAINTE-VICTOIRE
1904–1906. Oil on canvas. 25⅝ x 31⅞".
See color plate 23

Although Seurat and Cézanne were strong individuals, each following his own course, they shared the desire to make something lasting out of the discoveries of the effects of light and color. They based their work on direct observation of nature and they both used visibly separate strokes of color to build their richly woven surfaces of paint. Seurat's highly demanding method was not popular among younger artists. Cézanne's open strokes, however, were part of a fluid system of form-building that offers a whole range of possibilities to those who study his work.

Cézanne achieved a method of designing the picture's space by carefully developing exactly the right relationships between separate strokes of color. His approach gave a new life to the surfaces of his own paintings and to innumerable painted surfaces by other artists since that time.

Subject matter acted mainly as a point of departure for Seurat and Cézanne. This is not true of the work of Jacob Riis. While many of the great impressionist and post-impressionist painters of Europe were concentrating on the golden glow of casual human life, Riis armed himself with a camera in order to record the misery of a world no one really wanted to look at. For Riis, art was a way of calling attention to and thereby helping to change conditions of suffering that appalled him. In holding this attitude he was unique among the prominent photographers of the day, who sought merely to imitate the artistic effects of painters. Riis realized that the photographic medium would enable him to produce strong images of the actual living environment of New York's slum dwellers.

Like other painters at that time, Degas was strongly influenced by the asymmetrical compositions of Japanese prints and by photography, with its fragmented and candid poses (see page 169). Riis used the camera as a weapon of protest, whereas Degas used it as an aid in seeing contemporary life, including the sad, desperate side.

His painting, THE GLASS OF ABSINTHE, of 1876, shows the influence of photography. It was painted the same year that Renoir painted LE MOULIN DE LA GALETTE. Renoir gave us a happy crowd soaking up the sensual delights of the passing moment. Degas gave us two people experiencing a dead end. Absinthe is part wormwood, gall, and opium. It vegetablizes one's brain.

Degas had a broad range of subject matter. Often, as here, he was able to turn his great ability to the task of defining human character and mood in a given situation. In THE GLASS OF ABSINTHE he emphasized the bored apathy of the couple through his superb sense of composition. We enter the picture by way of the table tops, focus on the man gazing off to the right, then center on the woman staring blankly downward. The zigzag pat-

210 Jacob Riis
BANDIT'S ROOST. c. 1888.

tern of eye motion creates an unusual asymmetrical tension.

Toulouse-Lautrec went far into the underworld of Parisian night life, recording his keen sense of human character. His quick, long strokes of color define a world of corrupt gaiety that reveals deep human drama. The impressionists objectively painted the pleasant, uncomplicated life in sunlit exterior spaces. Toulouse-Lautrec found inspiration in the smoke-filled, gaslit interiors of Parisian night clubs. He employed the visual elements, particularly shape and line, in ways that heighten our feelings about the subject.

211 Edgar Degas
THE GLASS OF ABSINTHE
1876. Oil on canvas. 36 x 27".

212 Henri de Toulouse-Lautrec
AT THE MOULIN ROUGE
1892. Oil on canvas. 48⅜ x 55¼".

Edward Munch, a Norwegian, traveled to Paris to study and view the works of his contemporaries, especially Gauguin, van Gogh, and Toulouse-Lautrec. What he learned from them, particularly from Gauguin, enabled him to carry expressionism to an even greater level of intensity.

His great work, THE SHRIEK, was completed in two versions — as a painting and as a lithograph. It is difficult to imagine a more powerful image of anxiety. The major human figure could be anyone caught in complete isolation, fear, and loneliness. Despair reverberates throughout the picture, carried by continuous linear rhythms.

Auguste Rodin was one of the most important sculptors of the late nineteenth century. Rodin's work is part of a long tradition of sculpture based on the nude human figure. This tradition reached a high point in Greece in the classical period (fifth century B.C.) and in Italy during the Renaissance (fifteenth century), and was revitalized by Rodin.

Conceive form in depth.
Clearly indicate the dominant planes.
Imagine forms as directed towards you;
    all life surges from a center,
      expands from within outwards.
In drawing, observe relief, not outline.
    The relief determines the contour.
The main thing is to be moved, to love,
    to hope, to tremble, to live.
    Be a man before being an artist!

                          Auguste Rodin[35]

Two of his best known works are THE THINKER and THE KISS. In THE KISS, two life-sized human figures embrace. They represent ideals of masculine and feminine form. Their implied physical softness is accentuated by the roughness of the uncarved marble on which they sit.

By giving form to a concept of ideal love, Rodin was in tune with the romantic idealism found in most popular art of his time.

213 Edvard Munch
THE SHRIEK
1896. Lithograph. 20¹¹⁄₁₆ x 15¹³⁄₁₆″.

He stands out as one who was usually able to stay considerably above the general level of sentimental froth then being generated.

Rodin presented subjects suggesting deep meaning. He liked to suggest an idea in such a way that the viewer could complete the concept. Rodin's emotional force is background for German expressionist sculpture. The rapport between impressionism and Rodin's sculpture is felt in the fluid surface qualities commonly found in his later work.

With the Rodin sculpture we conclude the art of the nineteenth century.

214 François Auguste René Rodin
THE KISS
1886–1898. Marble. Height 5′11¼″.

215   Constantin Brancusi
THE KISS
1908. Limestone. 23 x 13", depth 10".

TWENTIETH-CENTURY ART

I can think of no way to present art history in the twentieth century as a single, chronological sequence. The art and the life that goes with it in any period are more like a collage than a line, particularly in a complex, contradictory time like ours. Only small indications of history are given here. In actuality, art falls into neat categories even less easily than other things.

Brancusi carved two figures kissing in a solid embrace. The work was originally commissioned as a tombstone by a couple who must have loved each other very much. The work does not portray an ego-building image of erotic love. Rather, it is a symbol of the inner union that occurs when two people love each other in such a continuing and unselfish way that they achieve oneness. THE KISS by Rodin and THE KISS by Brancusi represent either side of a major transition in the tradition of figurative art. One is representational; one is geometric abstraction. Rodin was the great master of sculpture in the second half of the nineteenth century, while Brancusi held the same position for the first half of the twentieth.

Brancusi's SLEEPING MUSE of 1906 has a similar quality to Rodin's romantic naturalism. In 1908 he completed THE KISS and in 1911 he finished a second version of the SLEEPING MUSE. THE NEWBORN, finished in 1915, has the refined simplicity of a powerful conception stripped to its essentials. Brancusi said, "Simplicity is not an end in art, but one arrives at simplicity in spite of oneself, in approaching the real sense of things. . . ."[36]

These three works span ten years of Brancusi's evolution toward the kind of elemental form for which he is known. Seen together they illustrate the transition between representational and nonrepresentational emphasis that occurred in much early twentieth-century art.

216 Constantin Brancusi
SLEEPING MUSE
1906. Marble. 6½ x 12".

217 Constantin Brancusi
SLEEPING MUSE
1909–1911. Marble. Height 11½".

218 Constantin Brancusi
THE NEWBORN
1915. Marble. Length 8½", height 6".

The break in Renaissance tradition from representational to abstract is bridged in another way by Gustav Klimt. In his painting, THE KISS, there is some of the abstract boldness that we find in Munch's final woodcut of the same name (see page 85), and some of the romantic representational quality of Rodin's sculpture (see page 181). It is unusual to find representational and abstract styles combined so effectively. Most artists would not attempt it. The heads, hands, and feet are realistically portrayed, while the bodies are only suggested beneath a rich color pattern that is organized within simple shapes against a plain background.

Between 1901 and 1906, comprehensive exhibits of the works of van Gogh, Gauguin, and Cézanne were held in Paris. Many young painters were deeply affected by their first views of these masters. Several of them consequently developed styles in which expressive distortions were emphasized by the use of violent color. When their works were first shown together in 1905, a critic angrily called them *les fauves* (the wild beasts). This pleased them greatly.

The leading figure in the group was Henri Matisse. His painting JOY OF LIFE is an important early work in his long career and a key masterpiece of fauvism. Pure colors vibrate across the surface. Matisse and the other fauve painters broke away from all prior rules and conventions limiting the free use of color.

This black and white reproduction of JOY OF LIFE can merely act as an invitation to see the original. The Barnes Foundation in Merion, Pennsylvania does not permit color reproductions of this painting. The only hint of Matisse's rich color comes from the bold rhythmic lines and shapes. The seemingly careless depiction of the figures is based on a profound knowledge of human anatomy and of drawing. The simple, child-like quality of the form serves to heighten the joyous content.

219   Gustav Klimt
THE KISS
1908. Oil on canvas. 71 x 71". *See color plate 24.*

NASTURTIUMS AND THE DANCE shows Matisse's fauve color and his radical new balance between the two-dimensional and three-dimensional aspects of painting. See color plate 3 and discussion on page 38.

220   Henri Matisse. JOY OF LIFE. 1905–1906. Oil on canvas. 68½ x 93¾".

221   Wassily Kandinsky
BLUE MOUNTAIN
1908. Oil on canvas. 42 x 38½". *See color plate 25.*

Wassily Kandinsky, a Russian, abandoned law to become a fauve painter. His paintings grew toward an absence of representational subject matter. He believed that a painting should be "an exact replica of some inner emotion."[37] In BLUE MOUNTAIN, painted in 1908, he created a "choir of colors,"[38] in which figures on horseback move through an imaginary landscape of rich color, as if they were calling our attention to the pure enjoyment of visual form existing for its own sake.

222   Wassily Kandinsky. WITH THE BLACK ARCH, No. 154. 1912. Oil on canvas. 74 x 77⅛".

By 1910, Kandinsky had abandoned representational subject matter entirely in order to concentrate on the expressive potential of visual form freed from associations. He tried to free painting to the extent that music was free. Of his completely nonrepresentational paintings, Kandinsky stated that their content is "what the spectator *lives* or *feels* while under the effect of the *form and color combinations* of the picture."[39]

Music does not have to be like something preexisting or already known to be great. In fact, representational music is rare. We enjoy music because of the rhythmic harmonies and melodies that it contains. The relationships created by the composer and given life by the performer are what please us about music. We would never think of asking a musician, "What is that supposed to be?", as is still often asked by people viewing abstract and nonrepresentational works of art.

By calling his painting WITH THE BLACK ARCH, No. 154, Kandinsky refers to the dominant visual element, which is the major subject of the painting. It is the same as a composer calling his work Opus No. 48 in C Minor.

In 1913 Kandinsky described how deeply he was affected by the discovery of subatomic particles. The realization was a shock and a prod in his search for independent visual form:

A scientific event cleared my way of one of the greatest impediments. This was the further division of the atom. The crumbling of the atom was to my soul like the crumbling of the whole world. Suddenly the heaviest walls toppled. Everything became uncertain, tottering and weak. I would not have been surprised if a stone had dissolved in the air in front of me and become invisible.[40]

The works just discussed represent some aspects of what was happening in the loaded years of transition at the beginning of the twentieth century. Major changes were taking place in the way man looked at the world. The physicist and chemist, Marie Curie, and her husband Pierre, discovered the radioactive element radium in 1898. Einstein changed the concepts of time and space with his theory of relativity, published in 1905. In 1908 the Wright brothers began modern aviation history by flying a power-driven glider. During this period artists were breaking down visual preconceptions. New styles now came forward in rapid profusion.

The year that Matisse completed JOY OF LIFE, Pablo Picasso painted a self-portrait that had a unique quality of simplicity not seen before in his work. Picasso had mastered techniques of representational drawing before he was fifteen years old. In 1901 he was twenty and living in Paris. His paintings showed that he had assimilated the influences of postimpressionist painters like Toulouse-Lautrec, Degas, van Gogh, and Gauguin. Yet his work was very much his own. Between 1901 and 1904 he painted the poor and suffering people who were his neighbors. Most of the many paintings of those years were done in blue tones that created a deep mood of sadness. By 1905 a softer, more lyrical feeling appeared in his work. Picasso began painting circus people rather than the destitute. Tints and shades of warm, delicate reds replaced the somber blues. Even in the black and white drawing of the circus woman and her infant (see page 29), the gentle lyric quality is apparent.

Then, at twenty-five, Picasso became fascinated with a way of painting having nothing to do with the Renaissance tradition of representational accuracy in which he was raised. His self-portrait is built with strong, simple, curved lines, which define the edges of flat planes. The bold, curving planes of the eyelids and sockets show Picasso's new approach most clearly.

In the year this painting was completed, Picasso began to emerge as a major force behind the numerous new styles that made painting into a series of unique and independent visual events.

223 Pablo Picasso
SELF-PORTRAIT
1906. Oil on canvas. 36½ x 28¾".

224 Pablo Picasso
DANCER
1907. Oil on canvas. 59 x 39¼".

Picasso moved into a new world of visual
images. His small painting called DANCER
was one of many studies made for the large,
more famous work known as THE YOUNG
LADIES OF AVIGNON. DANCER shows the
radical break Picasso made with the past.
Tradition required a depiction of objects
from one point of view. Here the angularly
shaped figure fuses with rhythmic curves
that activate the entire picture plane. It is
as if the dancer were but part of a dynamic,
overall pattern.

The shifting planes are Picasso's exaggerated
adaptation of Cézanne's restructuring of objects in space on a two-dimensional surface.
A large, retrospective exhibition of Cézanne's work was held in Paris in 1906, the
year before this work of Picasso's was completed.

225 CHIEF'S STOOL
Baluba, Belgian Congo
Probably 19th century. Wood. Height 21".

There is little feeling of a figure against a
background in DANCER. The figure operates
in a visual world of its own. Its bold angu-
larity reflects Picasso's interest in Spanish
pre-Christian "Iberian" sculpture, El Greco's
flickering shapes, and African and Oceanic
sculpture, which Gauguin and les fauves had
"discovered." Picasso blasted the accepted
European ideal of beauty by incorporating

226   Pablo Picasso. The Young Ladies of Avignon. 1907. Oil on canvas. 8′ x 7′8″.

the abstract power of primitive form. Picasso's closest friends were astonished by his new approach. Even Braque, who did as much to develop cubism as Picasso, was appalled when he first saw The Young Ladies of Avignon in 1907. Braque commented, "You may give all the explanations you like, but your painting makes one feel as if you were trying to make us eat cotton waste and wash it down with kerosene."[41]

227 Alfred Stieglitz. THE STEERAGE. 1907.

Alfred Stieglitz, an American photographer, was reconsidering the geometry of composition on the picture plane as Picasso began taking the steps that led to cubism. When Picasso saw Stieglitz' photograph THE STEERAGE he said, "This man is trying to do the same thing that I am."[42]

THE STEERAGE looked chopped up to many people. Some of the artist's friends felt that it should have been two photographs, rather than one. But Stieglitz was seeing the complex scene as a pattern of interacting forces of light, shade, shape, and direction. Aboard a liner headed for Europe, he saw the composition of this photograph as "a round straw hat, the funnel leaning left, the stairway leaning right, the white drawbridge with its railings made of circular chains, white suspenders crossing on the back of a man on the steerage below, round shapes of iron machinery, a mast cutting into the sky, making a triangular shape. . . . I saw a picture of shapes and underlying that the feeling I had about life."[43] He rushed back to his cabin to get his camera hoping the composition would remain. It had, and he made the photograph, which he considered his best.

Stieglitz made his own move toward realizing the potential of an overall picture-plane geometry, freed from the continuous, linear flow of Renaissance perspective.

At the same time, the American architect Frank Lloyd Wright was designing his prairie houses, in which the rigid boundaries between interior and exterior space give way to a spatial flow and interaction that has much in common with cubism.

In the Robie house of 1909, Wright created long, horizontal lines that end in exaggerated, overhanging roofs. The lines repeat an irregular pattern throughout the building, keeping the structure in tune with the flat land that surrounds it. The long eaves reach out into exterior space working with the diagonally placed windows and open floor plan, allowing interior space out and exterior space in, in a continuous exchange. To get a feeling of how far ahead of his time Wright was, imagine the new 1909 horseless carriage that might be parked in front of this house the year it was completed.

228 Frank Lloyd Wright. ROBIE HOUSE. Chicago, 1909.

229 Paul Cézanne
THE GARDEN
1885–1886. Oil on canvas. 31½ x 25¼".

As we have already noted, Cézanne combined direct observation of nature with a way of working that was based on a new respect for the flat character of the picture plane. European painters since the fifteenth century had been judged on their ability to give the illusion of actual depth on flat surfaces. Now this basic premise was challenged. The beauty and integrity of the surface itself was reaffirmed. Painters in Europe thus rejoined the majority of the world's artists who have worked on flat surfaces without any compulsion to create illusionary space.

Cézanne, Manet, and the postimpressionists led the way, and Picasso and many others picked it up and carried the idea even further. A comparison between Cézanne's painting of a hill town, finished in 1886, and Picasso's painting of a similar subject done in 1909, twenty-three years later, shows the progression from Cézanne's postimpressionist style into the cubist style developed by Picasso and Braque. In Cézanne's THE GARDEN, the planes shift and interweave. In Picasso's THE RESERVOIR AT HORTA DE EBRO, the planes are stripped of representational detail and act as elements in an almost independent pattern of geometric shapes.

230   Pablo Picasso. THE RESERVOIR AT HORTA DE EBRO. 1909. Oil on canvas. 31⅞ x 25¼".

The cubists were convinced that the pictorial space of the flat plane of the two-dimensional surface was unique — a form of space quite different from natural space. The goal was to develop a more honest method of picture design. Natural objects were a point of departure. Cubism sums up a unity of vision from different moments in time and different positions in space, and suggests a visual parallel to the concepts of relativity that Einstein proposed. Cubism depicts what the mind knows rather than what the eye sees.

By 1910, cubism was a fully developed style. Picasso's painting of a clarinet player, painted in 1911, is a fine example of what is sometimes referred to as analytical cubism. The word "analytical" is appropriate, because, in this phase of cubism, the two artists most deeply involved, Picasso and Braque, spent a great deal of time analyzing their subjects. They wanted to transform natural forms into works of art that were independent of the original subject. Numerous drawings were done from different points of view. The drawings are rectilinear, rather than curvilinear. These studies of the model provided a basis for multiple views of the subject that were spread out and woven together in the final painting. There is no separation between figure and ground. The painted surface seems to echo and unify the subject. The subject and the background interpenetrate one another in shallow space, which seems to move as much in front of the picture plane as behind.

In order to concentrate on the formal reconstruction of the subject, Picasso used a limited range of neutral tones. Any strong color would be entirely out of place in these intellectual translations of three-dimensional form. Restrained color was also a reaction away from fauvism. The surface of the painting is activated entirely by interpenetrating planes that often seem both opaque and transparent.

231   Pablo Picasso
THE CLARINET PLAYER
1911. Oil on canvas. 42 x 26½".

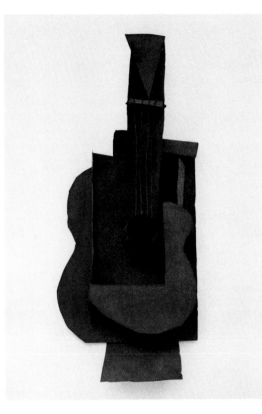

232   Pablo Picasso
GUITAR
1911–1912. Sheet metal and wire. 30¾ x 13¾ x 7¼".

In 1912, analytical cubism gave way to greater interest in textural surfaces and bold cutout shapes. Instead of representing surfaces with paint, actual two-dimensional objects were often used. Pieces of newspaper, sheet music, wallpaper, and similar items came into the work, not represented, but actually presented. Decorative aspects became more dominant than in analytical cubism. The design was flatter and used fewer shapes. Color was used more freely. These painted and pasted paper compositions were called *papier collé* by the French, and later became known in English as "collage," also known as synthetic cubism.

When Picasso constructed his GUITAR out of sheet metal and wire in 1911 or 1912, he began what has become a dominant trend in twentieth-century sculpture. Before Picasso's cubist GUITAR, most sculpture was modeled or carved. Now much of contemporary sculpture is created by assembling methods. According to Picasso, this sculpture was completed before he did any work with collage.

233   Pablo Picasso
SHEET OF MUSIC
AND GUITAR.
1912–1913. Gummed paper
with pastel. 21½ x 23".

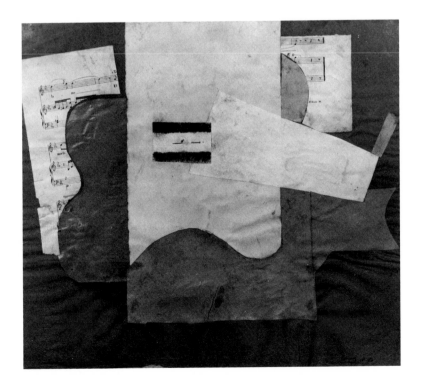

234   Marcel Duchamp. NUDE DESCENDING A STAIRCASE, #2. 1912. Oil on canvas. 58 x 35".

235 Jacques Henri Lartigue. Grand Prix of the Automobile Club of France.
Dieppe, France, 1912.

The French artist Marcel Duchamp and the futurist painters of Italy brought the dimension of motion to cubism. Creating a sense of movement and rhythm is as important in the art of the Western twentieth century as it was in India several thousand years ago.

Film is much better suited for depicting motion than is painting. However, Duchamp's Nude Descending a Staircase works well in a way that a film cannot. Utilizing sequential, diagonally placed, cubist images of the same figure, the painting presents the symbolic movement of a figure through space, seen all at once, in a single, rhythmic progression. Because of our sense of gravity, the diagonal placement intensifies the feeling of movement.

The Italian futurists were excited by the beauty of speed made possible by technology. In 1909, Marinetti, a poet, proclaimed in the Manifesto of Futurism: "The world's splendor has been enriched by a new beauty; the beauty of speed . . . a roaring motorcar . . . is more beautiful than the Victory of Samothrace."[44]

In 1912, the same year that Duchamp painted Nude Descending a Staircase, a young French photographer named Jacques Lartigue took one of many photographs of his father in action.

Cubism is a way of seeing. Cubism has been for the twentieth century what the development of linear perspective was for the fifteenth. After the original analytical phase of cubism, many painters adopted its basic spatial concept. One of them was Fernand Léger. In his painting called THE CITY, he used cubist overlapping planes in compact, shallow space to create a complex symbol of city rhythms and intensities.

In today's cities, the buildings, signs, people, and traffic crowd together between reflective surfaces, in a giant assemblage of

236   Fernand Léger
THE CITY
1919. Oil on canvas. 7'7" x 9'9".

overlapping, disjointed forms. To the eye, these phenomena join in a collage experience that is part of the same spatial awareness explored by cubism. Cubism has given us a relevant way of experiencing the world we live in.

In cubism, a painting became an object in its own right. The cubist approach led to further abstractions, and to nonrepresentational painting, although it was also used by painters for whom subject matter was important.

Feininger's painting of sailboats racing on open water is cubist in design. Geometric shapes, mostly triangles, move over the surface, woven into strong unity by straight lines of force that run from edge to edge across the picture plane. Size difference in the sails adds to the illusion of depth.

237   Duane Preble
REFLECTIONS
1972

238   Lyonel Feininger
THE GLORIOUS VICTORY OF THE SLOOP "MARIA"
1926. Oil on canvas. 21½ x 33½".
See color plate 26

239   Pablo Picasso. THREE MUSICIANS. 1921. Oil on canvas. 6′7″ x 7′3¾″.

The THREE MUSICIANS by Picasso is created in the flat, decorative style of synthetic cubism. The painting is an abstraction that acts as a culmination of cubism as a whole. Its form is heavily influenced by the cutout shapes of cubist collages. It was painted by Picasso at the same time that he was working with the style and subject matter of Greco-Roman antiquity, creating new figures with the appearance of great bulk and solid-ity. See YOUNG MAN'S HEAD, page 63.

Many historians find Picasso's work difficult to deal with, because he shifts from style to style, using one approach, and then another. Yet, now, as we look back over his career, the dramatic shifts in attitude all seem part of Picasso's fantastic inventive abilities.

Color plate 28   Kurt Schwitters. Construction for Noble Ladies. 1919. Mixed media assemblage of wood, metal, and paint. 40½ x 33″.

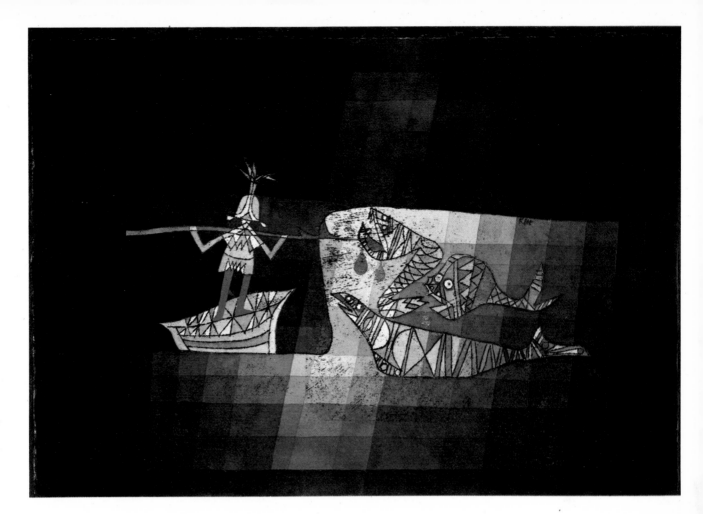

Color plate 29
Paul Klee
ᴌᴇ Sᴄᴇɴᴇ ꜰʀᴏᴍ
ᴇ Cᴏᴍɪᴄ Oᴘᴇʀᴀ
Tʜᴇ Sᴇᴀꜰᴀʀᴇʀ".
. Colored sheet,
ᴀtercolor, and oil
ings. 15 x 20¼".

Color plate 30
Hans Hofmann
Tʜᴇ Gᴏʟᴅᴇɴ Wᴀʟʟ
961. Oil on canvas.
60 x 72½".

Color plate 31   Willem de Kooning. WOMAN AND BICYCLE. 1952–1953. Oil on canvas. 76½ x 49″.

240 Jacques Lipchitz
FIGURE
1926–1930. Bronze. Height 85¼".

Two of the figures in THREE MUSICIANS are the traditional characters of French comedy — Pierrot, in white, playing a recorder, and brightly costumed Harlequin in the center, playing a guitar. The third figure wears a black monk's habit and a veiled mask, and sings from the sheet of music he holds. Behind the trio a black dog lies with tail raised. They might be happy figures, yet they become solemn and majestic because of the predominance of sombre colors and the monumental size of the picture.

For the sculptor Jacques Lipchitz "cubism was essentially a search for a new syntax."[45] He came to Paris from Poland just as cubism was developing. His seven feet, one and one-quarter inch FIGURE of the late 1920s, however, is not really cubist. The sculptor arrived at this form by digging beneath the surface of cubism. The figure's bold symmetry seems to have an organic rather than a geometric basis. But the sculpture could not have existed without cubism, just as van Gogh's THE SOWER (see page 174) could not have been created without impressionism.

The taller-than-lifesized piece has an awe-inspiring presence. It has the power we might expect to find in a votive figure from Africa or the South Pacific. Here the power comes from Lipchitz' sense of his own time. A viewer asked Lipchitz to explain his work. "It wouldn't help you," the sculptor answered. "If I were to explain it in Chinese, you would tell me you didn't know Chinese, and I would tell you to learn Chinese and you will understand. Art is harder than Chinese. Anyone can look— you have to learn to see."[46]

This is a symbol of inner man in the twentieth century. It seems closely related to the figure in Munch's THE SHRIEK (see page 180).

Picasso continued to produce a great volume of high-quality drawings, paintings, prints, posters, and sculptures throughout the 1920s and into the early 1930s. Many of these works were filled with distortions and metamorphoses. In 1937, while the Spanish Revolution was in progress, Picasso was commissioned by the Spanish democratic government to paint a mural for the Spanish government building at the Paris Exposition. For several months, he was unable to start work. Suddenly, on April 26, 1937, he was shocked into action by the experimental mass bombing of the defenseless Basque town of Guernica. To aid his bid for power, General Franco allowed Hitler to use his war machinery on the town of Guernica as a demonstration of military power. It was the first incidence of satura-

tion bombing in the history of warfare. The bombing occurred at night. According to witnesses, one out of every seven people in the town was killed.

Picasso was appalled by this brutal act against the people of his native country. In retaliation, he called upon all his powers to create the mural GUERNICA as a protest against war.

Although GUERNICA stems from a specific incident, it has universal significance, and is viewed today as a work of tremendous religious importance. It is a powerful visual statement of protest against man's inhumanity to man.

The painting covers a huge canvas measur-

241 Pablo Picasso
GUERNICA
1937. Oil on canvas. 11'5½" x 25'5¼".

ing twenty-five feet, eight inches in length and eleven feet, six inches in height. It occupies an entire wall in the Museum of Modern Art in New York City, where it has been on extended loan from the artist.

GUERNICA is done in somber blacks, whites, and grays, stark symbols of death and mourning. A large triangle is imbedded under the smaller shapes, holding the whole scene of chaotic destruction together as a unified composition. The predominantly triangular shapes and the shallow space are cubistic. Some of the textural patterns are reminiscent of newsprint.

For Picasso, cubism was a tool, not a master. He took the cubist concept from the early intellectual phase through its syn-

thetic period, and here uses it to create a symbol of great emotional intensity.

During the 1940s, while the Nazis occupied France, Picasso maintained his studio in Paris. For some reason, he was allowed to paint, even though his art was considered highly degenerate by the Nazis. The German soldiers harassed him, of course. One day they came to his door with a small reproduction of GUERNICA. They asked, "Did you do this?" Picasso replied, "No, you did."[47]

During the same war years, Picasso made this statement: "No, painting is not done to decorate apartments. It is an instrument of war for a means of attack and defense against the enemy."[48]

Piet Mondrian was much more concerned than Picasso with the beauty of pure visual relationships. He spent forty years perfecting images based on what he considered to be the most essential visual elements. Mondrian's attitude toward nonobjective form was similar to Kandinsky's. Yet Kandinsky's approach was romantic or emotional, whereas Mondrian's was more classical or rational.

In 1912, Mondrian's work was shifting from naturalistic, fauvist landscapes to a more abstract, analytical approach under the influence of cubism. When he painted Horizontal Tree, he concentrated on the rhythmic curves of the branches and on the pattern of the spaces created between the branches. Mondrian began to be more and more aware of the strong expressive character of simple horizontal and vertical lines, creating basic geometric patterns.

242   Piet Mondrian
Horizontal Tree
1911. Oil on canvas. 29⅝ x 43⅞".

243 Piet Mondrian
COMPOSITION WITH RED, YELLOW AND BLUE
1930. Oil on canvas. 19 x 19"
See color plate 27

From 1917 until his death in 1944, Mondrian was one of the major nonrepresentational painters and a leading spokesman in the search for pure visual form.

The new art has continued and culminated the art of the past in such a way that the new painting, by employing "neutral," or universal forms, expresses itself only through the relationships of line and color.[49]

For Mondrian, these universal elements were straight lines and primary colors. Mondrian was able to create major works using only black horizontal and vertical lines of varying width and the three primary colors, red, yellow, and blue, against a white background. One of these is COMPOSITION WITH RED, YELLOW AND BLUE, completed in 1930. It exemplifies his most mature style, in which three simplified elements—line, shape, and color—combine to create images of significance.

Mondrian distilled his sense of design from the complex relationships of daily visual experience. His style was a way of getting at the universal core of our intuitive experience of form. Mondrian felt that he was expanding the possibilities of visual expression by using elements which in themselves would evoke responses deeper than those coming from representations of specific objects. In his search, he reached for new ways to express the nature of man.

Mondrian's style was shared by his circle of friends. In 1917 they founded a magazine called DE STIJL (the style). The group and their work have been known by this name ever since.

Mondrian wanted the new art to be "collective, impersonal and international."[50] Although De Stijl's origins are found in painting, its influence was felt and can still be seen in the design of buildings, books, interiors, clothing, and many other articles of daily use.

The search for a language of visual form that was stripped to its essentials was carried on by architects as well as painters between 1910 and 1940. One of the leaders in the development of the international style was Le Corbusier. He was a painter, an architect, and a city planner. Like the masters of the Renaissance, he was a total artist and a major figure in the twentieth century.

With the simple drawing shown here, the young Le Corbusier demonstrated the structural skeleton of a reinforced concrete house. This idea made it possible to vary the placement of interior walls and the nature of exterior coverings, since neither one plays a structural role. Le Corbusier's sense of the beautiful was inspired by the efficiency of machines and a keen awareness of the importance of spaciousness and light.

244 Le Corbusier
DOMINO CONSTRUCTIONAL SYSTEM
1914–1915

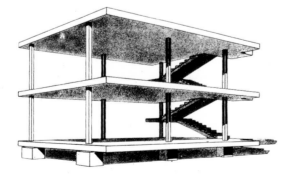

245 Walter Gropius
THE BAUHAUS. Dessau, Germany, 1925.

Also reflecting the influence of the De Stijl group are the buildings of the great German school of art called the Bauhaus, which were designed by Walter Gropius in 1925.

In this photograph, you can see how the reinforced concrete floors, supported by interior steel columns, allow for a curtain wall of glass, which reflects as well as transmits light.

The exterior and interior of the building are presented simultaneously in a design of opaque and transparent overlapping planes similar to the use of planes found in cubist and postcubist painting. Like Le Corbusier, Gropius deplored the use of excessive ornamentation. Simplicity is a major aspect in twentieth-century architecture and product design.

246 Ludwig Mies van der Rohe and Philip Johnson
SEAGRAM BUILDING
New York City, 1957

Much of twentieth-century architecture has lost almost all personal or locational identification in the quest for pure structural beauty. A major work built with this clean, functional approach is the Seagram Building in New York, designed by Ludwig Mies van der Rohe, with the help of Philip Johnson. The interior floor space gained by the height of the building allowed the architects to leave a large, open area at the base. The vertical lines emphasize the feeling of height and provide a strong pattern. The top was planned to give a sense of completion without suppressing the soaring height. Mies van der Rohe's famous statement, "less is more,"[51] is given full physical form in this austere, rectangular structure.

Dada is a word that identifies an art attitude that began to emerge during the nineteenth century and was finally christened in 1916. This attitude is different from the rational search for absolute or pure form. It is not a style.

Dada was not a school of artists, but an alarm signal against declining values, routine and speculation, a desperate appeal on behalf of all forms of art, for a creative basis on which to build a new and universal consciousness of art.

Marcel Janco[52]

After Duchamp painted the Nude Descending a Staircase (see page 196) in 1912, he became increasingly dissatisfied with the accepted framework for art. He said, "I have forced myself to contradict myself in order to avoid conforming to my own taste."[53] Duchamp was not alone. As European society moved inexorably into World War I, many people felt compelled to react. As the actual fighting began, artists counterattacked with their art.

While the thunder of guns rolled in the distance, we sang, painted, glued and composed for all our worth. We are seeking an art that would heal mankind from the madness of the age.

Hans Arp[54]

Dada began in poetry and painting, then carried into sculpture, architecture, photography, film, music, and graphic design. But more than an art form, "Dada was a metaphysical attitude . . . a sort of nihilism . . . a way to get out of a state of mind — to avoid being influenced by one's immediate environment, or by the past; to get away from cliches — to get free." (Marcel Duchamp.)[35]

In his effort to free himself from the past, Duchamp declared all art a swindle, and exhibited his first nonart "ready-made," Bicycle Wheel.

Duchamp felt that you cannot separate art from other man-made things. He recognized selection as the primary ingredient of art. In his Bicycle Wheel, an assemblage

of 1913, he applied both of these ideas to produce a work that has caused much controversy and has stirred considerable thought. Its components are simply a bicycle wheel and a kitchen stool. It is a conceptual work from Duchamp's fertile imagination. It took only a simple operation to join the wheel frame to the stool. The stool provides a static base for the movable wheel. This is the first mobile of the twentieth century.

247 Marcel Duchamp
Bicycle Wheel
Replica of 1913 original, 1951. Assemblage: metal wheel 25½", mounted on painted wood stool 24¾" high, overall height 50½".

The wheel and the stool still say whatever they said before, by themselves. Yet this expression is now subordinate to what they communicate as a combined form. Through their new association and by the placement of this work in galleries and museums as an art object, a strong change has occurred in the way we perceive them. Functional preconceptions have been cleared away. We now see the things themselves.

For Duchamp, mechanically produced, man-made things were a reservoir of potentially un-self-conscious art objects. In this view a reproduction of the MONA LISA was a "ready-made" thing, in the same class as bicycle wheels and kitchen stools and bottle racks.

L.H.O.O.Q. is a corrected ready-made by Duchamp. Corrections took the form of a moustache and goatee done in pencil and a

248   Marcel Duchamp. L.H.O.O.Q. 1919.

249   Man Ray
THE GIFT
Replica of 1921 original, c. 1958.
Flatiron with metal tacks. 6⅛ x 3⅝ x 4½".

new title. The unusual title gives a possible clue as to why the MONA LISA has been smiling all these years. It is a pun in French, comprehensible only to those who can say the letters in a flowing sentence with perfect French pronunciation. Translated into English, it reads, "She has hot pants." Duchamp's irreverence helps get art, and therefore life, back to a fresh start.

Man Ray, an American, was a friend of Duchamp's. His dada works include paintings, photographs, and assembled objects. In 1921, in Paris, Man Ray saw a flatiron displayed in front of a shop selling housewares. He purchased the iron, a box of tacks, and a tube of glue. He glued a row of tacks to the smooth face of the iron and entitled it THE GIFT. This particular dada assemblage tweaks the viewer's mind in a unique way. Utilitarian objects are transformed into useless irony.

In the past, the major subjects for art were gods (or God), nature, and man, and the interrelationships between them. It was not until the twentieth century that man-made things became a frequent subject for art.

It is not surprising that this shift in emphasis has occurred in art during an age when man has surrounded himself with objects of his own making, even objects that go on making objects. Modern man has spent more time, thought, and energy on the acquisition, use, and maintenance of manufactured things than he has on God, nature, or himself.

The twentieth-century emphasis on things has been apparent in art in two ways. First, as noted above, artists have ceased using traditional subjects that hold little meaning for them or for their public, and in some cases have even stopped using recognizable subjects altogether. To some, the appearance of the visual world has become either not to their liking or uninteresting, compared to the possibilities of independent visual form. Secondly, artists have confronted the most unlikely sources of inspiration. They have gone to man-made things themselves, to the most common artifacts of mass production, and have found in them symbols of crass materialism in some cases, and universal continuity and spirit in others. These attitudes have formed what has been called the art of things.

250   Hannah Höch. THE MULTI-MILLIONAIRE. 1920. Photomontage.

251   Kurt Schwitters
Construction for Noble Ladies
1919. Mixed media assemblage of wood, metal, and
paint. 40½ x 33". See color plate 28.

Rafael Squirru shed light on this subject when, in 1963, he wrote an article entitled "Pop Art or the Art of Things." "And we should not be surprised that a people that has become alienated from itself through things should seek to recapture its identity through its artists . . . ."[56]

Squirru went on to clarify the semantics relative to this style by pointing out that what has been called pop art in the United States is called l'art des objets (the art of objects) in Europe and el arte de las cosas (the art of things) in Latin America. Of these designations, the art of things may be the most revealing, since it calls attention to the common subject matter including styles ranging from synthetic cubism to pop art.

Paradoxically, the art of things has developed concurrently with the concept of a work of art as an independent thing, free to express itself without reference to external subject matter.

When Picasso and Braque put actual preexisting things, such as pieces of rope and scraps of newspapers, into their work, they began one development in the art of things, which includes works of collage and assemblage (see page 195). Things are not represented, but are themselves presented, in a new context.

Another direction moves from collage into photomontage. In The Multi-millionaire, by the dadaist Hannah Höch, man, the artifact-making industrialist, stands as a fractured giant among the things he has produced.

Kurt Schwitters was a master of dada collage. From 1917 until his death in 1948, he created images out of timeworn objects discarded by society. His assembled junk was designed to destroy the sacred standards of art. He asked us to look again at these cast-off objects. They are familiar old things returned to us, freed from their past functions and associations, and, therefore, visible again in a different context. Schwitters made his attitude clear in the following statement:

I could not, in fact, see any reason why one should not use the old tickets, driftwood, cloakroom numbers, wires and parts of wheels, buttons and old lumber out of junk rooms and rubbish heaps as materials for paintings as well as the colors that were produced in factories.[57]

Paul Klee intentionally freed himself from the accumulation of history by digging deeply into his own being in an effort to begin all over again. The self-portrait that he drew in 1919 goes well with this statement, written in his diary in June 1902:

It is a great difficulty and great necessity to have to start with the smallest. I want to be as though new-born, knowing nothing, absolutely nothing, about Europe; ignoring poets and fashions, to be almost primitive. Then I want to do something very modest; to work out by myself a tiny formal motive, one that my pencil will be able to hold without any technique.[58]

Paul Klee remained an independent artist all his life. He was creating fantastic images before surrealism became a group style. He was able to tap the resources of his own unconscious, years before the surrealist group was organized.

. . . . everything vanishes round me and good works rise from me of their own accord. My hand is entirely the implement of a distant sphere. It is not my head that functions but something else, something higher, something more remote. I must have great friends there, dark as well as bright. . . . They are all very kind to me.[59]

In Klee's painting of the BATTLE SCENE FROM THE COMIC OPERA "THE SEAFARER," Sinbad the Sailor fights three monsters of the unknown in a battle that has universal human implications.

The marvelous line patterns and rich color are common to Klee's small paintings.

252 Paul Klee
SELF-PORTRAIT
1919. Colored sheet, pen and wash. 9 x 5¼".

253 Paul Klee
BATTLE SCENE FROM THE COMIC OPERA
"THE SEAFARER"
1923. Colored sheet, watercolor, and oil drawings.
15 x 20¼". See color plate 29.

The Italian metaphysical painter Giorgio de Chirico is another artist who, on his own, anticipated surrealism. The playwright and critic Apollinaire used the word "surrealism" to describe de Chirico's works, which were shown in Paris in 1911 and 1912. In surrealism, the artist relies on the unconscious for inspiration.

THE MYSTERY AND MELANCHOLY OF A STREET, of 1914, is perhaps his greatest work. De Chirico used distorted linear perspective to create an eerie space peopled by faceless shadows. The painting speaks the symbolic language of dreams, mystery, and ominous silence. According to the artist:

Everything has two aspects: the current aspect, which we see nearly always and which ordinary men see, and the ghostly and metaphysical aspect, which only rare individuals may see in moments of clairvoyance and metaphysical abstraction.[60]

254 Giorgio de Chirico. THE MYSTERY AND MELANCHOLY OF A STREET. 1914. Oil on canvas. 34¼ x 28⅛".

255   Salvador Dali. PERSISTENCE OF MEMORY. 1931. Oil on canvas. 9½ x 13".

In the 1920s a group of writers and painters gathered to proclaim the omnipotence of the unconscious mind. Their goal was to make this aspect of the mind visible. The group was indebted to the irrationality of dadaism and the incredible creations of Chagall, Klee, and de Chirico. The movement was officially launched in Paris in 1924 by the publication of its first manifesto, written by the poet-painter André Breton.

Surrealism refers to the artists' concern for the superreality of the unconscious mind. Breton was a follower and patient of Freud. In the manifesto he asserts: "I believe in the future resolution of those two states which at first blush seem so contradictory — dream and reality — in a sort of absolute reality, a super-reality if one may so express it."[61]

The prominent members of the surrealist group were Tanguy, Ernst, Miró, and Dali. Although Dali is the best known of these men, he joined the group late and was considered by several surrealist painters to be too flamboyant and arrogant to be taken seriously. Picasso took part in the first surrealist exhibition, but he did not remain in the style long.

Miró and Dali, both Spaniards, represent two opposite tendencies operating in surrealism. Dali used illusionary deep space and representational techniques to make the impossible seem possible. This approach can be called representational surrealism. In contrast, Miró used abstract, suggestive elements, giving the widest possible play to the viewer's imagination. His style can be called abstract surrealism.

In PERSISTENCE OF MEMORY Salvador Dali evokes the eerie quality of dream experience. Mechanical time wilts in a deserted landscape of infinite space. The warped, head-like image in the foreground may be the last remnant of a vanished humanity.

b

256 Hieronymus van Aeken Bosch
THE GARDEN OF WORLDLY DELIGHTS.
(a) Detail of right panel. (b) Detail of center panel.
c. 1500. Oil on wood.

As surrealism expanded the horizons of the present, it found important ancestors in the past. One of the most imaginative of these was the Flemish artist Hieronymus Bosch, who was most active between 1488 and 1516. Bosch painted with equal care the delights of the garden of Eden and the horrors of hell. In his depictions of hell he made clear references to his own society, wracked by devastating plagues and the terrors of the Inquisition. What fascinated the surrealists was Bosch's ability to operate on several levels at once. In one sense his pictures are Christian allegories, in another they present seemingly endless symbolic events loaded with psychological overtones. These events may occur only in the world of fantasy and dreams, rediscovered in this century. It is common today to explain our actions by referring to subconscious forces. Many artists of the past and present have drawn on their images from this inner world.

a

In Belgium the surrealist movement was led by René Magritte, who based his work on an illogical form of magical realism, similar to Dali's in surface appearance, but quite different in content. In Magritte's paintings the macabre quality found in Dali's work is replaced by wit and playfulness.

Everything depicted in PORTRAIT is ordinary. The impact of the painting comes from the strange placement and perspective of these ordinary things. Is it possible not to react to PORTRAIT? Its quiet intensity is immense.

Joan Miró used free, evocative shapes to suggest beasts that seem both fearsome and enchanting. He referred just enough to monsters to evoke memories of the universal fears of childhood. Children respond easily to Miró's paintings.

The bold, organic shapes in NURSERY DECORATION are typical of Miró's mature work. The wild, tormented quality is unusual for this painter and probably reflects Miró's reaction to the times. This painting was completed within a year of Picasso's GUERNICA.

257   René Magritte
PORTRAIT
1935. Oil on canvas. 28⅞ x 19⅞".

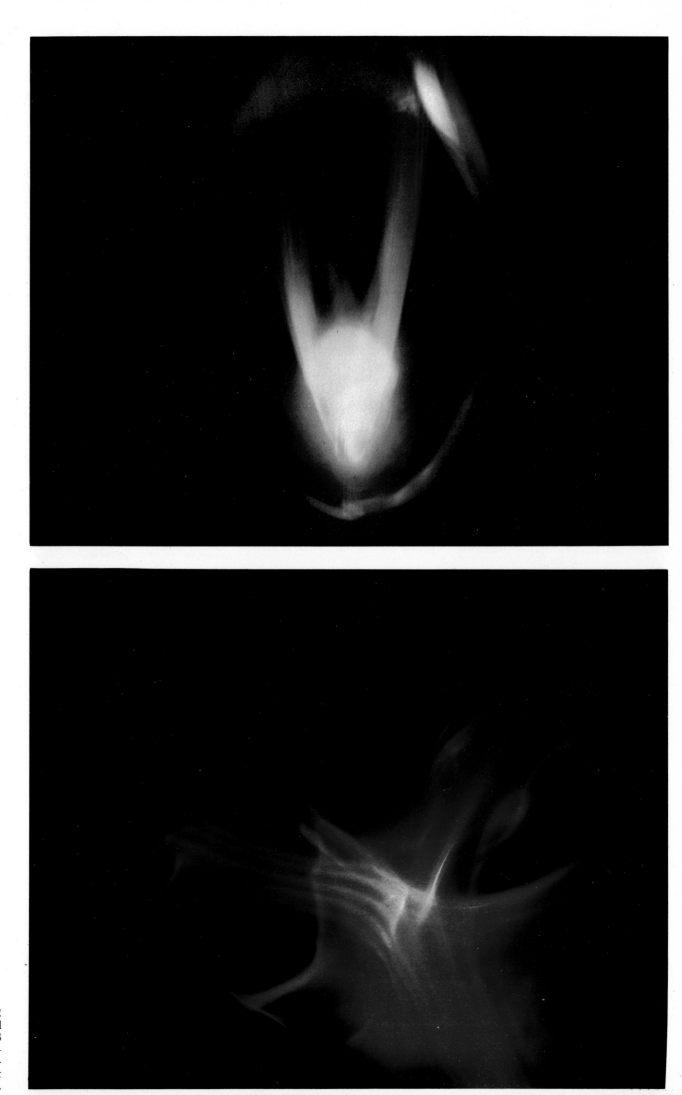

Color plate 32
Thomas Wilfred
ia Suite, Op. 158
two stages). 1963–
64. Light composi-
n projected against
a screen. 6 x 8'.

258   Joan Miró
NURSERY DECORATION
1938. Oil on canvas. 2′7½″ x 10′6″.

259   Willem de Kooning
THE MARSHES
c. 1945. Charcoal and oil on composition board.
32 x 23⅞″.

Nonrepresentational art came into its own in the United States during the 1940s. The expressive strength of van Gogh, the brushwork and rich color surfaces of Monet's late canvases, and, particularly, Kandinsky's rejection of representational subject matter and his expressive freedom, all formed part of the background against which abstract expressionism grew. Miró's abstract surrealism was a major influence on abstract expressionism.

By 1912 Kandinsky had painted abstract expressionist paintings long before the style had a name. The group that began to realize fully the potential of this mode came together in New York about 1943. Few young painters were as attracted to the austere, hard-edge abstractions of Mondrian and others of his age as they were to this more expressive approach. Many of these works are saturated with emotion because they were created as a spontaneous expression of intuitive, personal experience.

It is easy to see the influence of Miró's evocative shapes in de Kooning's THE MARSHES. The major difference between Miró's painting and de Kooning's is the dominant quality of restless energy that implies continual motion across the surface of THE MARSHES. Each brush stroke is the obvious record of an act.

De Kooning felt no compulsion to banish recognizable images from his work. After several years of working without explicit subject matter, he began a long series of paintings in which rather ferocious female figures appear.

These paintings are overpowering because of their size and the obviously slashing attacks by which they were painted. De Kooning began one of these woman paintings by cutting a gleaming artificial smile from an advertisement and attaching it to the canvas for the mouth of the figure. In WOMAN AND BICYCLE, the toothy smile is repeated in a savage necklace capping a pair of tremendous breasts. Everything in the painting is consistently outrageous.

260   Willem de Kooning
WOMAN AND BICYCLE
1952–1953. Oil on canvas. 76½ x 49".
See color plate 31

261   Jackson Pollock. No. 14. 1948. Enamel on wet gesso. 23¾ x 31".

The dynamic form of de Kooning's painting is closely related to the moving energy of Jackson Pollock's surfaces. The subject of Pollock's paintings is the act of painting itself and the energy of the paint. His painting, No. 14, was done by flinging paint onto the canvas rather than brushing it on. Because Pollock dripped, poured, and flung his paint, many people felt that he had no control. Actually, he exercised control and selection by the rhythmical, dancing movement of his body. Many of Pollock's followers did not do so well.

Mark Tobey was one of the oldest members of the abstract expressionist group. He studied Chinese art, and lived in the northwestern part of the United States, where he was physically and intellectually closer to Asia than to Europe. In 1947 he wrote a statement summarizing his position:

Our ground today is not so much the national or the regional as it is the understanding of this single earth . . . . America more than any other country is placed geographically to lead in this understanding, and if from past habits of behavior she has constantly looked toward Europe, today she must assume her position . . . toward Asia, for in not too long a time the waves of the Orient shall wash heavily upon her shores.[62]

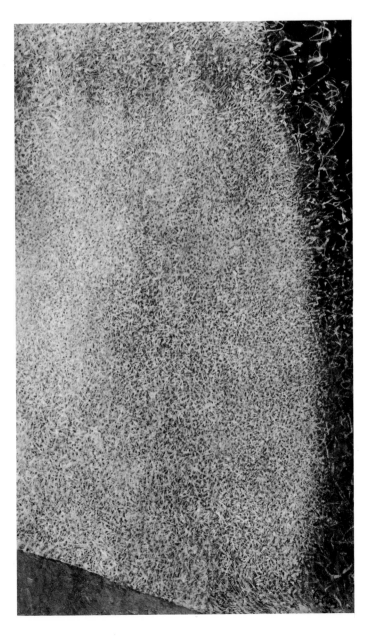

262 Mark Tobey
EDGE OF AUGUST
1953. Tempera on composition board. 48 x 28".

263   Yuichi Inoue
CALLIGRAPHY BUDDHA
1957

In addition to the influence of Tobey's out-
look, several of the New York painters were
fascinated by their own discoveries of Asian
art and religion. Zen Buddhism was particularly influential in their development.

A dominant element in much of abstract expressionism is the expression of the artist's
inner life through bold use of calligraphic
line. In this sense many of their paintings
are like giant signatures. This attitude toward line has been basic to Chinese and
Japanese writing, or calligraphy, for over
1,000 years.

Contemporary painters, like the Japanese
artist Yuichi Inoue, frequently develop their
own expressive visual language based on this
ancient art.

264   Franz Kline
HORIZONTAL RUST
1960. Oil on canvas. 86½ x 49".

The Japanese Buddhist scholar and master calligrapher Kazuaki Tanahashi recently traveled through the United States and felt particularly attracted to the paintings of Franz Kline.

There is a mutual influence going back and forth between Asia and the West that has been of great benefit to both cultures. The result is a growing international style based on shared beliefs, yet rich in its own variety.

265 Kazuaki Tanahashi
HEKI
1965

266 Hans Hofmann
THE GOLDEN WALL
1961. Oil on canvas. 60 x 72½". *See color plate 30.*

In speaking of artists like Rembrandt, it is common to use the phrase "old master." It may seem almost sacrilegious to some to call an abstract expressionist painter an old master. Yet to many young painters, Hans Hofmann is held in that esteem. Hofmann painted THE GOLDEN WALL in 1961 when he was 81 years old. He had been painting for sixty years at that point and had become not only one of the finest painters of the mid-twentieth century, but also one of the best teachers. Many of Hofmann's students have become major artists. Their works cover the whole range of contemporary styles from representational to nonrepresentational.

In THE GOLDEN WALL, warm, glowing color is set off by cool accents. Rectangles are played off against irregular shapes.

Hofmann was a father figure to the New York school following the Second World War. His influence as a teacher was based on a lifetime of experience. In the elements of his own past are roots for the entire American phenomenon called abstract expressionism. He lived in Paris from 1904 to 1914 when cubism was changing the concept of space within a picture. Hofmann had contact with Matisse, Picasso, and many others. Matisse's work attracted him the most. The more decorative side of abstract expressionism shows this influence. In New York in the 1940s, Hofmann was an innovator of action painting. He dripped and flung paint before Pollock made that his trademark. Hofmann based his spontaneity on years of visual experience. When he was over sixty, Hofmann began to produce his finest paintings. His large canvases glow with the power of his vision.

The major characteristic of art today is variety. We are still too close to know who the most important artists of the last twenty years are. Andrew Wyeth may well be one. His paintings are put together with great precision. He uses the old medium of egg tempera, which has not been widely used since its replacement by oil paints in the fifteenth century. In his painting called THAT GENTLEMAN, Wyeth has done what any master painter must do. He has constructed a painting in which each visual relationship works with the motivating concept to create an image of quality. Although every detail of this painting is highly representational, it is more than that. Wyeth has selected and defined the elements working together in THAT GENTLEMAN to make it much more than a mere copy of the subject. Much of the selection process started before Wyeth began to paint. "Just because something is tightly done doesn't mean anything," Wyeth explains, "but I feel that the more you get into the textures of things the less you have to clutter up the composition with a lot of props. When you lose simplicity, you lose drama."[63]

Everything that appears here has been carefully selected and placed in light and space by the painter. This is also true of the works of artists who choose not to reconstruct images of the everyday visual world.

267 Andrew Wyeth. THAT GENTLEMAN. 1960. Tempera on board. 23½ x 47¾".

268 Dolmen of Mané-Kerioned
Carnac, Morbihan, France, 3000–2000 B.C.

It is not difficult to find deep roots for today's art. There is a basic unity of expression influenced by the fact that man has always been surrounded by certain basic circumstances, such as sky and earth, light and dark, matter and spirit, solid and void, and life and death. With this in mind, compare the ancient European dolmen with the modern the chapel at Ronchamp.

In the late 1940s Le Corbusier reacted against the stiffness of the international style with his design for Notre-Dame-du-Haut. He was inspired by the shell of a crab as he began to develop a form that would fit the beauty of the site and the purpose of the building. The structure was built between 1950 and 1955 out of reinforced concrete, wood, and plaster. The walls are massive. Natural wood and rough

269a Le Corbusier. Notre-Dame-du-Haut. Exterior. Ronchamp, France. 1950–1955.

269b   Le Corbusier. NOTRE-DAME-DU-HAUT. Interior.

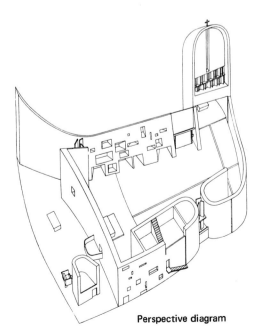

Perspective diagram

concrete and plaster are contrasted with bright accents of color. Light enters through corner slits and through funnellike windows that emphasize the thickness of the walls. The side altars are illuminated dramatically by sunlight slanting through tower openings.

Ideally, architecture is functional sculpture. A primary function of churches and other public buildings is to celebrate an idea. Because the Ronchamp chapel is a pilgrimage site, the building is used for both outdoor and indoor services. Inside and out, in every detail, Le Corbusier has provided a structure of expressive strength. It is one of the most revolutionary and influential pieces of architecture of the last twenty years. It has put emotion back into architecture.

270   Robert Rauschenberg
TRACER
1964. Mixed media. 84 x 60″.

Robert Rauschenberg was a leader in the trend toward what came to be known as pop art. In the mid-1950s, he began incorporating actual, identifiable, three-dimensional objects in paintings that were otherwise abstract expressionist in form. By so doing, he again brought attention to the aesthetic capacity of mundane things. He called these works combines.

Jasper Johns joined forces with Rauschenberg and began to create large paintings

271   Richard Hamilton
Just What Is It that Makes Today's Homes
So Different, So Appealing?
1956. Collage. 10¼ x 9¾".

that were based on common, flat symbols, such as targets, maps, flags, and numbers, that could be presented, but not represented. see color plate 8 and discussion on page 62. Both Johns and Rauschenberg remain outstanding individual artists of our time.

Rauschenberg's collages relate to the work of Kurt Schwitters. See page 211. About 1962 Rauschenberg began to reproduce borrowed images from art and life with the aid of the new photographic silk-screen printing. These he combined with brushwork on large canvases. His Tracer of 1964 is a key work of this type.

Soon Rauschenberg was joined by others who shared his dissatisfactions with the denial of common visual reality in abstract

expressionism. They rejected the very personal and emotional expressions of the action painters, and returned again to the visual environment that had been avoided by their predecessors. Instead of rejecting the mundane ugliness of the man-made environment, they accepted it. By so doing, they gave us a way of seeing that takes into account what is actually there for us to see.

The artifacts that are the dominant subject matter of pop art take a central position in our time similar to the position held by Christian subjects during the Renaissance. The difference is that Michelangelo was intensifying faith in a religion, while artists like Tom Wesselmann are exposing the shallowness of our faith in things.

The size of the paintings, and the boldness of single visual components within them, have carried over from abstract expressionism. Yet, in contrast to the emotional warmth of abstract expressionism, pop painters such as Lichtenstein, Rosenquist, Warhol, and Wesselmann use skill in creating cool, mechanical images by hiding evidence of their personal touch. They often use photographic silk-screen stencils and airbrush techniques to achieve their images. This impersonality links their work to the uniformity and banality prevalent in mass media.

Pop art's media sources include the comic strip, the advertising blowup, the branded package, and the visual clichés of billboard, newspaper, movie house, and TV. All of this material is present in a small collage done in 1956 by the English artist Richard Hamilton, called Just What Is It that Makes Today's Homes So Different, So Appealing? In spite of its small format, it was loaded with significance for the future. In it we see inspiration for the name as well as the attitude behind the pop style. Quite appropriately, Hamilton made his collage for an exhibition called "This Is Tomorrow."

272   Tom Wesselmann
STILL LIFE No. 33
1963. Paint and collage. 11 x 15'.

273   Bernie Kemnitz
MRS. KARL'S BREAD SIGN
1964. Billboard. 60 x 150'.

274 Claes Oldenburg. Sculpture in the Form of a Trowel Stuck in the Ground.
1971. Height 40′.

Artists have had the ability to awaken the senses of their fellow men since art began. Works like Tom Wesselmann's painting, Still Life No. 33 and Bernie Kemnitz' billboard, Mrs. Karl's Bread Sign, reveal the pop-art world in which we live.

It is fairly easy to divide artists into stylistic groups, but the practice is valuable only up to a point. Ultimately each person gives form to individual experience. Claes Olden-burg can be called a pop sculptor, but that label merely suggests his point of view.

Oldenburg calls our attention to the amazing character of ordinary man-made things by taking them out of context, changing their scale, or by transforming them from hard to soft. A garden tool becomes a monument in his Sculpure in the Form of a Trowel Stuck in the Ground.

275   Ivan Masser. THE PAUSE THAT REFRESHES. Kenya, 1964.

The Coca-Cola bottle has been designed with care. Its design evolved over a comparatively long period of time (see page 250). The Coke bottle is a most commonplace object in today's world. An archeologist of the future who digs up the remains of our present civilization will find so many Coke bottles that he may assume they were used in some sort of common religious ritual!

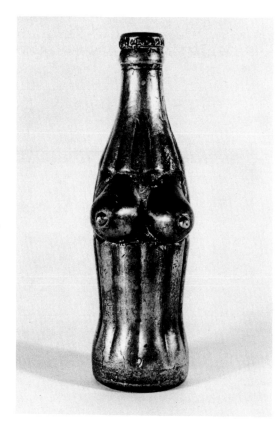

276   Charles Frazier
COKE BOTTLE
1963. Bronze. Height 7¾".

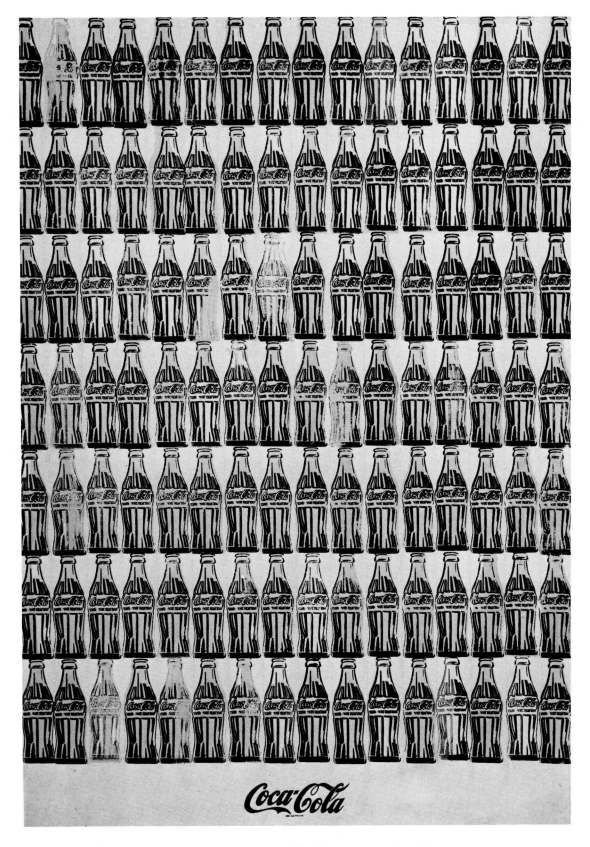

277 Andy Warhol. Green Coca-Cola Bottles. 1962. Oil on canvas. 82¼ x 57".

278 George Segal
Detail of THE GAS STATION
1963. Plaster and mixed media.
8'6" x 24' x 4'.

279   Marisol
LOVE
1962. Plaster. Life-size.

As paintings have become things themselves, rather than reflections of things, they have begun to function as environments, rather than as patches of decorative color. They are no longer representations of environments already existing elsewhere.

Ben Cunningham goes beyond the usual rectangular format for a painting in PAINTING FOR A CORNER. His combination of reflective and nonreflective surfaces creates a new kind of illusionary space. Numerous artists work with free-standing panels, reflective and relief surfaces, and with shaped canvases that move in three-dimensional space. Their work breaks down the line between painting and sculpture.

280 Ben Cunningham
PAINTING FOR A CORNER
1948–1950. Oil on canvas. 25½ x 36½". 25½ x 21½".

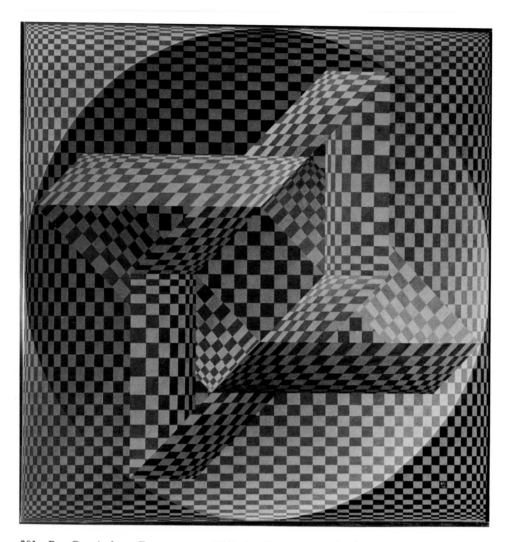

281   Ben Cunningham. EQUIVOCATION. 1964. Acrylic on composition board. 26 x 25½".

There is more than one way to make a surface come to life. The action painters used thick paint and bold brushwork to develop dynamic surfaces. Then a few painters began to create hard-edge images that were visually tantalizing in a new way. The paintings in this group are known as optical art, or op art. The concept of a painting as a thing is pushed beyond surface decoration. Images are more than what is actually on the surface. Their full dynamic tension exists only in the eye of the beholder. This can be seen in EQUIVOCATION by Ben Cunningham. Hungarian artist Victor Vasarely was a pioneer of this style. See color plate 39.

The op artist's emphasis on the scientific exploration of optical phenomena is even farther than pop from the idea of personal expression.

This movement brings together the work of artists who are exploring the field of pure optical experience with the cool precision and anonymity of engineers. Group creation and teamwork are common, as a means of seeking and sharing discoveries of optical phenomena. One primary aim is to stretch vision by producing kinetic visual sensations that are not actually present in the initial image. These eye movements are involuntary.

282   Wes Wilson. THE SOUND. 1966. Silk screen.

In the mid-1960s the drug culture produced a vibrant, emotional style of art that appeared most frequently in posters advertising rock music concerts and accompanying light shows. The flamelike curvilinear forms of turn-of-the-century art nouveau provided inspiration.

Psychedelic art grew out of drug use, yet provides the viewer with a drug-free "turn on." Works such as Wes Wilson's poster recreate through visual media the expansive experience of a "good trip." Psychedelic art was the popular informal partner of op.

Kinetic art is art that changes as you look at it or touch it. The term "kinetic" applies to a wide range of styles in which motion is an important element. Form and content in contemporary kinetic art ranges from the cool precision of Nicholas Schöffer's gleaming metal and plastic motorized constructions (see page 306) to the happy absurdity of Jean Tinguely's mechanical junk sculpture.

The Swiss sculptor Tinguely creates machines that do just about everything except work in the manner expected of machines. In 1960 Tinguely built a large piece of mechanized sculpture that he put together from materials gathered from junkyards and stores around New York City. The result was a giant assemblage designed to destroy itself at the turn of a switch. The sculpture was appropriately called HOMAGE TO NEW YORK: A SELF-CONSTRUCTING, SELF-DESTROYING WORK OF ART.

Another mixed-media art form that came into prominence in the early 1960s was the "happening." Artists, who saw easel painting and fixed-object sculpture as irrelevant, found they could involve their audience in works that can best be described as experimental participatory theater. The resulting dramas had dada and surrealist overtones.

The term "happening" was first used in the United States by Allan Kaprow. Like Duchamp, the creators of happenings wanted to force the viewer to be involved with his environment. No help is given to the viewer who is expected to find his own answers. Strictly speaking, happenings are drama with "structure but no plot, words but no dialogue, actors but no characters, and above all, nothing logical or continuous."[64] Unlike dada and surrealist events, the first happenings were frequently nihilistic without a relieving sense of humor.

Festivals of all kinds can be considered happenings. In a broad sense, if they contribute to human experience, they act as art. Street protests can work as happenings. If the participants have a sense of symbolic drama, the effect can be powerful.

283 Jean Tinguely. HOMAGE TO NEW YORK: A SELF-CONSTRUCTING, SELF-DESTROYING WORK OF ART. 1960.

284   ANTIAUTO POLLUTION DEMONSTRATION OUTSIDE COLISEUM, NEW YORK CITY, WHERE THE ANNUAL AUTO SHOW WAS ON. April 1971.

285   Geoff Manasse. MORATORIUM RALLY. San Francisco, April 1971.

286   Michael Salzberg. ANTIWAR VETERANS IN WHITEFACE. 1971.

287   Nora Scarlett
PEACE MARCH. San Francisco, 1971.

The tragic, seemingly endless Vietnam War has been shown in many aspects by artist-photographers, who often died in the process of trying to capture the most telling images of what they were experiencing.

The United States Army has collected paintings and photographs of American wars for a long time. In the past, many of these made war seem heroic. As the Vietnam War continued, the army began to send drafted artists to Vietnam to record their impressions. Much of what came back was superficial.

The work of John D. Kurtz is exceptional. In his painting, NINE SEATED INFANTRYMEN, he has created an image of futility and boredom that probably represents 90 percent of what soldiers have experienced there.

288   John D. Kurtz. NINE SEATED INFANTRYMEN. c. 1968. Oil on canvas. 40 x 52".

During the last ten years, a number of painters and sculptors have reduced the complexity of their designs to a minimum by
concentrating on simple geometric structures. By giving fewer elements to consider,
minimal art forces the viewer back on his
inner resources. Minimal artists often create
massive *things*, rather than sculptures or
paintings. Such objects invade space, con-
fronting the viewer with their presence.
There is nothing more to go on.

The sculptor and former architect Tony
Smith was one of the first to explore the
possibilities of large inert objects. He picked
up the telephone in 1962 and ordered a
steel cube six feet on each side. The size,
mass, material, and method go together to
make a heavy visual statement. Smith challenged another preconception about the
nature of art by removing himself completely from the processes of making the
work.

Continuous and accelerated change is an
ever-present phenomenon in late twentieth-
century art and life. The concept of obsoles-
cence does not provide for the development
of a tradition. Isamu Noguchi's CUBE relates
to the minimal trend, but immediately the
viewer is engaged in the dynamics of balance, bold color, and shaped space. Emphasis here is on a huge, simple, geometric mass.
The sculpture's massive proportions allow it
to interact with the skyscraper.

289   Tony Smith
DIE
1962

290   Isamu Noguchi
· CUBE
1969. Painted welded steel and aluminum.
Height 28'. *See color plate 40.*

The Russian painter Malevich was the grandfather of minimal art. He worked with cubism for awhile, then pioneered this purist approach in 1913, when he painted "nothing more or less than a black square on a white background. . . . It was not just a square I had exhibited," he explained, "but rather the expression of nonobjectivity."[65] A few years later, he painted SUPREMATIST COMPOSITION: WHITE ON WHITE, an ultimate demonstration of what he called suprematism (see page 93). He explained that by this term he meant "the supremacy of pure feeling or perception in the pictorial arts."[66]

Al Held cuts his shapes in such a way that they seem even more gigantic than they actually are. The figure in this photograph shows the scale of his painting, GREEK GARDEN.

291   Al Held. GREEK GARDEN. 1966. Acrylic on canvas. 12 x 56'.

Ever since cubism broke with the Renaissance concept of deep space, some painters have tried to push the limits of flatness, rather than depth. Almost any mark on a flat surfac will begin to give the appearance of depth. Frank Stella has tried to counteract that fact by building up surfaces that are made up entirely of parallel line patterns. More recently, he has begun to use interwoven bands of color. The interwoven pattern of intense color pulls together into a tight spatial sandwich. Although most of the colors tend naturally to appear to either advance or recede, each is pulled to the surface because of its placement in the overlapping visual weave.

The advent of acrylic paint has revitalized color in painting in recent years. Helen Frankenthaler's work evolved during the height of abstract expressionism. In 1952 she developed her stain technique as an extension of Jackson Pollock's poured paint. She spread liquid oil colors out across unprimed canvas, where they soaked in, becoming part of the fabric. Her main concern was the potential of colors and shapes. The new acrylic paints made it possible for her to cover huge canvases with thin layers of intense color. Today Frankenthaler is a leader in a direction called color field painting, in which fluid areas of paint provide an environment of color for the viewer.

Since Edison invented the electric light bulb in 1879, it has been possible to control light. Light is a medium, not a style. Its use in art is not a new idea. Twenty-five centuries ago Pythagoras visualized the silent motion of the heavenly bodies as visual music and called it "the music of the spheres." Isaac Newton speculated on a possible connection between the vibrations of sound and light in an art of "Color Music." This led to many futile attempts to assign a color to each note in the musical scale.

292 Frank Stella
SINJERLI VARIATION IV
1968. Fluorescent acrylic on canvas. Diameter 120″.

293 Helen Frankenthaler
INTERIOR LANDSCAPE
1964. Acrylic on canvas. 103¾ x 92¾″. *See color plate 41*

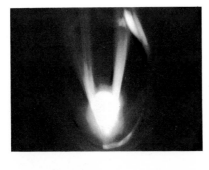

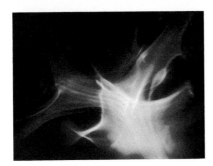

294 Thomas Wilfred
LUMIA SUITE, OP. 158 (two stages)
1963–1964. Light composition projected against a
screen. 6 x 8'. See color plate 32.

Thomas Wilfred was one of the first to conceive of light art as an independent aesthetic language. He called it "lumia." His experiments in 1905 led to the development of the "Clavilux Lumia," an instrument on which he played the first public recitals in 1922 in New York City, and later throughout the United States, Canada, and Europe. His recorded compositions are now exhibited in museums and art collections.

Wilfred's recent works have achieved rare quality. He has worked out a system for reflecting light from moving mirrors onto a translucent screen. From the front of the screen a continuously changing pattern of colored light appears. Light art has come into its own since 1960. The list of artists who have turned to the new medium is growing steadily.

Each person in the visual arts conceives his work on the basis of his own unique perception. This fact is readily apparent in the work of Don Eddy. There is nothing exotic about Eddy's subject matter. For each painting, he works from several of his own black and white photographs taken of subjects that excite him visually. The color is often inspired by his favorite artist, Hans Hofmann. Eddy's images are developed on fairly large canvases with a faultless airbrush technique. His father owned a car-painting shop, where Eddy worked in his youth. He became an expert at custom painting cars. While studying "fine" art, he rejected all of this visual experience and skill. Now he seems aware that it is part of him, and shares the insights gained from it with us. Eddy is particularly excited about what he can discover and make happen in terms of unique spatial tensions. On the flat painted surfaces, these tensions couple with ambiguous reflections, creating rich sensations for the eye. A sense of space and design, combined with the clarity and intensity of his perception, transform the ordinary subject into something quite extraordinary.

Eddy's work is part of an important style of the late 1960s and early 1970s, which can be described as cool realism. Charles Close represents another facet of this superreal photographic style. See page 274. Close uses a brush rather than an airbrush.

295 Don Eddy
PRIVATE PARKING X
1971. Acrylic on canvas. 66 x 95". See color plate 33.

Most of us have strong emotional attachments to the idea that a work of art is a unique object, an original, made only once by the artist's own hands. Actually, artists have been designing things that were made by artisans for thousands of years. Architects have rarely, if ever, tried to construct a building by themselves. In Japan, popular color woodcut prints have been produced by artist teams. The artist-designer, the publisher, the wood engraver, and the colorist were all responsible for the final print. Men like Hokusai, Hiroshige, and Utamura did nothing but the original design, yet we treasure their prints and call them originals. In filmmaking, large groups must work to produce the finished product. The idea of a single original created by the hands of one artist is irrelevant in this context.

We live in a world of reproductions. Nearly everything we come into contact with is designed by someone and then mass-produced by others. Do we enjoy these things less because of this? It is true that in an environment full of mass-produced things, a one-of-a-kind-thing, obviously made by hand, is refreshing. This is why the crafts are now enjoying greater and greater popularity.

The Swiss artist Max Bill is an artists' artist and a universal man as well. He is a painter, sculptor, architect, aesthetic theorist, teacher, journalist, and even politician. In 1927 he attended the great German art school called the Bauhaus (see page 206). Since then, his work has evolved in a way consistent with the rational approach he established as a student. From music Bill found inspiration for applying mathematical systems to the organization of visual form. The resulting works are crystallizations of his thought and intuition. Their purity seems to offer strength to those at hand, even without visual contact.

The multiple original concept has now grown from printmaking into sculpture (see

296 Max Bill
DOUBLEMENT
1970. Polished stainless steel. 15 x 15 x 15'.

Printmaking, page 279). Bill's sculpture of polished stainless steel, called DOUBLEMENT, has been produced by industrial methods in a numbered edition of 200 copies. This particular work can almost be considered a minimal multiple.

In the late 1960s many serious artists tried to abandon the established circuit of galleries, dealers, patrons, and museums by creating noncollectable works. The cult of the precious object was attacked. Permanence, long a major concern in the visual arts, had been losing importance for some time. In dada and surrealist works, chance frequently played a major role in determining composition. The process of creating art thus became as important as the product. This attitude was central to abstract expressionism and seems to have culminated in conceptual art.

In conceptual art, process is the birth of an idea or concept, which is then demonstrated and/or recorded in some way so that its existence is validated. A notable conceptual work was ICE by Rafael Ferrer. In the fall of 1969 Ferrer put together an assemblage of ice blocks and autumn leaves on the Whitney Museum's entry ramp. When collectors complained about the ephemeral nature of his creation, Ferrer suggested that the iceman's bill might do as a kind of drawing.

Conceptual art is part of a strong recent tendency to conceive works that relate to interior and exterior spaces, not as isolated wall pieces or floor pieces, but as environmentally inclusive forms. Such thinking is illustrated by one form of noncollectable work known as earth art. Artists such as Robert Smithson and Dennis Oppenheim manipulate the land. Whether this art is permanent or impermanent, beneficial or destructive to the land depends on the sensibility of the individual artist. As with happenings, some of the most beautiful earth

works have been done by people who do not consider themselves artists.

As we approach the last quarter of the twentieth century, artists continue to find ways to challenge and augment our experience. The gold frame and the pedestal that set art apart from the viewer are things of the past. Increased viewer participation is a major characteristic of contemporary art. Some artists, whose works would traditionally be found in galleries, museums, and the homes of wealthy collectors, are creating works designed for public indoor and outdoor spaces and for the homes of people with moderate incomes. This move away from exclusive art circles has been helped by the growing patronage of corporations and by the production of multiples, which can be sold at prices many people can afford. Rapidly growing interest in the crafts has greatly increased involvement in the visual arts.

297   Robert Smithson. SPIRAL JETTY. Great Salt Lake, Utah, 1970. Length 1500′, width 15′.

298   Dennis Oppenheim. CANCELED CROP. 1968.

Capsule histories of the visual arts, like this one and all others of which I am aware, barely mention or leave out the most nota-ble public arts of our time; photography, and its children cinematography and tele-vision. These arts play a major role in contemporary life, yet to weave them into this history of painting, sculpture, and architecture would cause considerable confusion. Although the histories of painting and photography have been intimately linked, cinematography and television have developed independently because of their strong relationship to drama. While the camera arts are the dominant popular forms of our time, their quantity makes it difficult to find those works that are of sufficient quality to be called art in the full sense of the word. Both cinema and television are kinetic forms that respond to the demands of mechanized urban life. Their transitory character fits with the complex technology that supports them. What will be their significance to future man?

The ability of primitive man to identify with his environment and to act out the drama of life in drawing, carving, mime, and song calmed his fears and hungers and intensified his joy. To create art called for imagination, memory, and the imitation of natural forms. Today we have the same human needs. Artists live in the present. It seems as if

they are ahead of their time, but actually they are among the few who are with their time. Some artists are especially concerned with bringing together the outer and the inner man, and with reasserting man's intimate relationship with his surroundings. And yet, it is no accident that the often abrasive quality of modern life has found full force in contemporary art.

Contemporary art reveals contemporary life, and vice versa. Boredom, cynicism, and mediocrity characterize much of what passes for art in today's affluent society. If we do not like what we see, perhaps we should take a look at ourselves and at what we have produced.

Works from the past that we consider great have been made available for our appreciation through repeated favorable criticism and frequent reproduction. It is easier to understand, and therefore enjoy, works of art from the past because they fulfill well-established preconceptions concerning the nature of art and reality.

Works of poor quality from the past have generally not been reproduced and therefore are removed from consideration. In contrast, we have a full array of works, good, bad, and indifferent, from our own time. History shows that artists who are best accepted in their own time are not necessarily the ones whose works are appreciated by future generations. Some artists, now unknown, and therefore "unsuccessful," may be the ones who make the most lasting contribution to humanity.

Society takes what it wants. The artist himself doesn't count, because there is no actual existence for the work of art. The work of art is always based on the two poles of the onlooker and the maker, and the spark that comes from that bipolar action gives birth to something — like electricity. But the onlooker has the last word, and it is always posterity that makes the masterpiece. The artist should not concern himself with this, because it has nothing to do with him.

Marcel Duchamp[67]

299   Sanford Darling
PAINTED KITCHEN
Photograph by Rafael Maldonado, Jr., 1971

What are the visual arts?

Years of direct observation and practical experience are necessary to understand thoroughly each discipline of the visual arts — the materials used, and the techniques appropriate to it. The development of a discipline is intimately connected with the limitations and possibilities inherent in the materials. A particular material, along with its accompanying technique, is called a *medium*. Wood, stone, plastic, metal, glass, paper, paint, and clay are all materials. Each material has its own unique properties. Artists often combine or mix many materials and their accompanying techniques in one work. The result is then referred to as mixed media.

Newspapers, magazines, books, and brochures are considered to be print media; television and radio are broadcast media. Marshall McLuhan has called attention to the importance of media by pointing out that the communicative form of a message is often more important than its given content.[1]

In each case, the artist seeks that medium which best suits the ideas and feelings he wishes to express. The starting point may be the desire to work in a particular way with certain kinds of materials.

DESIGN

Everything that man creates needs to be designed either before or during the process of its construction. This process is often spontaneous. After a work is finished, we respond to the quality or lack of quality in its design. We are frequently in contact with poorly designed objects that negate our own sensitivity. This is why it is important for each person who is responsible for designing anything to become conscious of and develop his design sense so that he may assume effective control over the quality of his work.

Design is also a professional discipline of the visual arts. Designers are paid to apply their sense of design to a wide variety of man-made objects and spaces. Design begins with small objects and interior spaces. The concept has now been extended to include large-scale environmental decisions.

Over 70 percent of the United States population now lives in urban centers, and a large percentage of the rest of the world is either equally urbanized or moving in that direction. By definition, an urban environment is largely man-made. Many people today, and most of our descendants, will spend their lives surrounded by objects designed by man. In areas where man-made designs are dominant, a struggle goes on between the demands of human sensibility and the demands of mechanical and economic expediency. In the United States, art, like religion, has been separated from

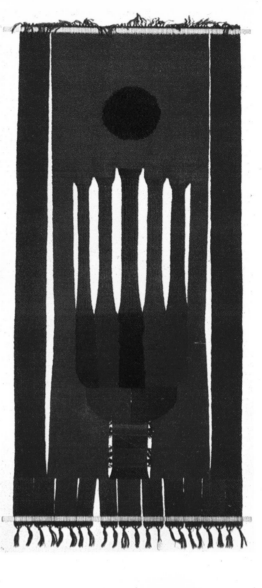

Color plate 35
Alice Parrott
Red Form
1967. Wool.
Approx. 36 x 70″.

Color plate 34
Toshiko Takaezu
Ceramic Pot
1971. Height 13″.

Color plate 36
Carol Summers
Cheops
1967. Woodcut.
29¾₁₆ x 21″.

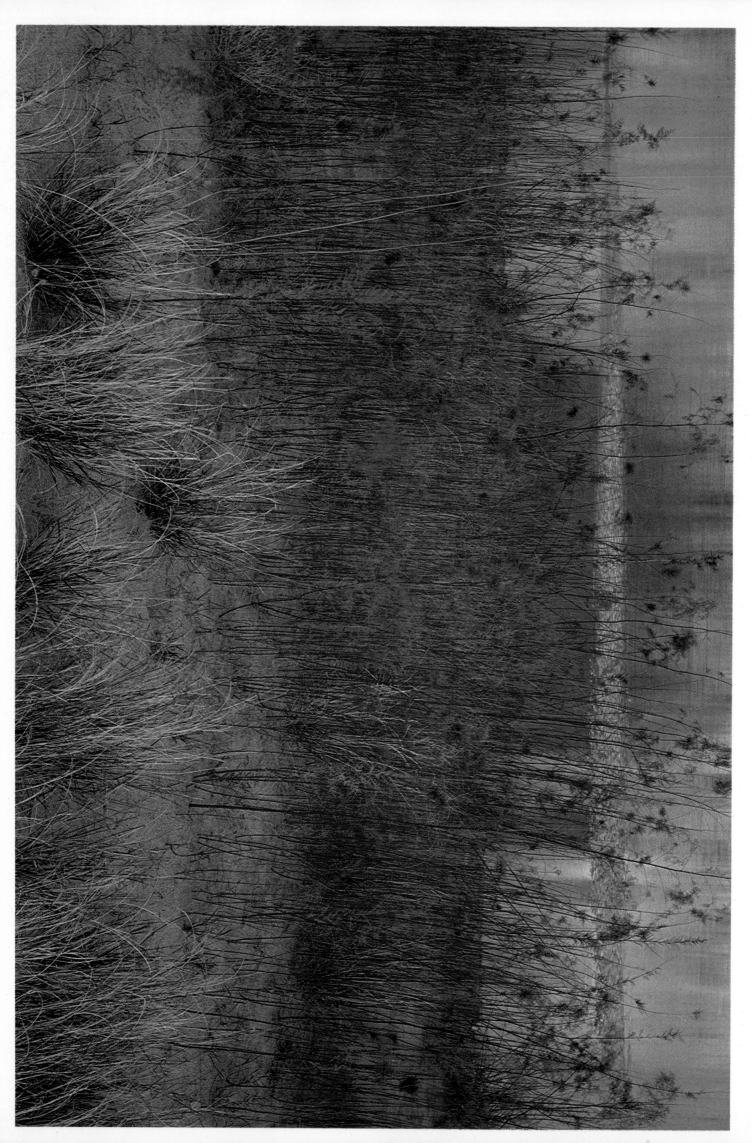

Color plate 37 Eliot Porter. TAMARISK AND GRASS. 1961.

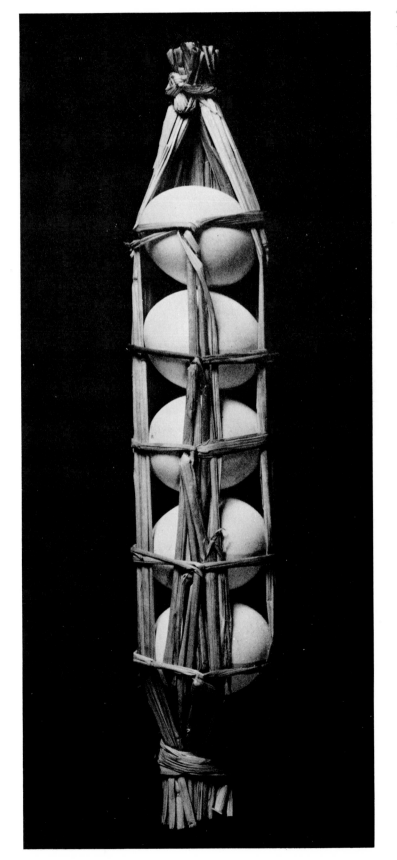

daily life. Recent concern about this separation is producing an increasing number of well-designed objects, made both by hand and by machine.

Preindustrial societies throughout the world frequently designed domestic utensils with such care that today we give these objects space in art museums.

The traditional, functional objects of Japan exhibit a high degree of design sophistication, even when the object is a disposable wrapping such as the one shown here.

300 RICE STRAW EGG CONTAINER
Yamagata Prefecture, northern Japan
Photograph by Michikazu Sakai

250 WHAT ARE THE VISUAL ARTS? / Design

1894-1906

301

1915 1923 1937 1956

Wrapping Coca-Cola is as difficult as wrapping five eggs. Between 1894 and 1915 the Coca-Cola bottle changed from an ordinary turn-of-the-century medicine bottle to more than just a bottle. Through design it took on some of the appealing curves of the female figure clothed in a long dress. The parts of the bottle began to interrelate to form a flowing design. By 1956 this design had evolved into the bottle that is so common today.

302 Ludwig Mies van der Rohe. BARCELONA CHAIR. 1929.

Chair design is important to us, both for visual appearance and physical comfort. The architect Ludwig Mies van der Rohe designed a chair in 1929 that has become a classic. It is sculptural and comfortable.

The beanbag chair is a different sort of concept. It provides comfort by responding to the form and position of the sitter. Visually it is a blob. Its soft spineless character makes it ideal for casual relaxation.

303 BEAN BAG CHAIR
Photograph by Rick Regan, 1972

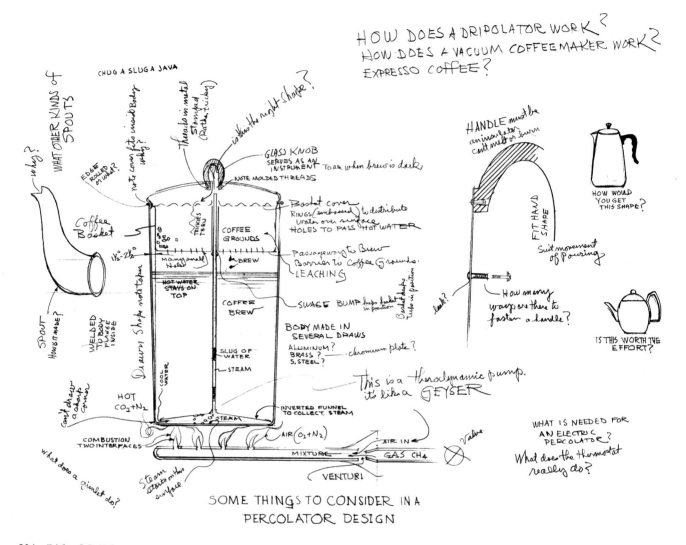

SOME THINGS TO CONSIDER IN A
PERCOLATOR DESIGN

304 Richard I. Felver. PERCOLATOR DESIGN. 1972.

INDUSTRIAL DESIGN

Industrial design is art working within industrial media. An industrial designer can work on things as simple as a bottle cap or as complex as an information-processing system. Always he needs to be able to learn anew, becoming familiar with how the object he is designing is fabricated and must work, and how it can become meaningful, economical, and a contribution to living processes. This means designing so that the relationship between the object and the people who use it provides a means, rather than a hindrance, to human fulfillment. Industrial design is an important and demanding field whose purpose is to make sense of technology.

This sketch shows a few of the specific details and possibilities that a designer must consider when trying to comprehend the design of any common yet always complex object, for example, the coffee percolator.

How much of the cost of a new car goes for visual design? It depends on the make of the car. It has been estimated that of the price paid for the average American car over the last twenty years, one-half to two-thirds has been for design alone. If this is true, millions of Americans have spent an average of about $2,000 apiece for "art" when they purchase a new automobile.

Because economy has been more important in automobile manufacturing outside the United States, the portion of the purchase price of a foreign car that pays for designing and redesigning is much less. The aspect of car design that is expensive is the retooling of the machinery that makes the car. Thus, it is the change in design, rather than the design itself, that costs so much.

305 TEAM OF INDUSTRIAL DESIGNERS AT WORK
Isuzu Motors Ltd., Tokyo

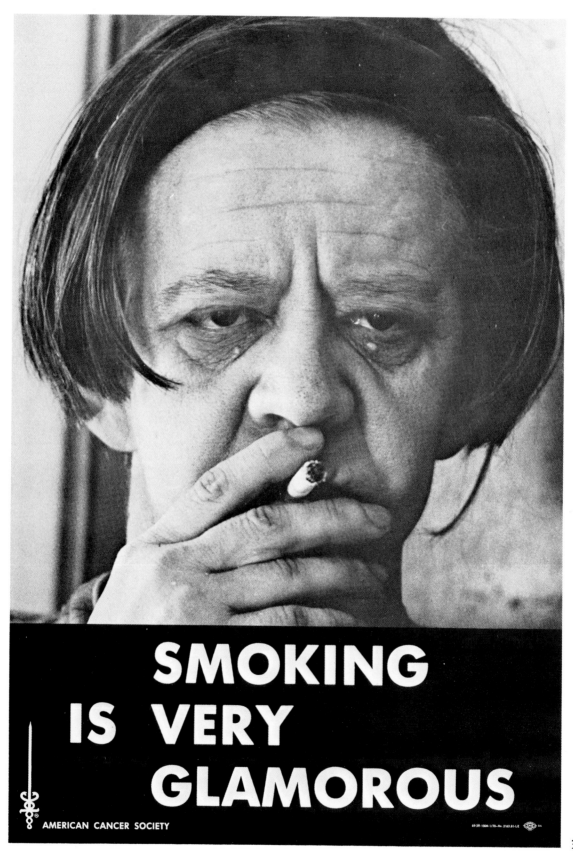

SMOKING IS VERY GLAMOROUS

AMERICAN CANCER SOCIETY

306

307

ADVERTISING DESIGN

Another field of work is advertising design. It has been estimated that the average American adult is assaulted by a minimum of 560 advertising messages each day. And we are building up our communications machinery in order to transmit an even richer array of images at an even faster rate.

"Commercial art" was a common term for this professional discipline. Now it is often called "graphics design" because it may involve more than the design of advertising images.

In advertising, the arts frequently work together. In that sense television advertising is a kind of operatic art form that calls upon writers, musicians, and actors, as well as directors, cameramen, and graphics designers.

Printed visual advertising was not widely used before this century. A writer, a designer, and often an illustrator or photographer work as a team to achieve the final ad. Both of the accompanying ads have been effective. They offer strong propaganda on two sides of an argument. One may have been designed to counteract the other.

INTERIOR DESIGN

Important considerations for any interior design include size, shape, arrangement of space, the relationship between inside and outside space, texture, and color. The theory is that a good interior designer brings out the inherent design wishes of his client and does his best to make these ideas work.

The life style of the individuals who will live in certain interior spaces should determine the design of those spaces. Because of this, some of the best interior design is done by individuals for themselves. When you know what you like and why you like it, there is no end to the quality that you can build into a home or work space.

Good designers know how indoor environments affect people who use them. The quality of the spaces we occupy can cause us to be cheerful or discouraged. Man enhances the quality of his living space by developing and utilizing his sensitivity to relationships in physical space.

The character of the living area of the Nicoll residence is largely determined by the architectural space. Structural clarity in the building is echoed in the strong simple forms of the furnishings.

Interior living spaces are designed consciously and unconsciously by the way of life of those who inhabit them. Compare the life style symbolized by Richard Hamilton's satirical pop collage on page 227 with the life style reflected in this photograph of the Libra Commune.

308   William Kenzler. Interior, Nicoll Residence. 1963.

309 LIBRA COMMUNE. Photograph by Dennis Stock, 1970.

hands to create objects for everyday use. This trend is evidently much more than a passing fad — it is part of the foundation of a new era. Ceramics and weaving have been the most widely practiced of the crafts, but the recent revival has reintroduced a wide variety of other crafts, including leatherwork, jewelrymaking, candlemaking, enameling, and glassblowing.

310 M. & T. Bass
WOMAN SPINNING
Kathmandu, Nepal, 1970

CRAFTS

The crafts practiced today link us with a long tradition. If the fossil fuels and metal ores that now support our industrialized society run out, we may again depend on the crafts to provide for our daily needs, as they have done throughout much of human history. A seemingly infinite variety of material goods, such as fabrics and dishes, are now produced in quantity by mechanical methods. This development has made it possible for many people to make objects in the craft disciplines without the pressures of earlier demands for quantity, economy, and practicality.

Handmade articles can have a quality that enhances the spiritual aspects of human life. Many people are discovering the lasting satisfaction that comes from using their own

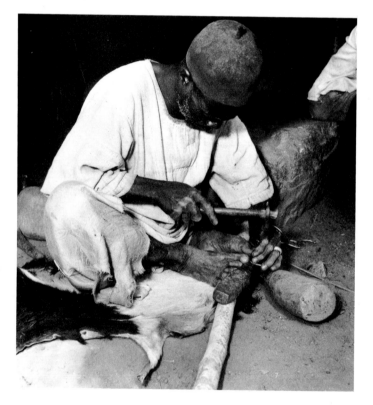

311 René Gardi
SMITH FROM NORTHERN DAHOMEY
1969

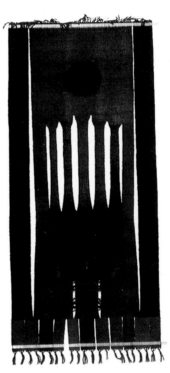

314 Alice Parrott
RED FORM
1967. Wool.
Approx. 36 x 70".
See color plate 35

315 LEATHERWORKING

312 JEWELRYMAKING

313 Toshiko Takaezu
CERAMIC POT
1971. Height 13".
See color plate 34

316 GLASSBLOWING

317 POTTING

318 BATIKING

CERAMICS

Ceramics is the art and science of making objects from clay. The earth provides a variety of clays that can be mixed with one another and refined in order to obtain the desired body and plasticity. Ceramics range from coarse raku and stoneware to fine porcelain. Clay has long been a valuable material for man. It offers ample flexibility and relative permanence because of its capacity to harden when exposed to intense heat.

A craftsman in clay is usually called a potter. Potters create functional pots or purely sculptural forms by hand building with slabs or coils of clay or by "throwing" forms on a hand-, foot-, or motor-driven wheel.

When a piece is thoroughly dry, it is chemically changed into a hard, stonelike substance by firing it in a kiln. Glazes for added color and texture can be applied before a single firing or between the first and second firings.

320 WEAVING

WEAVING

319 MACRAMÉING

Threadlike fibers, both natural and synthetic, are the basic materials for a variety of forms produced by processes such as weaving, stitching, knitting, crocheting, and macraméing (knotting).

Weaving, like ceramics, was developed when early man was forced to shift from hunter to farmer. Garments made from cloth became a necessity when skins were no longer available for warmth.

The basic processes of making cloth, from spinning to weaving, are relatively easy to learn, and materials can be inexpensive. Weaving may be complex or simple. A large floor loom capable of accommodating wide yardage can take several days to prepare. On a simple hand loom, a weaving can be finished in a few hours.

Processes such as silk-screen printing, batiking, and tie-dying enhance cloth surfaces in a variety of ways that cannot be achieved through any weaving technique.

DRAWING

Drawing is practiced by artists working in most disciplines as a basic means of expressing visual ideas quickly. The differences between drawing and painting are sometimes vague. In one sense painting is drawing with paint. Direct drawing is often necessary in the process of printmaking and in making relief sculpture. Cartooning is completely dependent on drawing. Drawing is also a separate discipline.

Line is the fundamental element of drawing. To draw, in the most elementary sense, means to pull, push, or drag a marking tool across a surface in order to leave a mark.

Anyone who is intrigued by the rich complexity of the visual world can develop that interest by drawing. Once involved, an artist draws whatever catches his eye or imagination. Many artists keep a sketch book to serve as a visual diary. From it ideas may develop and reach maturity as complete works, in drawing or in other media.

Giacometti drew his own face as he saw it reflected in a nearby mirror, using the materials at hand — a ball-point pen and a napkin. The idea of exhibiting or selling this drawing was undoubtedly far from his mind. His primary impulse was to satisfy his compulsion to record what he saw and felt.

321 Alberto Giacometti
SELF-PORTRAIT
1962. Ball-point pen on paper napkin. 7¼ x 5".

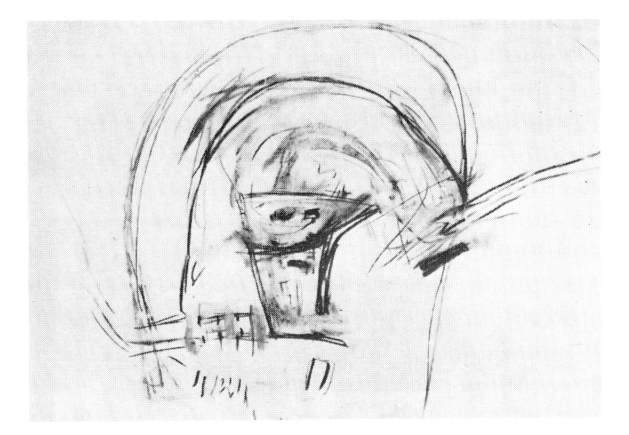

322 Le Corbusier
DRAWING FOR NOTRE-DAME-DU-HAUT
Ronchamp, France, c. 1949

323 Le Corbusier
NOTRE-DAME-DU-HAUT. Exterior.
Ronchamp, France, 1950–1955

A drawing can function in one or all of the following ways:

- as a notation or record of something seen, remembered, or imagined;
- as a study for something else (sculpture, film, painting);
- as an end in itself.

Many drawings can be seen and enjoyed as self-sufficient works of art, in addition to serving one or both of the first two functions.

A drawing can act as the embryo of a complex work. A simple drawing can be to a building or a painting what a melody is to a symphony. When Le Corbusier did his early drawings for the chapel at Ronchamp, he had the shell of a crab lying on his drawing board. This drawing and the roof of the finished building reflect the form of the shell.

324 Pablo Picasso. FIRST COMPOSITION STUDY FOR GUERNICA.
May 9, 1937. Pencil. 9⅛ x 17⅞".

GUERNICA is a very large painting, measuring more than eleven feet in height by twenty-five feet in length. Picasso did many preliminary drawings in preparation for the final painting. Forty-five of these are preserved, all but one dated to a particular day. Yet the overall concept of this complex work is contained in the very first drawing. If GUERNICA had never been painted, this drawing would have little significance. But as a study for such a painting, the drawing takes on meaning.

It is dominated by a woman with a lamp, which appears to be an important symbol to Picasso. She leans out of a house in the upper right. Below her the lines indicate a horse lying on the ground with its head thrown up in a gesture of agony. On the left a bull appears with a bird on its back. These major elements in the final painting are indicated with Picasso's rapid, searching lines. This study was probably drawn in a few intense seconds. It captures in sudden gestures the essence of the final painting. This drawing is the visual embryo of a complex work.

325 Pablo Picasso
GUERNICA
1937. Oil on canvas. 11'5½" x 25'5¼".
See illustration 241.

Two years before doing this drawing, Picasso wrote:

It would be very interesting to preserve photographically, not the stages, but the metamorphoses of a picture. Possibly one might then discover the path followed by the brain in materializing a dream. But there is one very odd thing to notice, that basically a picture doesn't change, that the first "vision" remains almost intact, in spite of appearances.[2]

When Michelangelo made studies for the figure of the Libyan Sibyl, he had no idea that reproductions of this sheet of working drawings would be seen and loved by perhaps as many people as have enjoyed the finished painting of the figure on the ceiling of the Sistine Chapel. The drawing is a record of search and discovery. Michelangelo carefully observed each part and put on paper a record of his observations. His understanding of anatomy helped him to define each part. The rhythmic flow between the head, shoulders, and arms of the figure is based on Michelangelo's feeling for aesthetic continuity as well as his attention to anatomical accuracy. The parts of the figure that were difficult to draw were done more than once. These include the muscles of the figure's left shoulder, the face, the foreshortened left wrist and hand, and the foreshortened big toe of the left foot, drawn three times on this one sheet.

326 Michelangelo Buonarroti. STUDIES FOR THE LIBYAN SIBYL IN THE SISTINE CHAPEL CEILING. c. 1508. Red chalk. 11⅜ x 8⅜".

327 Vincent van Gogh
Carpenter
c. 1880

Van Gogh, like Michelangelo, learned a great deal about visual form by drawing. Michelangelo had fully developed his artistic ability when he drew the studies of the Libyan Sibyl. Van Gogh was just beginning his short career as an artist when he completed this drawing of a carpenter. Both van Gogh and Michelangelo worked in ways that were true to themselves. They each left an account of their unique feelings and perceptions.

Any person who can learn to write can learn to draw. Learning to draw is in some ways easier than learning to write because it is less abstract. The most important factors in learning to draw are interest, integrity, and the ability to see. No one can pick up where someone else has left off. We must all begin in our own way at a beginning point. That is where Michelangelo, Hokusai, van Gogh, and Thurber all began.

James Thurber always said he could not draw, but he drew anyway. He could not draw if by drawing we mean drawing in a particular style. If by drawing we mean realizing our potential to make images of ideas or experiences, then Thurber could draw. See page 7.

328 Hokusai
TUNING THE SAMISEN
c. 1820–1825. Brush drawing. 11 x 8⅞".

The nineteenth-century Japanese artist, Hokusai, was a skillful draftsman. It is estimated that he created 35,000 designs in his lifetime. Yet his humorous statement about the development of his own ability reveals an attitude of struggle against the kinds of self-doubts that we all possess:

I have been in love with painting ever since I became conscious of it at the age of six. I drew some pictures which I thought fairly good when I was fifty, but really nothing I did before the age of seventy was of any value at all. At seventy-three I have at last caught every aspect of nature — birds, fish, animals, insects, trees, grasses, all. When I am eighty I shall have developed still further and will really master the secrets of art at ninety. When I reach one hundred my art will be truly sublime and my final goal will be attained around the age of one hundred and ten, when every line and dot I draw will be imbued with life.

(signed) Hokusai
"The art-crazy old man"[3]

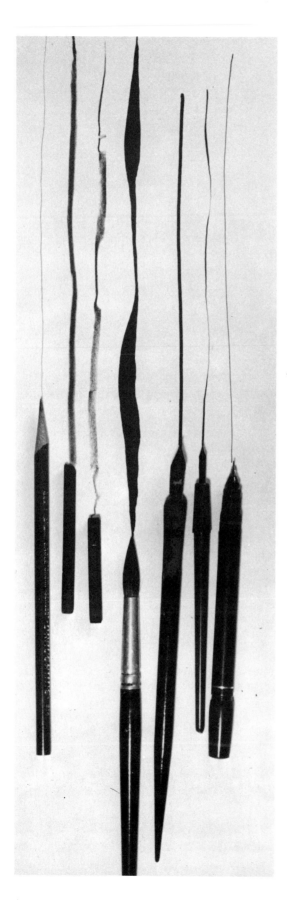

Each drawing tool and each type of paper has its own character. When they combine well with the character and skill of the person drawing, the result will have merit.

Charles Sheeler drew FELINE FELICITY with pencil on fairly rough paper (paper with tooth). The result is a very detailed image. Light and shade work together in an intricate pattern. This is a good example of a drawing done as a finished work, although drawings do not have to be this refined to be conceived as an end in themselves.

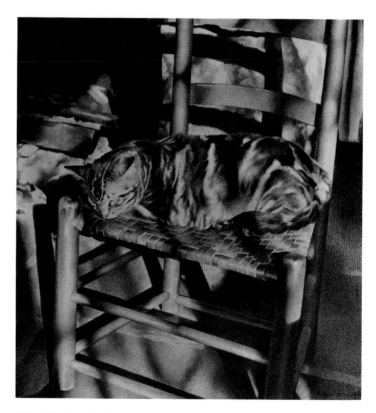

330   Charles Sheeler
FELINE FELICITY
1904. Crayon. 14⅛ x 13¼".

329

331 Alphonse Legros. HEAD OF A MAN. 1892. Silverpoint. 8¾ x 7".

The head study by Legros was done with *silverpoint*. No variation in width or gradation in value is possible with this medium. Value must be built up with parallel lines, called hatching, or with crosshatching. Silverpoint will only mark a specially coated surface. Lines are made of actual silver, giving an even grey line that soon darkens with oxidation. The line quality thus achieved goes well with a refined style of drawing.

The metal-point stylus was used for writing and drawing before the invention of the pencil. Silver was the favorite metal because it wore down slowly and produced an even line. Paper or parchment was coated with fine abrasive material, like bone dust mixed in thin glue, in order to give the proper tooth to the surface.

Legend has it that someone saw a portrait
drawing by Matisse done with great economy of line and asked with some disgust,
"How long did it take you to do this?"
Matisse answered, "Forty years."

332   Henri Matisse
PORTRAIT OF I.C.
c. 1935–1945. Drawing.

Rembrandt used brush, ink, water, and paper to draw his wife, Saskia. The result is at once bold and subtle, representational and nonrepresentational, finished and unfinished. As a total image, it is complete. His technique bears comparison to oriental brush painting.

333   Rembrandt van Rijn
SASKIA ASLEEP
c. 1642. Brush and wash. 9½ x 8".

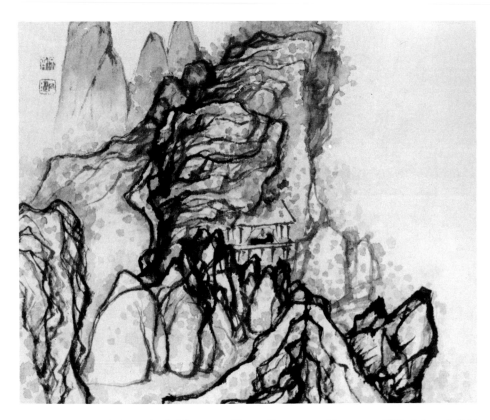

334 Tao Chi (Shih Tao). A Man in a House Beneath a Cliff. c. 1800. Ink and light color on paper. 9½ x 11".

The soft-hair brush is a flexible drawing instrument with considerable expressive potential. Tao Chi's drawing was probably painted with a single brush. The vigorous strokes symbolize a mountain cliff full of energy surrounding a house in which a man sits quietly in meditation. Because the work is completed by light color areas, yet emphasizes drawn lines, it can be considered either a drawing or a graphic painting.

PAINTING

The nature of paint makes it possible to do certain things that cannot be done with other media. Traditional painting media consist of *pigments* that provide the range of colors and a *binder* that holds pigments together in suspension so that they can be applied to surfaces. Pigments are the same in each medium; only the binder changes — the binder is sometimes called the medium. Paints are generally applied as a liquid or paste, but even dry color media such as crayon and pastel are referred to as paint media because they contain the same pigments found in liquid paint. Until recently pigments were earth colors and natural dyes. Today many pigment colors are produced synthetically.

Paints are usually applied to a flat *support*, such as stretched canvas for oils and paper for watercolors. The surface of the support may be prepared by *sizing* and *priming* to achieve a *ground* that will have the proper absorbency and permanence. A paper surface provides both the support and the ground for watercolor.

The development of painting media has determined to a large extent the evolution of various kinds of visual images. The following is a summary of major types of painting media and their dominant characteristics.

OIL

The paintings at Lascaux caves (see color plate 17) were made by mixing earth pigments with animal oils. During the Renaissance in Europe, painters began using vegetable oil made from the seed of flax, linseed, as a binder. Linseed oil paint has the advantage of not changing color as it dries. This factor plus its flexibility has made it a favorite medium for 400 years.

Oil paint is usually diluted for application with a mixture of linseed oil, varnish, and turpentine. It can be applied thickly or thinly, wet into wet or wet into dry. Applied thinly mixed with varnish, it is excellent for building up deep transparent surfaces through a technique called glazing. Oil paint can also be applied as a thick pastelike material, which may be given added body and texture with the addition of inert substances like sand. Thick application of paint, such as that used by Hans Hofmann in MEADOW SPLENDOR, is called *impasto*. See also Rembrandt's HEAD OF SAINT MATTHEW, page 87. The slow-drying time of oil medium allows for reworking and blending colors directly on the painting surface. The wide range of application possible with oil paint has led to personal styles of painting in which brush strokes act as a kind of signature for the painter.

335 Hans Hofmann. MEADOW SPLENDOR. 1959. Oil on board. 18 x 24".

336   Charles Close. FRANK. 1968–1969. Acrylic on canvas. 9 x 7′.

ACRYLIC

Several types of synthetic painting media are now available. The most popular of these are acrylics. In acrylic paints, pigments are suspended in acrylic polymer medium. Acrylic binders provide a fast-drying, flexible film that can be opaque or transparent, and which is relatively permanent, even out of doors. Such paints may be applied to a wider variety of surfaces than traditional painting media. Most acrylics are water-thinned and water-resistant when dry. Unlike linseed oil, acrylic binders will not darken or yellow with age. The rapid drying time of acrylics can be an advantage or a disadvantage depending on the manner of working.

The huge portrait of FRANK by Charles Close was painted on primed canvas, using a few tablespoons of black acrylic paint, water, and a brush.

New color brilliance has been achieved through the use of acrylic paints. See Anuskiewicz' INJURED BY GREEN, color plate 9, and Frankenthaler's INTERIOR LANDSCAPE, color plate 41.

TEMPERA

Tempera paint uses an emulsion (a mixture of oil and water) as a binder. This emulsion may contain glue, gum, casein, egg, or egg and oil. Most tempera paints are water-thinned, yet relatively insoluble when dry. They are good for working in precise detail and will not yellow or darken with age. Their main disadvantages are color changes during drying and difficulty in blending and reworking. The crisp, luminous quality of egg tempera cannot be matched by any other traditional painting medium. See Fra Filippo Lippi's MADONNA AND CHILD, page 27, and Andrew Wyeth's THAT GENTLEMAN, page 223.

WATERCOLOR

Watercolor paintings are made by applying pigments suspended in a solution of water and gum arabic to a white surface. Rag papers are the preferred supports. Paper quality is important because the whites in the painting depend on the lasting whiteness of the paper. Paint is laid on in thin transparent washes or in opaque strokes for detail. When employed carefully, watercolors provide a medium well-suited to spontaneous application. In spite of the simple materials involved, it is not an easy medium to handle because it does not allow for easy correction. Watercolor painting, like fresco, is essentially a one-way process.

Both transparent washes and opaque areas are used in John Marin's DEER ISLE — MARINE FANTASY. Foreground and distance merge in a pattern of dynamic dark and light shapes. Jagged edges play off against softer flowing lines. The fluid spontaneity of watercolor made it a favorite medium for Marin.

337 John Marin
DEER ISLE — MARINE FANTASY
1917. Watercolor. 19¾ x 16".

338 Fan K'uan
TRAVELERS
ON A MOUNTAIN PATH.
c. 990–1030. Hanging
scroll, ink on silk.
Height 81¼".

Chinese brush painting is a watercolor method employing ink and color. The viewer as well as the artist is expected to know the basic visual elements and the attitudes that animate them.

Subject matter is secondary to form. Poetry is frequently written on the surface. Brush techniques are highly developed, both for the written word and for the painted subject. The quality of each stroke is considered as important as the total design. Landscape strokes and their rhythms have names such as raveled rope, raindrops, ax cuts, nailhead, and wrinkles on a devil's face. Timing and speed add to the unrepeatable quality of each stroke. In order to paint a landscape the artist is expected to spend time in quiet meditation outdoors until he becomes one with his subject. The painting is then done from memory.

Traditional Chinese painting is based on values upheld for centuries, with emphasis on perfecting brush technique. In this, Chinese painting contrasts with Western painting in which changing values have brought about frequent changes in technique. Young painters spend several years copying the works of earlier artists in order to fully assimilate the rich tradition they inherit. Artists are also interested in adding their individual interpretation to traditional themes.

It is common to base a composition on the work of an earlier painter, as Tung Ch'i-ch'ang has done in his version of Fan K'uan's ink painting, TRAVELERS ON A MOUNTAIN PATH. The title guides the viewer to the essential man-nature relationship.

With humility, human travelers traverse the horizontal earth, while behind them mountain cliffs rise vertically toward heaven. Brush work suggesting trees creates textural shapes that emphasize the powerful structure of the mountain. The stylized waterfall acts as an accent in the design.

339 Tung Ch'i-ch'ang
TRAVELERS ON A MOUNTAIN PATH
c. 1368–1644. Hanging scroll, ink on silk. Height 24".

FRESCO

Fresco painting is an ancient technique in which pigments suspended in water are applied to a damp lime-plaster surface. The plaster is the binding agent. This medium is suited to painting on walls where permanency is desired. Wall paintings of this type are called fresco murals. See Giotto's THE DESCENT FROM THE CROSS, page 144. In fresco painting as in watercolor, pigments are applied in a rapid staining process that makes changes difficult or impossible. In order to change the painting it is necessary to remove the plaster surface and start over.

ENCAUSTIC

Encaustic is another ancient technique in which pigments are suspended in hot refined beeswax. Encaustic paintings have a lustrous surface which sets off rich warm color. Encaustic is not a popular medium, due to the difficulties involved in keeping the wax binder at just the right temperature for proper handling. The results seem to justify the effort, however. The PORTRAIT OF A MAN from Egypt was painted in encaustic on wood. Its lifelike vigor and individuality remain strong after 1800 years. See also the contemporary encaustic painting by Jasper Johns, color plate 8.

340 PORTRAIT OF A MAN
Fayum, Egypt, 100 A.D.
Encaustic on wood. 13¾ x 8".

PRINTMAKING

Printmaking began with the desire to make multiple images of a single work of art. It is now a creative medium in its own right. Because our lives are full of images that are printed as multiples, it is difficult for us to imagine a time when the only pictures ever seen were one-of-a-kind originals.

The words and pictures in this book were reproduced by a mechanical printing method called offset lithography. The basic concept of lithography was not put to use until early in the nineteenth century, but multiple printing was in use in China as early as 200 B.C. and was widely used in Europe by the end of the fifteenth century.

Until this century, multiple image-making was carried on with semimechanical procedures by groups that usually included artist, artisans, and laborers. As photo-mechanical methods of reproduction developed, handwork by artists played an increasingly minor part in the process. Images of original works were no longer drawn or cut into the printing surface by hand copying. Artists, however, have themselves continued earlier printmaking processes. Their goal has been to take advantage of the unique properties inherent in the printmaking media and to make their works less expensive and more readily available to the public by designing and printing "multiple originals." The two distinguishing words are "print," signifying the artist's handmade multiple impressions, and "reproduction," signifying copies of originals.

Reproductions may look better or worse than the original. Often a reproduction of a two-dimensional work looks different because the visual qualities of the reproduction are affected by such factors as paper, printing method, cropping, and size. Only within the last ten years have high-quality color reproductions become commonplace. The art of the world comes to us through these reproductions. As the French critic André Malraux has stated, "A museum without walls has been opened to us . . . ."[4]

Some artists now use photo-mechanical means to reproduce their own works, which are then sold as signed original prints. This attitude is based on the feeling that it is most important to get one's work seen and to make a profit from selling it.

In the mid-1960s young people began covering their walls with popular art posters, many of them conceived as advertisements for rock concerts and given away at the door. Some of the best poster artists became well-known, Wes Wilson among them (see page 235). Few care whether these posters are original prints or reproductions. They are simply enjoyed for the images they present.

There are four basic printmaking methods: *relief, intaglio, planographic,* and *stencil.* All except stencil will produce a reversed version of the original image. Printmaking techniques are continually changing and expanding in capability as printmakers combine traditional methods and add new ones.

RELIEF

In a *relief* process the parts of the printing surface not meant to carry ink are cut away, leaving the design to be printed in relief at the level of the original surface. This surface is then inked and the ink is transferred to paper with pressure. Relief processes include *woodcuts, wood engravings, linoleum cuts,* and *metal cuts.* An enjoyable way to make relief prints is with cut potatoes.

341 Toshusai Sharaku. The Actor Otani Oniji III as Edohei. 1794. Color woodcut. 14¾ x 9¾".

The woodcut process lends itself to designs with bold lines and large areas of dark, light, and color. The multiple blocks necessary for most color prints require careful *registration* to ensure that each color is exactly placed.

Woodcuts have been made in quantity in Japan since the sixteenth century. Many of the printmakers who are well-known today created prints as guides to popular enter-tainment. The prints were often portraits of famous geishas or actors. Sharaku's print achieves visual impact by exaggerating the character of Edohei, as played by the actor Otani Oniji. The print is a color woodcut done with a block for each color. Such color prints can utilize as many as twenty blocks cut to achieve the final print. The original image was cut into cherrywood, which has fine, hard grain, making crisp edges possible.

342 Emil Nolde
PROPHET
1912. Woodcut. 12⅝ x 8⅞".

German artist Emil Nolde made a woodcut print called PROPHET in 1912. Each bold cut in the block reveals the expressive image of an old man and also the natural character of the wood itself.

The contemporary artist Carol Summers produced another kind of woodcut image. His bold shapes and rich colors work together with assurance. The character of cut wood is not a significant aspect of this image.

343 Carol Summers
CHEOPS
1967. Woodcut. 29³⁄₁₆ x 21".
See color plate 36

INTAGLIO

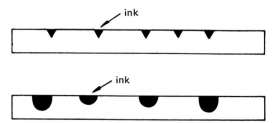

Intaglio printing is in a sense the reverse of relief because areas below the surface hold the ink. The design to be printed is either etched into a metal surface by "biting" with acid or incised by "engraving" lines into the surface with sharp tools. The plate is coated with ink using a dauber. The surface is then wiped clean, leaving ink only in the cuts. Intaglio processes most frequently used are *etching* and *engraving*.

An etching is made by drawing lines through a soft material made of beeswax and lamp black, which covers a copper or zinc plate. The plate is then placed in acid. Where the lines expose the metal, acid eats into the plate, making a groove that varies in depth according to the strength of the acid and the length of time the plate is in the acid.

In metal engravings, the lines are cut into the plate with a tool called a burin. This process takes strength and control. The pre-

cise lines of an engraving are not as fluid or relaxed as etched lines due to the differences in the two processes. See diagram.

Compare the line quality in Rembrandt's etching, Christ Preaching, with the line quality in Durer's engraving, Knight, Death and Devil. The hard precision of Durer's lines seems appropriate to the subject of the print. It is an image of the Christian soldier going with steadfast faith to the heavenly city of Jerusalem, seen in the upper background of the print. The dog, the central vertical position of the knight's figure, and the smooth, geometric contours of the powerful horse assure us that the knight will arrive at his destination in spite of the grotesquely shaped figure of the devil and the snake-entwined figure of death.

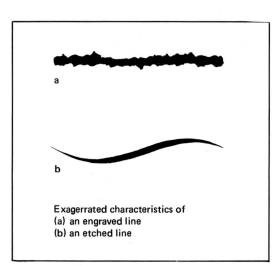

Exagerrated characteristics of
(a) an engraved line
(b) an etched line

344 Albrecht Dürer
Knight, Death and Devil
1513. Engraving. 9¾ x 7⅜".

Rembrandt's gentle compassion is evident in the relaxed quality of his etched lines. In the seventeenth century woodcuts and engravings were commonly used to reproduce paintings. Creative printmakers, such as Rembrandt, preferred etching, often adding drypoint lines for additional subtle effects. In his depiction of Christ preaching, he worked in a wide range of tonal values, creating variety within each value area. The strong light and dark pattern is typically baroque and a major component of Rembrandt's style. It adds clarity and emotional feeling to his sympathetic portrayal of the religious story.

345   Rembrandt van Rijn
CHRIST PREACHING
c. 1652. Etching. 6⅟₁₆ x 8⅛″.

PLANOGRAPHIC

In the *planographic* method the printing surface is left flat, as the name implies. The process lends itself well to a direct manner of working because the image is created on a single plane. *Lithography* is the major form of planographic printing.

It is often difficult to distinguish a lithograph from a drawing because the image is drawn on the surface of the stone or plate without any biting or cutting of lines. This directness makes lithography faster and more flexible than other methods.

346 Honoré Daumier. TRANSNONAIN STREET. 1834. Lithograph. 11¼ x 17⅜".

A print can be pulled from a single plane because of the chemical antipathy of water and grease. Lines or areas are drawn or painted on smooth, fine-grained, Bavarian limestone or a metal surface developed to duplicate the absorbent character of the stone. An image is created with crayons, pencils, or inks containing a greasy substance. The surface is then chemically treated so that the drawing is etched or fixed to become part of the upper layer of the stone. The surface is dampened with water and inked. The ink is repelled by the moisture, but adheres to the greasy area of the image. When this surface is covered with paper and run through a press, a printed image of the original is produced.

Honoré Daumier made his living drawing lithographs for the French newspapers. His bold personal style was well-suited to the direct quality of the lithographic process, a relatively new technique at that time. Rembrandt's influence is felt in the organization of strong light and dark areas. Political cartoons have become an important means of social satire and criticism, thanks to the sensitivity, skill, and integrity of artists like Daumier.

In TRANSNONAIN STREET Daumier reconstructed a contemporary event that greatly angered him. During a period of civil unrest in the 1830s there had been trouble in the streets of Paris. The militia, called out to keep things under control, claimed that a shot was fired from a building on Transnonain Street. The soldiers responded by entering an apartment and killing all the occupants. Daumier's lithograph was published the following day.

STENCILS

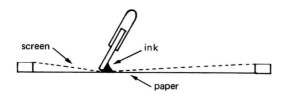

Stencils are familiar as a means of transferring letters and other shapes to a flat surface. An *aperture* is cut in a nonporous material, then held firmly against a surface and pigment is brushed through the opening, leaving a corresponding image. Complex shapes must be planned so that connecting links prevent parts from dropping out. This problem was solved centuries ago by Japanese artists who backed stencils with silk threads. Early in this century, the technique was further developed by adhering the stencil to the underside of silk fabric stretched across a frame. Colored inks are forced through the open pores of the fabric from the top, leaving the design on the paper or cloth below. No press is necessary. The term *serigraph* is used to distinguish an artist's print from a commercial reproduction. which is called a *silk-screen process print.*

Serigraphy, or silk-screen printing, is well-suited to the production of multiple color images. Each separate color change requires a different screen, but registering and printing are relatively simple. Victor Vasarely's nonrepresentational geometric paintings and prints used optical illusions to create impressions of rhythmic movement years before op became a named style. Such kinetic effects are produced in the eye of the viewer.

The latest development in screen printing is the photographic stencil or *photo silk screen,* achieved by attaching light-sensitive gelatine to the screen fabric. A developing solution and exposure to light make the gelatine insoluble in water. The gelatine is exposed to light through a film positive or drawing on acetate. The soluble, unexposed areas are then washed away, leaving open areas in the fabric that allow the ink to pass through to

the print surface. See Rauschenberg's mixed media painting with photo silk-screen images, page 226.

347 Victor Vasarely
UNTITLED
1967. Serigraph. 23½ x 23½".
See color plate 39

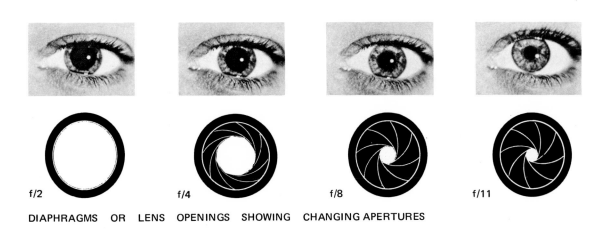

f/2 f/4 f/8 f/11

DIAPHRAGMS OR LENS OPENINGS SHOWING CHANGING APERTURES

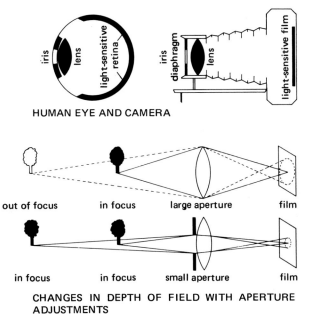

HUMAN EYE AND CAMERA

out of focus   in focus   large aperture   film

in focus   in focus   small aperture   film

CHANGES IN DEPTH OF FIELD WITH APERTURE ADJUSTMENTS

PHOTOGRAPHY

Photography means light-writing or light-drawing. We are so constantly bombarded by a flood of photographic images that we are not aware of the effect this medium has had on our ways of seeing. Much of our view of life — and, therefore, our way of life — is recorded, challenged, and changed by that relatively simple device, the camera. The camera has provided a profusion of ready-made images, which may dull our vision. Yet, it has also made fresh ways of seeing possible. In spite of the fact that many people now own cameras, it is rare to see an original photographic print of high quality.

The basic concept of the camera preceded actual photography by more than 300 years. The development of photography was motivated by the Renaissance desire to approach nature scientifically, to capture on a flat surface particular aspects of visual reality at a given moment. The camera is like a mechanical replica of the human eye. The major difference is that the eye brings a continual flow of changing images which are recorded by the brain, whereas the camera depends on light-sensitive film to record an image, and only one still image at a time can be picked up.

The camera is a scientific device and an artistic tool. It can record the surface of the moon, the interior of the human heart, or the exact visual details of some unrepeatable moment in history. It can bring to any subject the aesthetic sensibilities of the person who selects and captures the particular image. When this happens, the image created clarifies and intensifies reality so that the visual idea is communicated and retained by the viewer. The artist-photographer seeks significant form in the shifting images that pass before him. Looking through the camera, he seeks aesthetic reality within the actual world. He is able to clarify and enrich the personal experience of others by presenting images that come from his own personal experience. With the aid of the camera, he reveals and interprets what he sees.

A work of art is created by a subtle, complicated process of selection based on knowledge, feeling, and intuition. When Michelangelo carved a figure, he made thousands of decisions as he sought to find that figure in the block of marble. When a photographer like Henri Cartier-Bresson or Edward Weston creates a photograph, he makes thousands of choices in order to arrive at the point at which he releases the shutter and thus captures a memorable image. Cartier-Bresson calls this the "decisive moment."[5]

In the 1930s the photo essay became an important part of journalism. The factual images presented in the form of documentary photographs have had impact on society. Many photographers have led the way, as artists, toward a renewed concern with social reform.

In AT THE TIME OF THE LOUISVILLE FLOOD, Margaret Bourke-White confronts us with the brutal difference between the glamorized life of advertising promises and the actual reality people faced.

The airplane and the space vehicle have provided a new vantage point from which to see the natural beauty of the earth and the creative and destructive patterns of human enterprise.

Margaret Bourke-White brought her full artistic perception to the creation of the photograph CONTOUR PLOWING. The large curving shape that dominates the composition is powerful enough to make a lasting impression. The rhythmically vibrating furrow lines and the tiny scale of the plows add a human element.

349   Margaret Bourke-White. AT THE TIME OF THE LOUISVILLE FLOOD. 1937.

350   Margaret Bourke-White. Contour Plowing. 1954.

351　Eliot Porter
TAMARISK AND GRASS
1961
See color plate 37

Color becomes a liability for many photographers. It can weaken a photograph by acting as a superficial afterthought, or it can so tantalize the man behind the camera that he forgets about the other aspects of form, without which color has no meaning.

Eliot Porter sees color and light as integral aspects of form. In his photograph, TAMARISK AND GRASS, the two elements produce a subtle pattern of horizontal and vertical lines. This segment of nature would usually go unobserved.

Gordon Parks does many things well. He is a poet and a musician as well as a photographer. He was a professional basketball player and piano player before he bought his first camera. In the photograph reproduced here, Parks' enthusiasm for life is readily apparent. Through color and selective focus, he brings attention to that singular moment when the whole world was centered on a pet beetle crawling across the landscape of a boy's face.

There are some things that we could not see at all without photography. The exposure time for Harold Edgerton's photograph of a milk splash was 1/100,000 of a second. He dropped a ball and lit the event with the intense light of a stroboscopic lamp for a microsecond, thereby stopping the action.

352　Gordon Parks
BOY IN GRASS
1968
See color plate 38

353　Harold Edgerton
MILK SPLASH RESULTING FROM DROPPING A BALL
1936

CINEMATOGRAPHY

The art of motion pictures is the art of making pictures move. Whether they are in black-and-white or color, silent or accompanied by sound, animated or live-action, movies are essentially thousands of little pictures projected on a screen so fast that they give us the illusion of movement. Movies seem to move because of the function of the eye known as the *persistence of vision*. When we look at a bright light and then close our eyes, we seem to be able to see the light after our eyes are closed. What we are seeing is an *afterimage* (see page 62). Afterimages occur when the retinas of our eyes retain for a moment the image we were experiencing. If the succeeding image is only a little different from the one that went before, we might get the impression that what we are looking at is moving. This happens when we turn the pages of a flip book. Each picture differs only slightly from

those that precede it — just enough to give the illusion of movement when the book is flipped. Flip the top lefthand corners of pages 272–292 for this effect.

Eadweard Muybridge first put this discovery to use. Muybridge was a photographer who was engaged by Leland Stanford to settle a disagreement Stanford had with a friend. Stanford believed that when a horse trots there is a point at which all four hooves are off the ground at once. Stanford's friend disagreed.

Muybridge lined up twenty-four still cameras alongside a race course. Each camera was fixed with a wire to be tripped by the horse's front hooves, causing the horse to be photographed twenty-four times as he trotted. Stanford was only interested in the photograph that proved him right. But in settling the disagreement, Stanford helped introduce a revolutionary idea — that of the motion picture. For Muybridge found that if he projected all twenty-four pictures in rapid succession, the horse seemed to move!

354   Eadweard Muybridge
GALLOPING HORSE
1878. *See illustration 200.*

That was in 1877. Soon others began to film with motion-picture cameras. The new cameras were equipped to take several pictures in a row printed on long strips of flexible film. When the strips of film were developed and projected at the same rate of speed at which they were taken, the subjects photographed seemed to move naturally. One such early film is of a man named Fred Ott, sneezing. It is called, appropriately, FRED OTT'S SNEEZE, and in 1894 was among the first motion pictures to be granted a copyright by the Library of Congress.

The motion picture camera became the biggest sensation in the United States. People flocked to circuses and amusement parlors to see scenes of foreign lands and famous people they had heard about. They watched Theodore Roosevelt and his Rough Riders charge up San Juan Hill, followed the events of the Spanish-American War, and even got a glimpse of a lady named Little Egypt doing her exotic dance.

Early newsreels were similar to the reports we see on television today. Early fiction films, however, were quite different from today's movies. Like many new art forms, cinema in its infancy was not considered respectable. In order to make up for this slight, early filmmakers tried to make their movies look like filmed theatrical performances. Actors made entrances and exits in front of a fixed camera as though it were the eye of a great audience watching them on stage.

355 W. K. Dickson. FRED OTT'S SNEEZE. 1894.

One such film was AT THE CROSSROADS OF
LIFE (1907). It starred a young actor from
Kentucky, Lawrence Griffith. The fact that
he used the name Lawrence instead of his
real name, David, indicates how disreputa-
ble films were believed to be. Besides, Griffith thought of himself as a playwright. His
first play failed. It was not to be theater in
which David Wark Griffith was to make his
name.

Between 1907 and 1916 Griffith helped
bring the motion picture from its infancy
as a nickelodeon amusement to full stature
as an art. He was responsible for developing
most of the basic elements of the art of
film, among them the following:

• *The mobile camera.* Not a kind of motion picture camera, but a way of using one.
Griffith took the camera out of its fixed,
stagebound setting, and filmed on location
— out of doors, from moving trains, in au-
tomobiles, even in balloons.

• *Parallel editing.* Switching back and forth
between two events. The events may be occurring at the same time, as in THE LONE-
DALE OPERATOR, when Blanche Sweet is
trapped in a railroad station between two
menacing thieves while her boyfriend steams
to save her in a locomotive. The events may
be set at different times, as in INTOLERANCE,
in which Griffith cut back and forth between four stories set in different periods of
history. The former device builds suspense,
the latter lets us compare events occurring
at different times. Parallel editing is a refinement of narrative editing, which was introduced by Edwin S. Porter in his 1903
film, THE GREAT TRAIN ROBBERY. Porter
set up his camera in several locations to
film parts of the story of a train robbery.
Each camera setup is called a *shot.* Porter
glued all the shots together and projected
them in succession. Cutting and reassem-
bling is called *editing.* Since the assembled
shots told a story, his film is an example of
narrative editing. Any grouping of shots

within a film is called a *sequence.* Shots
make sequences. Sequences make movies.
These are the basic elements of dramatic
film.

356 Edwin S. Porter.
THE GREAT TRAIN ROBBERY. 1903.

• *Fade-in and fade-out.* Quite by accident, Griffith discovered the best way to divide films into sequences. His cameraman, Billy Bitzer, accidentally let the shutter of his camera close slowly, causing the light to gradually darken. On viewing this, Griffith remarked that it might be a good way to begin or end love scenes. Fading in or out remains the most common way of dividing films into scenes.

• *Flashback and flashforward.* Griffith admired the novels of Charles Dickens, especially A TALE OF TWO CITIES, in which Dickens moved backward or forward in time to tell the story. Griffith made the same thing happen in movies.

• *Close-up and long-shot.* While filming
FOR THE LOVE OF GOLD (1907), Griffith
astounded his cameraman by asking him to
move the camera closer to the actors to
film their faces. Since movies were stagebound at the time, Bitzer felt that doing
anything less than showing the full body of
an actor would surprise the audience. When
Griffith made his request, Bitzer replied,
"What? You mean you want a head with
no body?"[6] That was exactly what Griffith
wanted. He knew that movie audiences
would permit anything on film that the
mind was capable of imagining. Although
some were surprised at the dramatic close-up,
most people accepted it as a way of seeing
the actor's face. It was a logical step to the
use of long-shots to film whole armies in
battle, as Griffith did in 1915 in THE BIRTH
OF A NATION.

• *Montage.* Taken from the French word
monter, meaning "to mount" or "to assem-
ble," montage is the editing together of a
number of shots of a single event to give a
sense of heightened importance and drama.
The murder scene in the modern story of
INTOLERANCE (1916), for example, is com-
prised of over twenty-five shots. There is a
shot of the murderess peering in the window of the victim's room, of the victim
struggling with the villain, the frightened
wife standing by, the murderess leaning in
with the gun, a close-up of the gun firing,
the victim's surprised face, his fall to the
floor, the police arriving, the murderess es-
caping, and so on, all shown within the
space of one minute. In montage, a great
deal seems to happen in little time, much
more than could happen in real life in the
same period of time.

Griffith also worked to introduce other elements, which, although not essential to
film as art, are nonetheless strong technical
additions. He recognized early that movie
screens might be wider. Lacking the means
of doing that himself, he compensated by
masking the top and bottom of some of

his shots to give the impression of width.
Now we have Cinemascope, Panavision, and
Cinerama.

Griffith pioneered the use of music with
films. He helped write the musical score for
THE BIRTH OF A NATION, which opened in
New York in 1915 accompanied by the full
orchestra of the Metropolitan Opera. And
he knew that color film photography would
someday become a reality.

The coming of sound in 1928 added a new
dimension to cinema. Many actors who did
well in the silent period failed to make the
transition into sound. John Gilbert, the
great silent star, was discovered to have a
rather squeaky voice. And the art of slap-
stick comedy was lost in the craze to hear
people talk on the screen. However, sound
did not change the fundamental grammar
of film art. That had been set by 1925,

357a D. W. Griffith. THE BIRTH OF A NATION. 1915.

357b THE BIRTH OF A NATION

largely by Griffith. Color photography, sound, widescreen processes, and other innovations of later years were to be mere additions to the art developed in the silent years.

Cinematography and television have made the photographic image move. The camera is still the basic tool. All of the visual elements previously discussed (see pages 52–91)² occur in films. The major elements in cinema are time, motion, and space. There is also the very important nonvisual element of sound. In the twentieth century, when time consciousness has become acute, film media has added to that awareness. Cinema time is flexible, like mental time. Film can compress and expand time and can go forward and backward in implied time.

By creating the effect of motion with photographic images, films produce the most vivid appearance of visual reality since art began. Motion greatly increases our sense of participation. When motion is synchronized with sound, two major facets of total sensory experience are joined. The photo-graphic image, plus sound and motion, make cinema and television highly persuasive media. These media convince us that we are actually seeing events occur as they do in life.

TELEVISION

Television is the electronic transmission of still or moving photographic images with sound by means of cable or wireless broadcast. Today it serves primarily as a distribution system for the dissemination of advertising, news, and entertainment — in that order in importance. Television has its own characteristic advantages and disadvantages. Like photography and cinematography, it uses light impulses collected by a camera. The television camera is unique, however, because it converts lightwaves into electricity. Most of the visual arts produce images manually or mechanically; television produces and transmits images electronically. Lightwaves collected and converted by television cameras can then be stored on magnetic *video tape* for instantaneous or later transmisison to receivers. The images thus received appear on the face of a cathode-ray tube.

Multiple audio-visual equipment can be mixed instantaneously with live elements on television. This, along with the modification of images through such methods as electronic feedback, gives TV the potential for even greater flexibility and more complex and immediate forms than cinema. Television time can incorporate cinema time and can also bring us events instantly.

The first memorable live broadcast occurred in 1939 when President Roosevelt spoke to a gathering at the World's Fair in New York, appearing on about 100 monitors situated on the fairgrounds and in the city, thus demonstrating a major characteristic of television — its *liveness*. Television has made it possible for the people of the world to share events as they happen. An estimated 400 million people experienced man landing on the moon.

The potential of television as a creative medium of communication has barely been explored. Network television most often sacrifices imagination for saleability. Commercials get the most attention because they are where the money is. For higher levels of television communication, television's ways of creating form need to be separated from its use as a way of making money.

Like photography and cinema, television has created new ways of seeing, but it has eclipsed its predecessors in its ability to deluge the viewer with a continuous outpouring of canned images that must ultimately dull perception. The thirty-second TV commercial is a prime example of careful design and clear communication without lasting value. "A major portion of America's creative energy is siphoned off into television's exploitation of the profit motive. . . ."[7]

The average American spends about twenty hours a week watching television. It is easy to feel that these are wasted hours. A young adult has probably spent more time watching TV than in school. University students are less inclined to read because of their television habit. Children of nursery school age are more sophisticated than those of previous generations because of television. These are just a few examples of the immense effect of this medium.

The space exploration program has speeded up the development of lightweight television cameras and recording and transmission equipment. What television will be like in the future may well depend on this new lightweight gear. It offers the chance to break with the traditional heavy equipment and with the economic demands of network broadcasting. With this equipment a more direct approach is possible. It is now feasible to leave the studio more easily. Team work is becoming less necessary. Ex-

perimentation and individual expression are facilitated. Television is expected to replace much of what cinematography is now doing because it is less expensive and more flexible. Many filmmakers are already using TV as a kind of sketch pad.

358a   Apollo 16 Astronauts Saluting Flag on the Moon. April 1971

358b   Prelaunch News for Apollo 16 April 1971

359 APOLLO
c. 415 B.C. Silver coin. Diameter 1⅛".

SCULPTURE

Freestanding sculpture seems more physically real than any of the visual arts existing on a two-dimensional plane, because it occupies actual three-dimensional space.

When sculpture projects from a background surface, it is not freestanding, but *in relief*. In *low-relief* sculpture, the projection from the surrounding surface is slight and no part of the modeled form is undercut. In *high-relief* sculpture, at least one-half of the natural circumference of the modeled form projects from the surrounding surface. High-relief sculpture begins to look like sculpture that is freestanding. As sculpture enters the fully three-dimensional space that we occupy, it appears to change as we move.

A piece of sculpture may be small enough to hold in the hand and admire at close range, such as a coin or a piece of jewelry. Most coins are small works of low-relief sculpture. Sometimes sculpture is hand-sized and designed to be touched, yet has a monumental quality because of its design. This is true of much prehistoric sculpture. Or, sculpture can actually be monumental in size. The Sphinx of ancient Egypt is a good example. Colossal Buddha figures of China, Japan, and Southeast Asia are equally impressive.

Traditionally, sculpture has been made by modeling, carving, casting, assembling, or a combination of these processes. Modeling is an *additive* process in which pliable material such as clay or wax is built up from inside to a final outer form. Sagging can be prevented by starting with a rigid support called an *armature*.

Noguchi began his expressive figure, BIG BOY, with an armature. He rolled and pinched clay to form the hands, legs, and feet, and rolled out a slab of clay, which became the garment worn by the child. This slab was pressed into the other pieces of clay to form a single unit. Modeling, cutting, and assembling were used to achieve the final result.

360   Isamu Noguchi. BIG BOY. 1952. Karatsu ware. 7⅞ x 6⅞".

361 Michelangelo Buonarroti
UNFINISHED SLAVE
1530–1534. Marble. Life-size.

The process is *subtractive* when sculptural form is created by cutting or carving away material. Michelangelo preferred this method. For him, the act of making sculpture was a process of finding the desired form within a block of stone. In his UNFINISHED SLAVE, it seems as if this process is continuing as we watch. The figure symbolizes the human spirit as it struggles against the marble that imprisons it. Close observation of the chisel marks on the surface reveals Michelangelo's steps toward more and more refined cutting.

It takes considerable foresight to work this way. Each material has its own character and must be approached on its own terms. The stonecarver must apply his strength and endurance to unyielding material. In wood carving, grain presents special problems and unique results. Both wood and stone must be carefully selected beforehand if the artist is to realize his intended form.

362 IFE KING
Ita Yemoo, Ife, Nigeria
c. 12th–14th centuries, discovered 1957

363 CASTING IN BRONZE
a A model is drawn and her measurements taken.
b An armature, a skeleton of wire, provides support. Wood crosspieces help to anchor the clay.
c The clay figure takes shape. The artist establishes the major volumes and their overall rhythms.
d The balance, masses, and details of the figure are compared to the live model and final corrections are made.
e Plaster is spread over the clay in thin layers until a substantial shell is created.
f To remove the clay without damaging the plaster, the mold is made in sections (separators are visible along head, shoulders, and forearms).
g The plaster mold is removed by sections, revealing the damaged, but no longer needed, clay figure. Further work will be based on the plaster mold.
h The inner surfaces of the mold are painted with shellac and a greasy or gelatinous substance to prevent sticking. It is then filled with semi-liquid plaster.
i Once hardened, the plaster figure can be carefully removed from the mold. Its surface is a pure, pristine white.
j After careful inspection the sculptor smooths

Carving is usually slower and more difficult than modeling. But work in clay, wax, or plaster does not have the strength and permanence of stone or metal sculpture. For this reason the process of metal casting developed. The basic casting technique has remained unchanged for thousands of years. In China in the Shang dynasty, circa 1200 B.C. (see pages 114–115), and in the Ife Kingdom in Africa, circa 1200 A.D., casting techniques were highly developed. Works from these cultures have a degree of perfection unsurpassed in this century. The usual steps in the casting process are illustrated here.

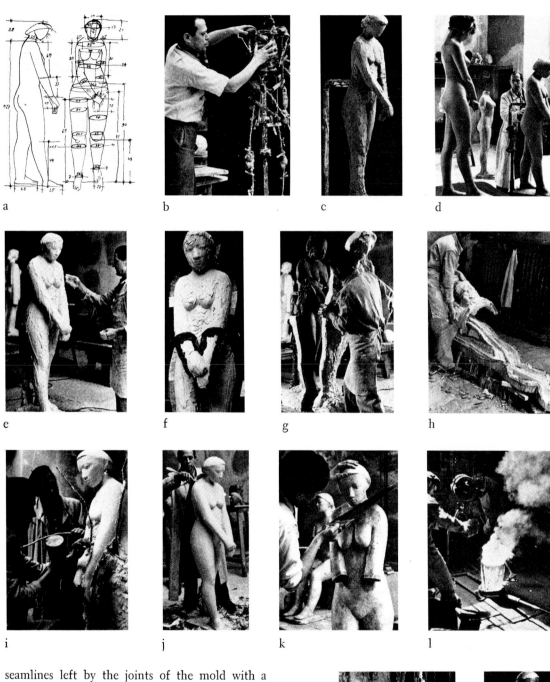

a   b   c   d

e   f   g   h

i   j   k   l

seamlines left by the joints of the mold with a
rasp and removes all blemishes. The surface can
be filed smooth to any desired finish.

k For the casting in bronze, the plaster is sec-
tioned. Head and hands are removed to facilitate
pouring.

l The mold is made in sections of damp, firmly
packed sand and reassembled in the casting frame
with an inner core. Metal is poured into the
¼-inch space between. The figure will be hollow.

m & n After pouring and cooling in the foundry,
sand and bronze residues are removed and the
figure is tooled to its final surface.

m   n

Before this century the major sculpture techniques were modeling and carving. Since Picasso constructed his cubist GUITAR in 1912 (see page 195), assembling methods have become widely used. In some cases preexisting objects are brought together in such a way that their original identity is still apparent, yet transformed when seen in a new context. This type of sculpture is called *assemblage*.

In Picasso's BULL'S HEAD, the creative process has been distilled to a single leap of the imagination. The components of this assemblage are simply a bicycle seat and handle bars. Almost anyone could have done the actual work of putting them together. Yet the finished work is based on a particular kind of empathy with things, which is far from common. The metamorphosis of ordinary manufactured objects into animal spirit is still happening for the viewer.

364   Pablo Picasso. BULL'S HEAD. 1943. Bronze. Height 16⅛".

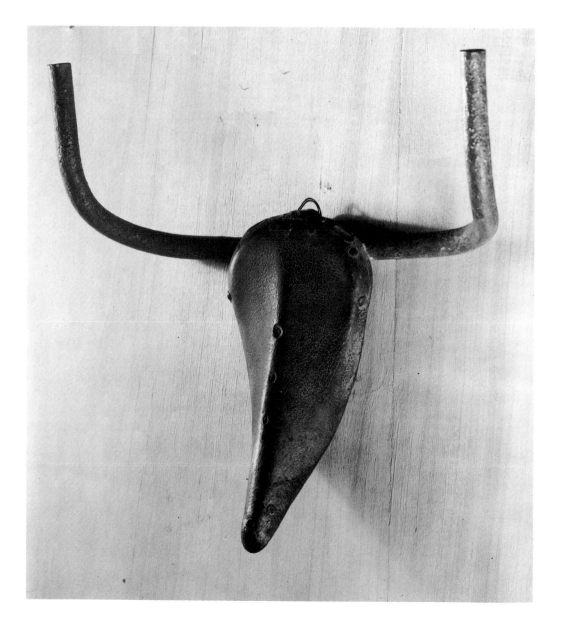

365 Richard Lippold
VARIATION WITHIN A SPHERE, No. 10: THE SUN
1953–1956. Gold-filled wire construction, 22k.
11 x 22 x 5½'.

Lippold's THE SUN is a beautiful and technically amazing piece of work. Its complex linear form is assembled from several thousand feet of gold-filled wire. The eleven foot height puts the center of the structure at about eye level. Light is reflected from the shimmering gold surfaces and translucent planes built up with wire. The pure mathematical precision of this construction ultimately creates a symbolic image of radiant energy.

The form of sculpture changes as technology develops new materials and processes and makes them available to imaginative sculptors.

Nicholas Schöffer's Microtemps G is a visual event in which projected light and motorized plastic and metal parts provide a continually changing pattern of light, color, and moving surfaces.

Live energy in the form of magnetic force plays an important role in the kinetic work of Takis. In Electromagnetic Sculpture, a sphere, suspended from the ceiling by an almost invisible fine wire, moves and pauses in an orbital pattern around an upright electromagnet that automatically turns on and off. The duality of stillness and motion is reminiscent of the alternating rhythms implied by the multiple arms of the dancing Shiva (see page 117).

366 Takis
Electromagnetic Sculpture
Paris, 1960, modified 1965. Metal.

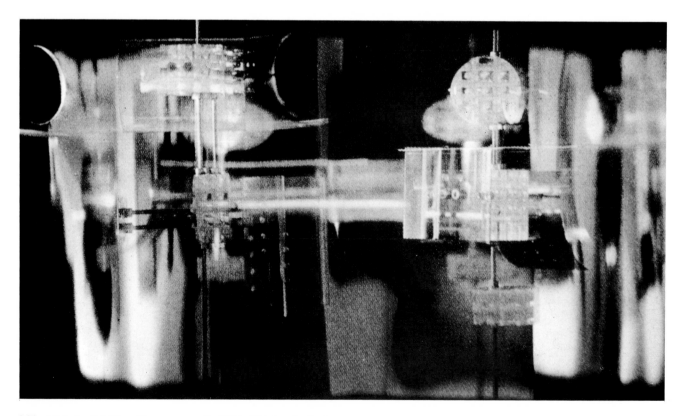

367 Nicholas Schöffer. Microtemps G. 1965. Metal and plastic.

368 Alexander Calder. THE GATES OF SPOLETO. 1962. Steel. Height 65'7", width 45'11", depth 45'11".

The direct use of metal as a material for sculpture has been minor until the twentieth century. Since 1930, cutting and welding metals such as iron, steel, and aluminum developed and became widespread. Equipment such as the oxyacetylene torch greatly facilitated these developments.

Alexander Calder was among those who gave renewed life to the blacksmith's ancient craft. Calder's father and grandfather were both sculptors who worked within the Greek and Renaissance tradition of subtractive figure sculpture. By the time the tradition reached the twentieth century, it was exhausted. Attempts at revival have rarely been successful. Calder feels he would not have become a sculptor if he had had to follow this withered path.

Calder pioneered kinetic sculpture. Since 1932 he has designed wire and sheetmetal constructions that are moved by natural air currents. Duchamp christened them "mobiles." The traditional emphasis on mass is replaced in Calder's work by an emphasis on shape, space, and movement.

THE GATES OF SPOLETO has shapes related to Calder's early mobiles. He calls this type of structure a "stabile." The cutout sheetmetal pieces are motionless planes, yet their shapes set up directional forces that intersect and project, giving the whole sculpture a lively quality. Monumental scale and openness invite the viewer to move through the work. Sculpture becomes architectural.

ARCHITECTURE

Architecture, like sculpture, is three-dimensional form, and both disciplines utilize space, mass, texture, line, light, and color. While sculpture is most often seen from the outside, architecture is experienced from the inside as well as the outside. The sculptural form of a building works best when generated from within — determined by those functions that the structure intends to serve.

Sculpture can be small and rarely needs a consistent structural system. Architecture, on the other hand, employs a structural system in order to achieve the size and strength necessary to meet its purpose.

369   Charles Sheeler
Bucks County Barn
1923. Tempera and crayon. 19¼ x 25½".

Natural forms exhibit high design quality because their perceivable characteristics and their function are aspects of a single form. In each natural substance that we perceive, process or function brings the form into being and is in turn made possible by the form. In architecture, man gives form to shelters, which in turn express and enhance their functions. Architecture, then, is the art and science of designing habitable, sculptural structures in which appearance is just one of many inseparable functions.

In a world sense, most man-made structures have been built without the aid of architects. Structures such as barns and factories are usually produced without the interference of style or the eccentricities of personal mannerisms. In their purity, such forms are seen by some contemporary architects as inspiration for a style of architecture that is honest, functional, and even playful.

Charles Sheeler was an American painter who was fascinated by structures that were designed by functional necessity and were free of all pretension. He painted them with loving precision. His paintings of barns and industrial constructions depict indigenous modes of building that developed from within.

370 Charles Sheeler
CITY INTERIOR
1936. Painting on fiberboard. 22⅛ x 27".

To be architecture a building must achieve a working harmony between the factors that call it into being and are in turn affected by its existence. We instinctively seek structures that will shelter and enhance our ways of life. It is the work of architects to design these structures. Such buildings are not simply inert enclosures; they are as communicative to the perceiver as other visual arts.

Buildings contribute to human life when they provide durable shelter, augment their intended function, enrich space, complement their site, suit the climate, and stay within the limits of economic feasibility. The person who pays for the building and defines its function is an important member of the architectural team. That person is the client. Often his understanding of architectural possibilities is so limited that he becomes a liability. In any creative effort in which more than one individual is involved, the weakest link is the person who is unaware of what is possible. Thus, clients must bear partial responsibility, along with architects, for the often mediocre design of contemporary buildings.

Of all the visual arts, architecture affects our lives most directly. It determines the character of the human environment in major ways. As you read the words printed here you are probably within a man-made structure. How does it feel? How does it look? Does it provide for and enhance the function for which it was intended?

The experiences offered by architecture begin with an awareness of how structures feel to the senses. Basic physical sensations related to up and down, in and out, high and low, narrow and wide come into play. After developing your own sense of architecture, you may be able to contribute to the form of future buildings.

In the past, architecture in Europe and the United States was dominated by the revival of Greek, Roman, Gothic, Renaissance, and Eastern styles. Ornamental decoration was applied to all types of architecture, from public buildings to factories and homes. Sometimes a complete copy of an earlier building was constructed. More often, architects borrowed elements from a variety of sources to meet their needs. The best of these buildings had distinctive qualities of their own. The worst were designed from the outside in, with more thought given to the façade than to the function of interior spaces. Architecture as a whole was out of touch with the needs of the times.

371   Louis Sullivan
WAINWRIGHT BUILDING
Saint Louis, 1890–1891

New building techniques and materials, as well as new functional needs, demanded a fresh approach to structure and form. The men who met this challenge during the last 100 years were strong, articulate thinkers, who developed a philosophy of architecture closely linked in their minds to social reform. The movement began to take shape in commercial architecture, became symbolized by the skyscraper, and found its first opportunities in Chicago where the big fire of 1870 had cleared the way for a new start.

One of the architects exploring striking new forms was Louis Sullivan (1856–1924). He was Frank Lloyd Wright's teacher and did more than anyone to develop that unique twentieth-century form, the "skyscraper," or "highrise" as we now know it. Although these names suggest severity of an inhuman scale, Sullivan's work does not have that character.

The Wainwright Building in Saint Louis was Sullivan's first skyscraper. It breaks with nineteenth-century tradition in a bold way. The exterior design reflects the internal steel skeleton and emphasizes the vertical height of the structure.

Lever House in New York shows a much later version of the multistoried office building. The austerity of the structure is softened by the open, parklike space provided in the setback.

372   Gordon Bunshaft of Skidmore, Owings, and Merrill
LEVER HOUSE
New York City, 1950

To achieve their purposes, architects manipulate solids and voids. As solid masses change in form, our feelings about them change. Straight edges tend to feel hard, curving edges soft. The brick and concrete architecture of the Romans was composed of many solid masses, in contrast with the lighter, more airy qualtiy of Gothic masonry. Traditional Japanese houses have sliding screens for both interior and exterior walls, providing flexibility in the flow of space according to seasonal changes and the desires of the householder. Contemporary architects have available many strong yet light weight materials that make it possible to enclose space with minimal structures of considerable flexibility.

The interdependence of form and function is basic to nature and to all well-designed human forms. Louis Sullivan's idea that "form follows function"[8] helped to clear away reliance on past styles and made it possible for young architects to rethink architectural design from the inside out.

More recently, Sullivan's formula has been employed with varying results. On the one hand, it has become a sterile formula for many architects today, who make design decisions purely on the basis of order books and profit margins. On the other hand, it is the basis of the continuing integration of design and industrial production for small-scale industrial objects and for larger environmental forms. During the last decade or so, there has been a growing interest in the methodology of environmental design, leading to several techniques of programming, in which an attempt is made to list and respond to as many functional influences on the form as possible. This school contends that if the needs and behaviors of the users of something to be designed are well-enough understood, the structure almost designs itself.

There is an unhealthy division between art and engineering. A few structural engineers, such as Pier Luigi Nervi and Buckminster Fuller, are leading the struggle to bridge this gap by developing architectural forms that will be appropriate to the human situation in the immediate and long-range future. Underlying the work of these men is the feeling that structural necessity and beauty must be considered simultaneously.

Methods of support utilized in architecture determine the character of the final form in major ways. These methods are based on physical laws and, for that reason, have changed little since man first started to build.

Architecture is *construction* and as such it cannot evade obedience to all the objective limitations imposed by the materials it uses and to those laws, not made by men, which govern their equilibrium.

Pier Luigi Nervi[9]

The world's architectural structures have been devised in relation to the objective limitations of materials. Structures can be analyzed in terms of how they deal with downward forces created by gravity. In the effort to enclose space, they may be designed to withstand primarily the stresses of compression (→ ←), tension (← →), bending (( )), or the combination of these in different parts of the structure. There are dozens of basic variations of these structure types, such as shells, folded plates, domes, hanging roofs, tents, and free-form castings. A few diagrams illustrate the main ideas.

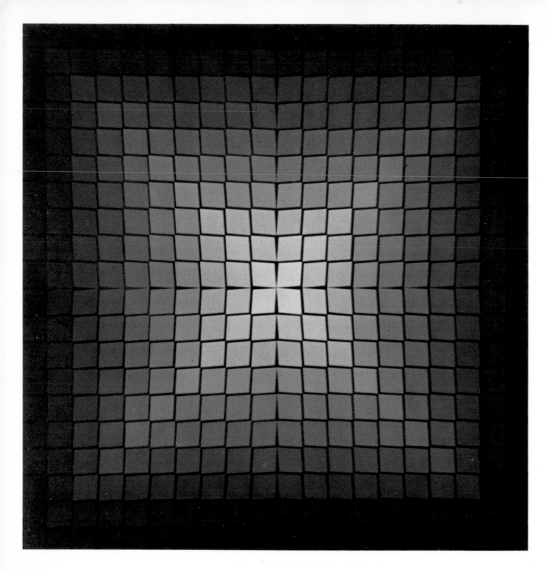

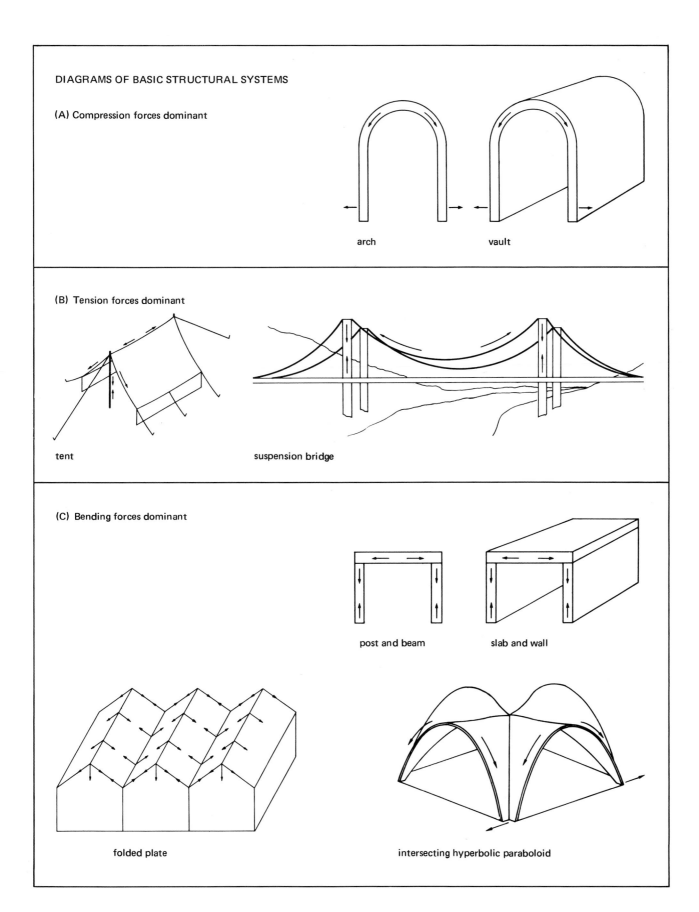

DIAGRAMS OF BASIC STRUCTURAL SYSTEMS

(A) Compression forces dominant

arch   vault

(B) Tension forces dominant

tent   suspension bridge

(C) Bending forces dominant

post and beam   slab and wall

folded plate   intersecting hyperbolic paraboloid

A radical innovation in structure was originated by Buckminster Fuller when he developed the principles of the *geodesic dome*. Exploring these principles has led to the construction of domes for many purposes.

Geodesic domes are designed according to Fuller's own system of mathematics, which he calls "energetic-synergetic geometry."[10] A Fuller dome can be erected from lightweight, inexpensive materials in a very short time. Usually a skeleton is constructed of small, modular, linear elements joined together to form single planes, which in turn join together to form the surface of the

dome. The resulting structure can be covered with a variety of materials to make the enclosed space weatherproof.

Fuller believes that all aspects of life can come together in a mutually beneficial pattern if the principles of structural design are applied to society as a whole.

Many critics evaluate Buckminster Fuller as one of the most forward-thinking men of our time. Significantly, the physical projections of his thoughts reach far ahead into the future, yet are in harmony with structures in nature and in the human past.

373   R. Buckminster Fuller. U. S. PAVILION, EXPO-67. Montreal.

374   KALAPALO INDIANS HOUSE. Aifa, central Brazil, 1967.

The Kalapalo Indians of South America build their own type of domelike structures. The house under construction shown here is in Aifa, a village in central Brazil. The house will hold several families, each with its own hammock space and cooking fire. It has already taken several months to curve these saplings in an arc fastened to giant posts.

Some of the values behind Japanese culture can be traced to neolithic times. Shinto beliefs have provided a frame of attitudes within which man works in harmony with nature. The Shinto temple complex at Ise embodies these values and has acted as a prototype for later Japanese architecture. The reconstruction of the neolithic house shows the origin of this temple architecture.

The shrines at Ise were built at least as early as 685 A.D. and have been rebuilt every twenty years since then. Wood for the structure is taken from the surrounding forest with gratitude and ceremonial care. As a tree is cut into boards, the boards are numbered so that the wood that was united in the tree is together in the building. No nails are used. The wood is fitted and pegged. Surfaces are left unpainted. The main shrine of Ise combines heroic simplicity with rich subtlety. The refined craftsmanship, sculptural proportions, and spatial harmonies are rooted in a seemingly timeless religious and aesthetic discipline.

A valuable comparison can be made between the architecture of Ise and that of the Parthenon (see page 133). Bauhaus architect Walter Gropius once asked, "What are the deep shadows hanging over Ise as against the limitless radiance of the Parthenon?" The Japanese architect Kenzo Tange answered:

This question . . . touch[es] upon the essence of Japanese culture as compared to Western culture, namely the contrast between an animistic attitude of willing adaption to and absorption in nature and a heroic attitude of seeking to breast and conquer it.[11]

375   Reconstruction of NEOLITHIC HOUSE
Kyokodan, Musashino, Japan
3rd century B.C.–6th century A.D.

376   SHRINES AT ISE
Main Sanctuary from northwest
c. 685, rebuilt every 20 years

a
b
c

377 Kenzo Tange. OLYMPIC STADIUMS. Tokyo, 1964. (a) Exterior, Natatorium; (b) Aerial view; (c) Interior, Natatorium.

Tange's own work includes the design of many single buildings and, recently, the design of cities.

The indoor stadiums built in Tokyo for the 1964 Olympics, show the harmony Tange achieves between spatial, structural, and sculptural requirements. The main building houses a huge swimming pool. With the aid of structural engineer Yoshikatsu Tsuboi,

Tange created an open interior space with a seating capacity of 15,000. The roof is suspended from cables carried by huge concrete abutments at either end of the building. Pipelike forms in the end wall are for air-conditioning the interior. They act, along with the diving boards, as sculptural accents to the sweeping curves of the hanging roof.

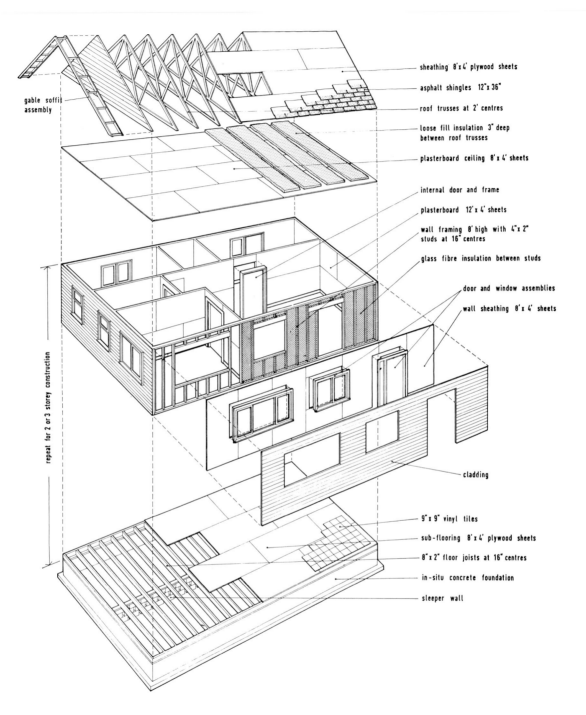

sheathing 8' x 4' plywood sheets

asphalt shingles 12" x 36"

roof trusses at 2' centres

loose fill insulation 3" deep between roof trusses

plasterboard ceiling 8' x 4' sheets

internal door and frame

plasterboard 12' x 4' sheets

wall framing 8' high with 4" x 2" studs at 16" centres

glass fibre insulation between studs

door and window assemblies

wall sheathing 8' x 4' sheets

gable soffit assembly

repeat for 2 or 3 storey construction

cladding

9" x 9" vinyl tiles

sub-flooring 8' x 4' plywood sheets

8" x 2" floor joists at 16" centres

in-situ concrete foundation

sleeper wall

378 PREFABRICATED PLATFORM CONSTRUCTION

In this century, a great deal of effort has gone into the development of prefabricated housing as a major aspect of the transition of architecture from handcraft to industrial production. Although prefabrication still offers the major hope for combining quality with low cost, poor design has been common in most prefabricated houses. There remains, however, an urgent international need for both high quality and low cost housing. In the United States alone, if the present birth rate continues, the equivalent of one new city for 200,000 people will be needed every month by 1980.

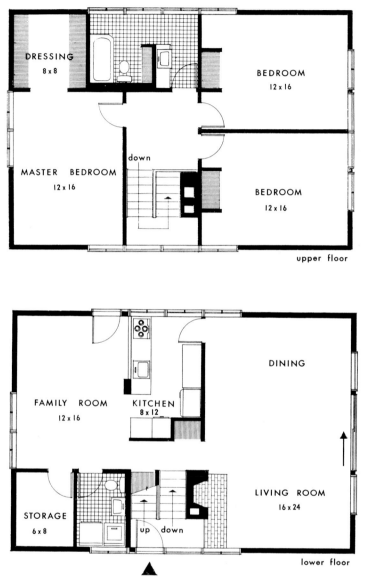

upper floor

Form and function are handsomely joined in the adjustable prefabricated houses produced by Techbuilt Corporation of Cambridge, Massachusetts. Many floor plans are possible because flexibility is built into each model. In the model shown here, the two upper floor bedrooms over the living room can be omitted if the family has no children. If the family has children, these rooms can be added. The floor plan can be changed again after the children are grown.

lower floor

379   Techbuilt Corporation
PREFABRICATED THREE-BEDROOM HOUSE
24 x 36', 1728 sq. ft.

380   Cortez Corporation. MOTORHOME. 1972.

Many people in this changing society are seeking the flexibility of a house that can be moved. The "mobile home" is in fact rarely mobile. In its common use, the mobile home is a poorly designed prefabricated house that is never moved after initial installation. Mobile architecture is in great demand today in the United States. The 1970 census showed that about 3 percent of the population now live in mobile homes.

In most cases, a trailer park or mobile-home community is a blight on the landscape. Even the heavy planting that is now encouraged in such places cannot hide the fact that the units themselves were designed to cash in on a booming mass market, with little thought given to aesthetics. Mobile homes could be movable and well-designed so that they would enhance rather than detract from the areas in which they are placed.

Actual mobility has been achieved with converted trucks, vans, buses, campers, and motor homes. Such vehicles were originally promoted for vacationing, but an increasing number of people are using them for permanent homes.

Although our society is undergoing a period of rapid change, much contemporary architecture is inflexible and permanent. Flexibility and impermanence might be more appropriate to the changing patterns of use for residential, commercial, and institutional structures.

381   HOME-BUILT CAMPER. 1972.

Educational buildings are a case in point. Expensive monumental school buildings are still being built, resulting in campus architecture that is too rigid to meet the changing needs of education. Campus buildings are built to last a century, whereas educational programs are being increasingly challenged and revised.

There is universal need for inexpensive, flexible, and disposable architecture to meet the demands of cultural change and increasing population.

ENVIRONMENTAL DESIGN

As we move outside of buildings, it is apparent that the general accumulation of man-made structures creates a landscape that frequently demonstrates lack of harmony with itself and with the natural setting.

The man-made environment is all the objects and places built or shaped by man. As such it is a composite design — an environmental design that includes indoor and outdoor spaces and the organization of objects within those spaces. We build the larger components of this environment to provide shelter from the elements; privacy; places and facilities for our activities; the manufacture of goods; and the transportation of people, things, and utilities.

The life of the human body depends on fuel, energy, and waste systems. The man-made environment extends these biological systems on an immediate scale in buildings and on a larger scale in cities, states, and countries.

The form of the environment is determined by our size, needs, desires, activities, cultural premises, and life styles, as well as the land on which we build, the climate, the materials with which we build, and our methods of construction.

We continually make changes in our environment by moving from place to place and by adding to or demolishing parts of it. Planned environmental changes must be based on geographical, biological, and sociological information.

382a BEFORE UNDERGROUND TELEPHONE AND POWER LINES.

382b AFTER UNDERGROUND TELEPHONE AND POWER LINES.

Environmental design is a broad category of interdependent planning and design disciplines that includes architecture, landscape architecture, urban planning, and regional planning. These disciplines ultimately depend on politics.

In the past, urban centers grew slowly to meet needs for protection, trade, and communication. Unchanging life styles and firm traditions kept these bits in harmony. Now, urban areas are rapidly growing and changing within. Ready-made suburban areas annex to the central city practically overnight. If any life-enhancing order is to come from this frantic growth, planning must be done and put into effect.

383 Detail of FORTIFICATIONS AT SACSAHUAMAN Cuzco, Peru, c. 1450

384 AERIAL VIEW OF MACHU PICCHU RUINS. Peru, c. 1500.

385 Ambrogio Lorenzetti. VIEW OF A TOWN. c. 1338–1340. Painting on wood. 9 x 13⅛".

Without the inclusion of aesthetic concerns, planning is a hollow shell. The growing complexity of urban fabric must be seen as a whole.

Environmental design now covers the design of subdivisions, new towns, master plans for cities, and regional plans. Some thinkers like Buckminster Fuller are asking us to think of design in a global sense. This does not mean that we should redesign the world. It means that we must think of our designs as part of a total world harmony that begins with the natural order.

The environmental design professions try to utilize man's highest sensibilities and applied knowledge to create and interrelate man-made and natural environments and systems in a way that provides a beneficial setting for human life. Environmental designers work with urban and regional planners in all phases of the planning process, from initial policy formulations through development of the design proposals, to the implementation of final plans.

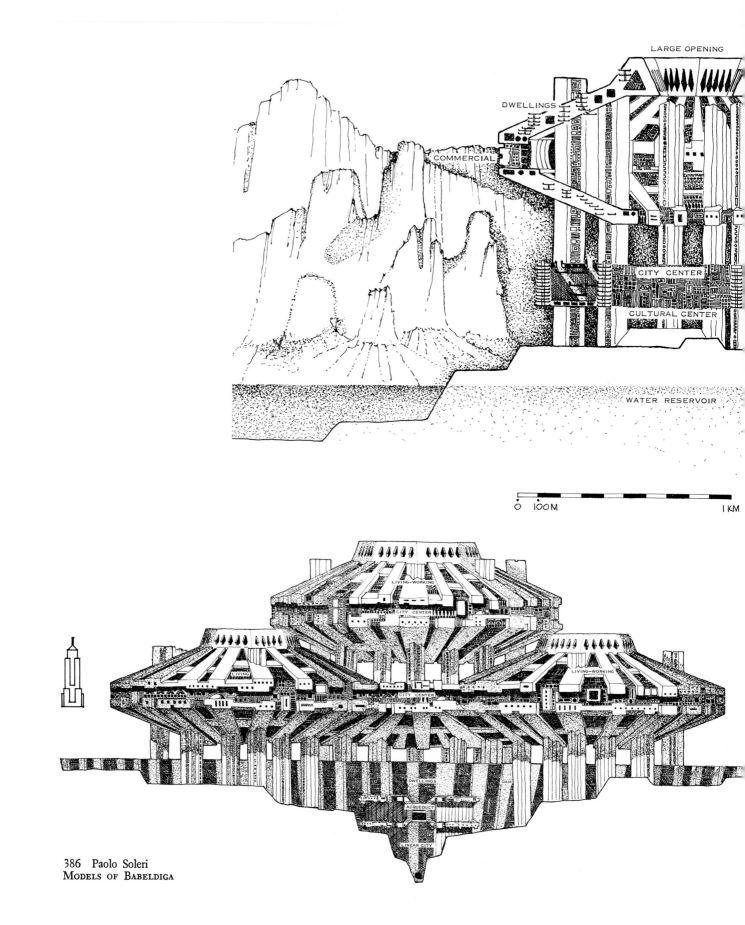

386 Paolo Soleri
MODELS OF BABELDIGA

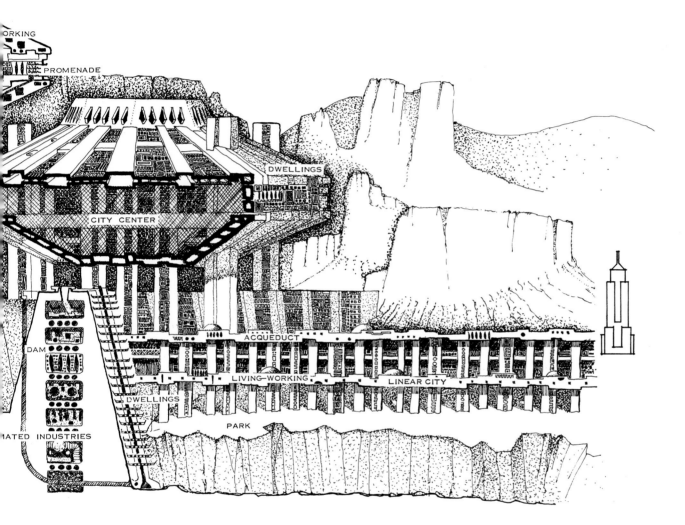

Babeldiga is a city that contains its own dam and supplies all of its power. It is designed for 1,200,000 people. The structure measures over a mile high, from its underground base to its cliff-level top. The urban environment is largely inside. Housing is situated on outer surfaces; residents may view an untouched wilderness outside. Within the structure a large variety of environments at different levels is produced. Scale is 1:10,000.

The visionary drawings of Paolo Soleri portray cities as single, self-contained structures.

387 Kenzo Tange. Plan for Reconstruction of Skopje, Yugoslavia. 1965.

Kenzo Tange and his assistants designed this model as a plan for Skopje, Yugoslavia.

Contemporary needs for protection are very different from those of medieval times. Patterns of commerce and methods of communication have changed radically. New transportation systems must be accommodated in ways that are harmonious with the general urban fabric.

Some environmentalists have suggested that we do not need concentrated urban forms, since they no longer offer protection, are not as necessary for commerce, and are hardly needed at all for communication. Other environmental designers point out that dense urban complexes are necessary to save agricultural, recreational, and wilderness land.

389 Moshe Safdie
MODEL OF HABITAT ISRAEL
1969

388

Moshe Safdie has designed new answers to urban housing problems. His first notable work was the apartment complex, Habitat, built at Montreal's Expo '67. Safdie's primary concern is for structures that meet human needs in humane ways. In his Habitat Israel, he uses prefabricated modular apartment units that can be stacked in different configurations. Private garden terraces, walkways, and covered parking areas are included. The design allows for a dense population, yet provides many of the advantages of single, unattached dwellings.

Environmental designer Constantinos Doxiadis points out the need for housing the world's growing population. Showing the accompanying photograph, he says, "The greatest part of humanity lives in conditions similar to these. This is the main architectural problem."[12] It is estimated that 90,000 people live on the sidewalks of Bombay alone.

A city is more than an architectural composition. It is a system within which variety should be able to exist harmoniously.

The radial plan has been used as a basis for numerous communities, including early village forms and large cities. Compare the radial pattern of a human center with a magnified cross section of a twig. Both show patterns of movement and growth within which variety can exist.

390 CLEMATIS VIRGINIANA
Transverse section of a young stem showing combination of hexagonal, radial, and concentric symmetries.

391 KRAHÔ INDIANS VILLAGE
Pedra Branco, central Brazil, 1965

393 AERIAL VIEW OF PALMANOVA, ITALY
1593

SCALE 0 2 4 6 MILES

LEGEND
A Airport
— Railroad
▪ Industrial Area
- - - - Rapid Transit

● Urban Centers
CR Connections with National
    Railroad-Network
CH Connections with National
    Highway-Network

▪ Regional Parks
  City Recreation } Open Space
  Local Recreation

City Planner Victor Gruen has diagramed a possible future city that would function as a cellular structure, radiating around a central core. Broken lines indicate mass transit leading out from urban centers represented by clusters of black dots. Speckled areas are for park areas.

392 Victor Gruen and Associates
METROCORE AND ITS TEN CITIES
1966

There is a variety of ways in which human communities can expand, change, and diminish without causing the kind of destructive chaos that we so often see today. The rapid, unplanned growth of human centers needs to be controlled.

Doxiadis feels that the typical growth of a city is outward in concentric circles. If the city is allowed to grow unchecked, its center finally strangles. To avoid this he suggests that we first recognize the fact that cities are not static, then plan their growth along an axis, creating a dynamic city with a parabolically expanding center.[13]

If we can think three-dimensionally in our planning for environmental changes, the expense in terms of land will not be so great.

The complexities of contemporary urban life make sophisticated environmental planning an extremely demanding task. As an inspiration for that task, we can note that the smallest units of natural structures that we know are quite similar to the largest. In both the microcosm and the macrocosm, nature exhibits three-dimensional structures to which we can turn for clues to the future of environmental design.

Environmental design specialists need to be backed by a public educated in environmental awareness and ready to become involved in participatory planning. Without the benefit of the ideas and feelings of the citizens who will ultimately live in the environment, plans become constricting and detrimental to life.

394

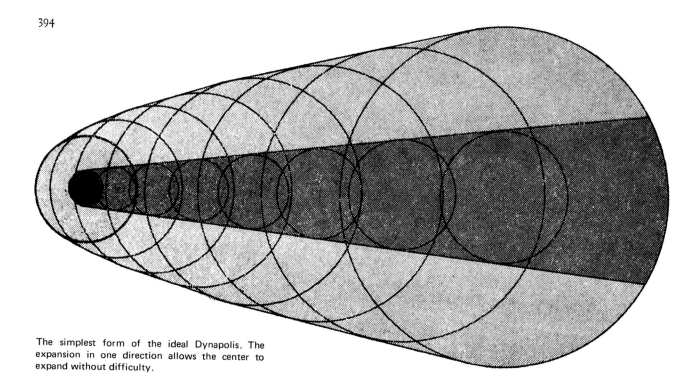

The simplest form of the ideal Dynapolis. The expansion in one direction allows the center to expand without difficulty.

How can art
serve the future?

Design, the act of putting constructs in an order, or disorder, seems to be human destiny. It seems to be the way into trouble and it may be the way out. It is the specific responsibility to which our species has matured, and constitutes the only chance of the thinking, foreseeing, and constructing animal that we are, to preserve life on this shrunken planet and to survive with grace.

Richard Neutra
Survival Through Design[1]

Art is who we are. It is how we manifest our being in the world. What we create indicates our states of mind and our value systems. Art objects are an extension of ourselves and what we feel about our environment. Man-made environment is a collection of objects — they are the art that we create. They represent our collective selves. That is why it is an important process to extend our awareness into the environment, to see how it reflects ourselves. If we do not like what we see, we need to find ways to change the image. Man creates art creates man.

Necessity encouraged early man to develop and apply his imagination. The problem was survival. Man began to make things in order to meet the need for food, shelter, and protection. From these beginnings we have gone on inventing and constructing at an ever-increasing rate, building up around ourselves an accumulation of artifacts that has set us apart from what Walt Whitman called "the primal sanities of nature."[2] This proliferation of material goods has become so dominant in the world that it has caused the extinction of over 300 species of animals, and now threatens many more, including man. "Only within the moment of time represented by the present century has one species — man — acquired significant power to alter the nature of his world." (Rachel Carson, Silent Spring.)[3]

Because of this power, we now have a colossal array of goods and technologies, supported by historically unprecedented levels of resource and energy use. But in the haste and challenge to develop such impressive displays of technology as the SST and the digital computer, one vital fact has been forgotten: that man has evolved as an integral part of a natural system. The earth was not made *by* or *for* us, we grew *from* it, part of an evolutionary continuum more than a billion years old.

Although man exists within supportive biological systems, his cleverness has led him to forget it. Gradually man has learned to manipulate nature's rules to his own advantage, to move from creature to creator, to make things in order to survive, and to move beyond physiological survival to a civilized life of leisure and culture. Yet our powers of selection and manipulation are such that in exercising them we have denied and, in some cases, destroyed the sources of life.

395 Lucas Cranach the Elder
ADAM AND EVE
1526. Oil on wood. 117 x 80.5 cm.

Western civilization has been trying for centuries to bring about a separation between
man and nature. This drive even seeks a
separation between man and himself by dividing body, mind, and spirit. Our arrogant
conquest of earth seems based on a literal
interpretation of the biblical injunction in
Genesis:

And God blessed them, and God said to them,
"Be fruitful and multiply, and fill the earth and
subdue it, and have dominion over the fish of the
sea and over the birds of the air and over every
living thing that moves upon the earth."
                                    Genesis 1:28[4]

The Old Testament description of the fall
of man may symbolically portray man's mental separation from his natural home. According to the Old Testament, the fall of
man occurred when Adam decided to bite
the apple. The apple symbolizes conscious-

ness, the fruit of knowledge. This painting
by Lucas Cranach the Elder shows Adam
scratching his head in doubt as Eve tempts
him with the forbidden fruit. After they in-
dulged, their transgression was discovered
by the Lord and they were expelled from
Paradise. Masaccio's work shows eloquently
their pain, alienation, and disgrace.

396 Tommaso Guidi Masaccio
EXPULSION FROM PARADISE
c. 1427. Fresco. 15 x 6⅛".

Now, nearing the end of the twentieth century, the problem is not only physiological survival, which men have always been faced with, but it is also the survival of a life with personal and social fulfillment. At least for humans, mere survival is not enough, but even to achieve that requires the survival of complete ecological systems, not merely of one species. In an ecosystem, bacteria and worms are as important as any other species. No ecosystem, no human existence.

How can man have dominion over a system of which he is merely a part? Systems do not work that way. Our lives depend on a finite supply of air and water enclosing the earth, an equivalent in proportion to the skin on an apple. The life-sustaining capacity of this biosphere is based on a set of complex relationships of cause and effect. Health of the individual and of his environment depends on the harmonious operation of the whole.

Once we understand the interdependence of all things, we can understand why cooperation is more important than competition. A dynamic, yet balanced relationship between the various environmental elements is crucial to our well-being and ultimately to our survival. While man's environment since primitive times has been both natural and man-made, the man-made factors are now becoming increasingly out of harmony with the natural order.

397 Warren Roll. TWO MOUNTAINS. 1972.

We are now at a crossroads between natural evolution and man's technological progress. Man-centered attitudes and values have created an explosive growth in technology and an accompanying emphasis on material wealth and physical security. The changes accompanying this growth have led to a re-examination of basic human values. A major struggle is going on between those who believe that the highest quality of life will be obtained by continuing the drive toward greater control over the physical world and those who would like to abandon this direction in order to move toward a more spiritual and natural style of life. A possible solution appears to be *not* simply to abandon the mental and physical environments produced by industrial technologies, but to select technologies with great care. Selection of technologies should be based on the ideal of bringing human endeavor into equilibrium with the natural order.

Art could act as a tool in encouraging equilibrium between human efforts and the order of natural systems. In the past art has brought together man with man and man with nature. Art refers to human creations (acts, ideas, constructions) that fuse matter with spirit. Art is inspired by nature in a way that few people understand. The artist uses his abilities to create something, as nature does; that is, not to do what nature has done, in the sense of a replica, but to move with nature, to do as nature does.

The man-centered approach to nature is arrogant and full of conflict: man against nature. The nature-centered approach is humble and based on unity: man is nature. The two views can be seen in the following poems:

Flower in the crannied wall,
I pluck you out of the crannies;
Hold you here, root and all, in my hand,
Little flower — but if I could understand
What you are root and all, and all in all
I should know what God and man is.
                                        Alfred Lord Tennyson[5]

Not knowing
The name of the tree,
I stood in the flood
Of its sweet smell.
                                        Matsuo Basho
                              (translated from Japanese)[6]

In the few small areas of the earth where modern civilization has not made strong inroads, man's physical unity with the natural world still acts as a spiritual basis for daily life. Many traditional cultures have based their value systems on reverence for the natural world. People who have been native to a particular area of land for many generations frequently hold certain outstanding features of their landscape in particularly high esteem: such as a lake, river, mountain range, or peak. These landmarks act as a symbolic link between the known world of their everyday life and greater unknown spheres.

Diamond Head, the famous Hawaiian volcanic mountain, was named *Leahi*, the place of fire, by the Hawaiians. It was a sacred place and was a home of the fire goddess Pele. This photograph, taken about 1880, shows how Diamond Head gave a unique character to Waikiki Beach.

By necessity preindustrial societies have consciously maintained a harmonious relationship with the sources of life around them. When outsiders bring in manufactured goods and new technologies, the apparent necessity for harmony is broken. Few traditional societies have been able to keep their values intact when faced with the attractiveness of modern industrial products.

When Europeans first "discovered" the Hawaiian Islands in the eighteenth century, an estimated 400,000 Hawaiians were living there in ecological harmony with the land. For centuries they had maintained both the natural resources and the beauty of the islands. Today, the population is about double its earlier level, and the islands' natural wealth are being rapidly depleted. The

398 WAIKIKI BEACH. c. 1880.

people are no longer self-sufficient, and the Hawaiians are no longer influential in terms of either beliefs or numbers. The islands cannot feed their occupants and the original practicing ecologists have succumbed to a culture devoted to modern industrial production.

One reason for this situation is that Hawaii's motto has been profoundly ignored in the physical and economic development of the state. The motto is: Ua mau ke ea o ka aina i ka pono, and its meaning, from ancient Hawaiian tradition, is: The life of the land is preserved in righteousness (or right use). Before exposure to Westerners, Hawaiians preserved the land by obeying a firm tradition of religious laws called kapus. As principles about man's relation to the natural environment, these kapus did not urge

dominion, but required humility. For instance, one of them required an Hawaiian to ask forgiveness before cutting a canoe log.

The environmental humility of religious beliefs like these is beginning to be appreciated again. There is a growing realization that the people throughout the world whom Europe and the United States first tried to "save" with missionaries, then with military efforts and certain foreign aid programs, may indeed have some knowledge and beliefs for salvation. In the United States it seems very likely that some Indian, Eskimo, and Hawaiian citizens are still able to teach essential attitudes of humility and rapport with the natural world. Value change in this direction will be necessary if man, especially industrial man, is to live on the earth without destroying it.

The *quantity* of people and their things threatens the earth. It is now time for growth in the *quality* of people and their things.

As human beings we are more responsible for our choices than other species because we are more conscious. Our consciousness makes it possible for us to select the wrong choices as well as the right ones, to be awkward as well as graceful. The price of consciousness is responsibility for choices.

One of the major choices that we must make is to limit our numbers. If we do not control population, nature will do it for us in ways that we will find hard to accept. The accompanying population graph shows our present position. Environmental problems start here.

399

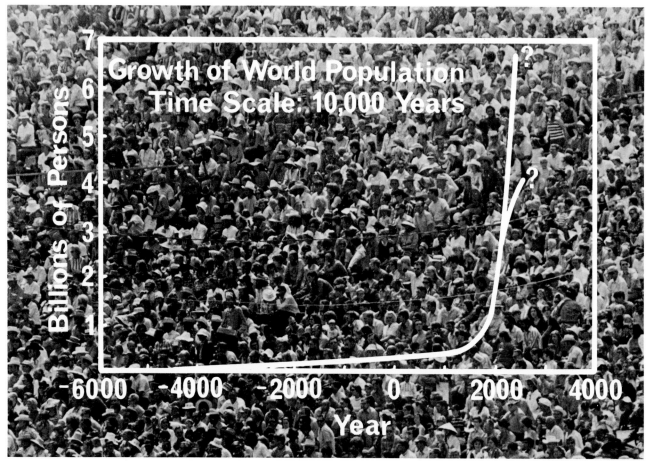

As a graphic example of the environmental impact of virtually unbounded growth, here are photographs of Waikiki, taken exactly ten years apart.

400 WAIKIKI. August 1961.

401 WAIKIKI. August 1971.

With this background in mind, let us look at some visual images of man's relationship to environment in the United States.

The painter George Catlin had great respect for native Americans. He spent considerable time in the West painting them and their life style, just before their land was taken over by settlers. Catlin was the first to conceive of a national park. As he expressed it, such a park would not only protect the great beauty of the land, but also the people who lived there in harmony with it. The artist recorded the idea in his journal in 1832.[7]

With the establishment of Yellowstone National Park in 1872, Catlin's dream became a reality and the United States became the first country in the world to set aside national land purely to preserve its natural beauty. There are now a total of thirty national parks. Among these, one of the best known is Yosemite in California.

402 George Catlin
ONE HORN (HA-WON-JE-TA),
A DAKOTA (SIOUX) CHIEF.
1832. Oil on canvas. c. 28 x 23".

403 George Catlin. A BIRD'S-EYE VIEW OF THE MANDAN VILLAGE. 1832. Oil on canvas. 19½ x 27⅝".

404   Ansel Adams. Moon and Half Dome, Yosemite National Park, California. c. 1960.

The need for such protected areas was stated with amazing clarity in 1898 by John Muir, naturalist, conservationist, pioneer spokesman for the national parks, and founder of the Sierra Club:

"Thousands of tired, nerve-shaken, over-civilized people are beginning to find out that going to the mountains is going home; that wildness is a necessity; and that mountain parks and reservations are useful not only as fountains of timber and irrigating rivers, but as fountains of life."[8]

Contrast these protective attitudes with the attitudes underlying much land use in twentieth-century America.

When Alfred Stieglitz took the photograph called THE HAND OF MAN in 1902, the progressive deterioration of the environment was already under way in the United States. It had occurred before in other times and places, but never with such relentless speed and over so vast an area.

405   Jean Coté
LITTERED LANDSCAPE
1970

406   Alfred Stieglitz. THE HAND OF MAN. 1902.

407 Rondal Partridge
HIGHWAY 64
Arizona, 1962

Since Stieglitz' picture of seventy years ago, man has built a lot of housing. Jammed together in a flattened, treeless landscape, great stretches of identical, stereotyped houses and apartments amalgamate into the pattern of land use known as urban sprawl. It is awkward, ugly, distressing, and unnecessary. Better methods of urban development are available, but they are rarely used because population pressures keep land speculators and developers well-supplied with clients who are either too ignorant or too much in need of housing to demand more. Land speculators, acting as land wholesalers, often force land prices to soar far beyond fair value.

As a pattern of land use, urban sprawl is the rule, not the exception. Daly City, just south of San Francisco along the California coast, represents thousands of places where urban sprawl continues to roll across the land.

408 Donald W. Aitken. DALY CITY. c. 1960.

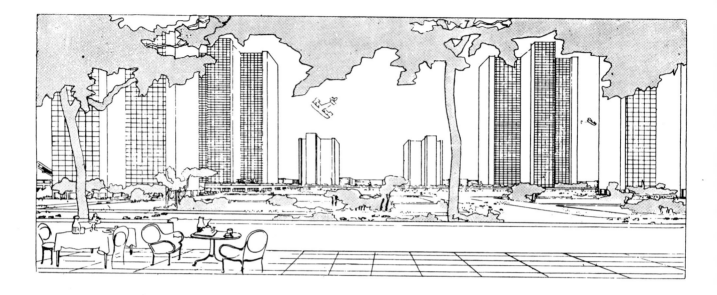

There are alternatives to uncontrolled horizontal growth. Le Corbusier's visionary plan
of 1922, City of Three Million, sought "to
de-congest the centers — to augment their
density — to increase the means of getting
about — to increase the parks and open
spaces."[9] In Le Corbusier's plan, housing is
split between widely spaced tall towers (at
the subway stops) and low–level garden
apartments. Industry is banished to the out-
skirts, and business occurs in towers at the
center.

Le Corbusier's idea solves many urban problems. It provides for a dense urban population while allowing for ample green space.
Pedestrian space is separated from automobile space as much as possible.

It took several decades for this idea to be
put to actual use in a few locations. Shallow
versions of it have appeared repeatedly during the last twenty years in major urban renewal projects.

This photograph reveals the great difference
between the original concept and its usual
present application.

409   Le Corbusier
DRAWING FOR CITY OF THREE MILLION
1922

"We are in the very center of the city, the point of
greatest density of population and traffic; there is any
amount of room for both. . . . Theaters, public halls,
etc., are scattered in the open spaces between the sky-
scrapers and are surrounded by trees."[10]

410   HYGIENIC APARTMENTS IN
THE MAN-MADE DESERT.

Although this advertising rendering looks superficially like Le Corbusier's idea, the building is a single tower, unconnected to any overall plan. It does not approach the ideals of Le Corbusier; in fact, quite the opposite. The building has been designed to offer views to those inside, but has, by its height and location, blocked several major view corridors within the city of Honolulu, including many views of Diamond Head.

413 RENDERING OF THE CONTESSA
Honolulu, 1970

411 HARTFORD, CONNECTICUT CENTRAL CITY
1953

412 CONSTITUTION PLAZA
Hartford, Connecticut, 1964

Although no city like Le Corbusier's has been built, a few large building complexes have been successful. One of them is Constitution Plaza in Hartford, Connecticut, finished in 1964. The project was designed to renew the central city, and it has. A greater number of people are now using the area, yet they are enjoying their time there more because of the greatly improved use of the space. Open space is increased and pleasantly varied. Pedestrian areas are removed from vehicular traffic. Here is a completed renewal project that measures up to the intention of Le Corbusier's original idea.

The tremendous urban growth in America in the last twenty-five years has given cities new kinds of pressing problems. Many people wished to live near the city, but not in it. As new shopping and business centers grew around the central city, the old city centers decayed. The photograph taken of Hartford in 1953 shows the decaying downtown area before Constitution Plaza was built.

The central area of New York City is now so crowded with tall buildings that improved spacing is almost impossible. The demands of a growth economy designed this incredible human construction.

Rockefeller Center, built in 1932, was an early demonstration of the fact that tall buildings can be interrelated to create pleasant space, even when population density is extremely high. But this exceptional venture has remained just that. Midtown Manhattan is a colossal concentration of uncontrolled vertical growth. Crowding and pollution problems have brought the city close to being uninhabitable.

414 ROCKEFELLER CENTER
New York City, 1933

415 MANHATTAN. 1966.

Color plate 42   NASA. THE WORLD. North and South America photographed from
Applications Technological Satellite at a 22,300-mile altitude, November 18, 1967.

416 Bernice Abbott
EXCHANGE PLACE
1933

New York City is the epitome of environments made by industrial man. Because it brings together in one place much of the best and the worst of human life, it can be both exhilarating and depressing.

In the seventeenth century, New York (then called New Amsterdam) was a small town occupying the southern tip of Manhattan Island. The town's northern boundary was a wall similar to those surrounding many European medieval cities. The wall formed a protective division separating the inhabitants from the dangerous wilderness. This site has been transformed from a wall against the wilderness to a canyon in the heart of a new kind of wilderness.

Lack of the adequate space that nature requires for man to be physically and psychologically healthy leads both to social and personal disorders. The beginning of Ian McHarg's film, MULTIPLY AND SUBDUE THE EARTH, shows that overcrowding in rats causes a higher-than-normal percentage of deviant behavior.[11] In addition to a variety of sexual deviations, rats experience a high incidence of withdrawal. The withdrawal tendency may have particular application to humans. A study of midtown Manhattan, done over a period of eight years and completed in 1962 by Columbia University Medical College, determined that in Manhattan less than one in five people is mentally well. The norm is abnormality.[12]

Cities in general are suffering from an increase in crime. An incredible pall of fear permeates much of New York City. The saying used to be, "It's a great place to visit, but I wouldn't want to live there." Now even visitors are affected by the city's declining quality of life. If you stay in a New York City hotel, regardless of the price of your accommodations, you will find this notice prominently displayed in your room, courtesy of the Hotel Association of New York City, Inc.:

TO INSURE A MORE PLEASANT STAY, WE SUGGEST THE FOLLOWING: KEEP DOOR LOCKED WHEN IN ROOM. DO NOT DISPLAY VALUABLES IN ROOM. PLACE THEM IN HOTEL SAFE DEPOSIT BOX. CLOSE DOOR BY HAND WHEN LEAVING HOTEL. NEVER ADMIT PERSONS WITH UNSOLICITED DELIVERIES. DO NOT REVEAL NAME OF HOTEL OR ROOM NUMBER TO STRANGERS. DEPOSIT KEY WITH DESK CLERK UPON LEAVING OR CHECKING OUT. NEVER ADMIT REPAIRMEN TO ROOM WITHOUT CHECKING WITH MANAGER. NEVER DISCUSS PLANS FOR STAYING AWAY FROM HOTEL IN FRONT OF STRANGERS.[13]

Ghetto people are most affected by the poor quality of many urban environments. They are forced by economic necessity to live in the marginal areas where the worst aspects of bad planning or no planning accumulate. They cannot afford to leave. Every day their physical and social environment tells them they do not count, and they lack the power to change their environment. The resulting downward spiral is powerful and self-perpetuating.

417 George Tooker
The Subway
1950. Egg tempera on composition board. 18⅛ x 36⅛".

418 Roy DeCarava. Untitled. c. 1950.

Man-made chaos and ugliness are the symptoms and causes of cultural disease. What happens to our senses when we must constantly react to a hostile environment? It seems that when our senses are so accosted, we try to turn them off as much as possible —as a partially deaf person turns off his hearing aid when the audible world becomes unpleasant to him. This reaction may be natural and unavoidable, yet it is also disastrous in light of our current environmental crisis. Our sensory equipment must be fully working in order for us to make the choices necessary to improve the quality of our surroundings. Without being sensitive, we cannot recognize the changes that are needed. In fact, the more our senses are bombarded, the more we withdraw. The more our environment defines our lives and weakens our initiative, the less able we are to make any change. Our ability to adapt can work against us. We become increasingly tolerant of surroundings that deny human needs.

The regular occurrence of open space combined with vegetation can help to meet the city-dweller's need for relief from pollution of the senses. In a park, he can open ears, eyes, and nostrils without fear of being overwhelmed. In such a place, the surroundings confirm the significance of the individual. One of the most dangerous aspects of concentrated urban environments is the lack of confirmation of the worthwhile self. Living in a dingy apartment in a crowded neighborhood sends the message that a person is not worth much. A low opinion of oneself may ultimately result in destructive behavior. This opinion, spread through a city's population, can produce what anthropologist Edward T. Hall described as "a series of destructive sinks more lethal than the hydrogen bomb."[14]

419   M. Paul Friedberg and Associates
VEST POCKET PLAYGROUND
AND NATURE STUDY CENTER.
New York City, 1968

420 Le Corbusier. PLAYGROUND ON ROOF OF UNITY HOUSE. Marseilles, 1947.

Children are particularly affected. Their open spirits are hammered on by surroundings that offer too few positive relationships. Nature can be found here only in the form of other wilting, dying members of one's own species.

Attempts have been and are being made to turn all of this around. The design of a "vest pocket" park and nature study center by M. Paul Friedberg and Associates offers New York children an area of hope. Small parks can be liberally sprinkled throughout the city, offering safe park space near all residences. Vest pocket parks can be created in only one lot or partial lot.

In dense cities, the tops of buildings offer a major quantity of open space. Le Corbusier has demonstrated that these rooftops need not be ugly leftovers. His playground on the roof of Unity House in Marseilles, France, incorporates stacks and air conditioning equipment into a pleasant outdoor space for the families living in the highrise building below. This building was designed with plenty of open green space on the ground level as well. Unity House is supported by piers acting as legs or feet for the building, lifting it off the ground so that it does not block pedestrian space.

421 RIVER WALK. San Antonio, Texas, 1969.

Our attitudes about the basic natural elements of an urban site are very important. How important to us are waterways, hills, and climate? If we respect and try to retain and enhance the character and advantages offered by natural preconditions, the urban centers that we create will better meet our needs for comfort and delight.

In San Antonio, Texas, there was much argument about how to deal with the San Antonio River that flowed through the heart of the city. Some said that it should be encased in concrete and built over in order to provide more commercial space. Others wanted to take advantage of its inherent charm by providing park space, a continuous walkway, boating facilities, and restaurants along the river's edge. Fortunately for the city, the people who held this image of the river's potential won the argument. In many other cities of the world, rivers and streams are simply convenient places to dispose of waste.

Signs are a dominant form of visual pollution. The most obtrusive signs are designed to catch the eye of the passing motorist, who has become increasingly immune to their demands. The faster he goes the larger the sign. Products vie with one another for attention. The pedestrian is a minor element in this garish man-made jungle.

422 Herbert Loebel. AVENUE U. 1961.

Henry Ford had little idea of the kind of world his product would help create when he wrote:

I will build a motor car for the great multitude. . . . But it will be so low in price that no man making a good salary will be unable to own one — and enjoy with his family the blessings of hours of pleasure in God's great open spaces.[15]

The automobile industry has grown in a great spiral, passing the point where the birthrate for cars became double that for humans. As more and more people take to the highways the great open spaces shrink accordingly.

Vast amounts of land continue to be consumed by the ever-increasing demands of this tool of man. Urban areas are frequently designed not by urban designers, but by the needs of the automobile. Cars beget highways and highways discourage other means of transportation in a vicious cycle.

424   Elliott Erwitt
HIGHWAYS
1968

423   Dorothea Lange
U. S. HIGHWAY #40
California, 1956

425

Alternatives to our overreliance on automobile transportation are being found. After years of talk and political setbacks, a few cities are putting efficient mass transit systems into operation. The Bay Area Rapid Transit system is one of them.

426

The environmentally aware are rediscovering the clean, quiet, economical transportation offered by bicycles. It is estimated that the sale of bicycles will soon surpass the sale of cars. Bikeways encourage this environmentally responsible change in transportation habits. On bikes and on foot one stays in full contact with surroundings while in motion.

The automobile, like most homes, apartments, schools, and workplaces, is a capsule designed to shield us from the larger environment. While providing protection, it also cuts us off from things outside itself. Driving along with windows up, and air conditioner and radio on, the closed capsule is a world of its own.

427

Although the phenomenal mobility created by our habits of car use has indeed brought some benefits, the other side of the coin, generally unrecognized, is experiential insulation. In a car we experience environments fast, passively, and superficially. We do not extract a rich variety of stimulation, but the minimal visual cues needed to navigate toward a destination.

The visual world, as experienced from inside a car is "out there," beyond a glass barrier, silent and bland. The net effect is as if there were several coordinated movies being shown in each of the windows of the car. Such passive reception of a series of visual scenes has been compared to the passive viewing of scenery done by people on canned tours.

428 Saul Steinberg

Capsule living raises the question: How can we improve our environment if we are passive and out of contact with it? There are alternatives to knowing the world from inside a capsule, and they are obvious ones. Try walking or bicycling around your neighborhood or to school. Touch and smell and look at things you encounter. Try to see the details and differences among the various environments you find yourself in. If you can break out of encapsulated encounters with the sensory world, it can become a playground. Try to be as attentive and curious about the visual world as a child. The possibility is there for all of us, but it requires a little encouragement and retraining.

The noncapsule way of knowing the world brings us into contact with the astonishing diversity of the physical world and the body's ways of learning about it. Intimate familiarity with the processes and possibilities of your own body is identical to familiarity with an amazing ecological system;

it is a vital process in the total encounter between man and nature. This kind of knowing is knowing through direct, active, participatory experience and exploration, rather than through passive reception of stimuli.

What has been happening to the descendants of Adam and Eve as industrial man has been developing a steadily declining relationship with natural environments? We are those descendants and it seems that we are still wandering around trying to buy our way back into the Garden of Eden. Industrial man's values are largely centered on the notion that getting the proper possessions, or getting to the proper places, will magically and automatically create bliss.

In the process of this self-centered quest to find the Garden, industrial man has become a perpetual tourist, always seeking an external paradise. He is restless and constantly mobile, and has developed a way of relating to the world in which he experiences objects, places, and other people for what they can contribute to his search, rather than what they are in themselves. His experience of people and environments is constantly filtered by a distant ideal which can never be realized.

Because he never reaches the Garden, but strives to, man's experience of people and environments is shaded, as if by a tourist's sunglasses. Even without his automobile, he travels in an insulating capsule of limiting experience. As a result, industrial man's contact with the world is a perfect metaphor for the tourist's real experience of Waikiki. Because Waikiki is neither Hawaii nor paradise, the search must go on to other places. Similarly, industrial man's images of the world are idealized, incomplete, and unsatisfying, like the tourist's postcards. He experiences predigested fragments rather than whole systems. In these ways, industrial man is not a unique perceiver and shaper of his experience and environments, but rather a passive and alienated searcher.

Since man lives in a series of environments that are partially or totally man-made, it is fair to ask: Where does environmental form come from? The origin of man-generated physical form, whether it is a sewing needle or a megalopolis, lies in the interaction of human needs, attitudes, and values with natural laws and materials. Both man-made and natural objects can be read as a record of the forces that introduced them.

One of the fundamental values underlying industrial society is the belief that the growth of populations and economies is synonymous with increasing human welfare and happiness. Our built environments often reflect this value distinctly. For a long time environmentalists have felt that our present growth patterns will ultimately lead to disaster. Recently the scientific evidence which irrefutably documents this belief has been accumulating. One recent study that integrates much of the scientific work is THE LIMITS OF GROWTH, a study initiated by an international group of scientists, educators, industrialists, and humanists called the Club of Rome. Carried out by a team of scientists at the Massachusetts Institute of Technology, the study came to this conclusion: unless we find ways to stop the growth of industry in this century and population soon thereafter, mankind faces a worldwide economic collapse and an international epidemic of deaths within three generations.[16]

The implications are profound. Although the concept of a society in economic and ecological equilibrium may appear simple and readily understandable, the study points out that "the reality is so distant from our experience as to require a Copernican revolution of the mind."[17] The report goes on to discuss the obstacles to implementing a society based on the principle of equilibrium, the principle that bigger does not mean better:

Translating the idea into deed, though, is a task filled with overwhelming difficulties and com-

plexities. We can talk seriously about where to start only when the message of THE LIMITS OF GROWTH, and its sense of extreme urgency, are accepted by a large body of scientific, political, and popular opinion in many countries. The transition in any case is likely to be painful, and it will make extreme demands on human ingenuity and imagination. As we have mentioned, only the conviction that there is no other avenue to survival can liberate the moral, intellectual, and creative forces required to initiate this unprecedented human undertaking.[18]

Confronted with this colossal challenge, we cannot allow ourselves the luxury of despair.

How can art help transform society into a social structure whose values and physical forms are rooted in the biological requirements for survival? One obvious approach might be simply to make things and places prettier. But remember that environmentally we are dealing with cancer and not acne. If the human values behind environmental forms are destructive or false, no amount of "beautification" will help. As in other forms of illness, it is the disease, not the symptoms, which must be stopped, and pollution, noise, ugliness, and related conditions are but symptoms. Application of a concealing cosmetic will only delay the process of solving the deeper problems.

If beautification is skin deep, art may contribute to survival in two less superficial ways: by training perceptions and by guiding the process of formmaking. In both cases values require change, like the change from growth to equilibrium, and from arrogance to humility. Sensory experience can provide the awareness and imagination necessary for value changes. Intense aesthetic experiences break the habit of taking things for granted, and thus are an important tool in the nurturing of necessary new perceptions.

Changed values result in changed actions. If we learn how to design *with* and not *against* the natural order, our actions in the physical world will be markedly different than they are presently. Translating new

429 Russ Kinne. DAISY PETALS. 1962.

values into new actions entails design problems of two types: the design of new life styles and the design of physical environments for human use. When both types of design occur with respect and understanding for the laws of nature, making form can be a deeply aesthetic act, not merely another accommodation to an endlessly expanding industrial society. To do that, we need to abandon the shortsighted "practicality" that characterizes the socio-economic thought of consumer-oriented societies and adopt a more profound pragmatism based on consideration of the long-term meaning of human action in biological and social systems. If we can design our lives and physical surroundings genuinely *with* nature, we will stop being tourists in our own lives. If we cannot do that, we will leave our children a barren earth.

The possibilities are open for richer and less stressful experiences and for design that is *for* survival. We have the option of working for life styles and techniques of environmental design, which not only assure biological survival, but also provide individual fulfillment. To design with nature means to design in harmony with natural form and the forces that bring it into being.

The idea of designing *with* rather than against nature is presented not as an activity for elite specialists, but as a process and a way of looking at the world that everyone can understand and do in his own way.

As we have seen, a variety of professions deal with the technical details of object- and environment-making. As a social subgroup, these specialists are being confronted with a reexamination of values. They must learn how to incorporate biological criteria into their work in order to meet the requirements of the systems that sustain life on earth. An innovative, ecologically literate planner, Ian McHarg, has clearly stated this point:

If one accepts the simple proposition that nature is the arena of life and that a modicum of knowledge of her processes is indispensable for survival and rather more for existence, health and delight, it is amazing how many apparently difficult problems present ready resolution.[19]

When fully understood in the environmental design professions, McHarg's reasoning will help generate new methodologies for creating form for human use. It is a hard lesson for many tradition-oriented professionals to learn, but no harder than the lesson all of us are now presented with. If it can be learned by the specialists, it will lead to many intriguing and ecologically responsible strategies for the design, construction, and relationships of objects, buildings, and land use. Also, it seems clear from ecological understanding that the professions concerned with large-scale building must wrestle with the new ethical problem that

their work to *accommodate* population growth may only worsen matters in the long run by *encouraging* that growth.

The formmaking professions need to be backed by an aware public. Otherwise, their decisions can be ignored, forgotten, or imposed on by existing life patterns, with little benefit and frequent detriment. Just because someone calls himself a planner cannot guarantee that his plans will be beneficial. Those who are to be affected must be able to effect the character of their surroundings.

Current experiments with citizen participation in planning and design processes — such as "advocacy planning" and "participatory planning" — are a step in the direction of extending environmental awareness to larger and less specialized groups of people. A more significant step will be taken as more people realize that we are not facing questions about the color of public buildings, but of life and death.

The ultimate responsibility for responding to these questions lies within each of us. Labeling some professions "concerned with the environment" does not change the fact that human actions always exist in the context of biological systems.

To act effectively as agents in our own survival, we must first *see* and *feel*. To be aware of only that which is immediate and proven is not enough. More than the practical details of working in various media, art provides the tools for going beyond the bald facts of the world. If understood and employed by many, the ideas, values, and approaches that constitute the basis of the visual arts could *help* transform our manmade surroundings into something viable and satisfying. Art verifies and encourages man's expanding awareness. As the creature with the most advanced consciousness, man has been described as nature becoming aware of itself. Man creates art creates man.

430   NASA. The World. North and South America photographed from Applications Technological Satellite at a 22,300-mile altitude, November 18, 1967. *See color plate 42.*

List of color plates

Chronological guide
to works of art

1884–1885   Thomas Eakins, NUDE ATH-
             LETE IN MOTION, 170

1884–1886   Georges Seurat, SUNDAY AFTER-
             NOON ON THE ISLAND OF LA
             GRANDE JATTE, 176, color plate
             22

1885–1886   Paul Cézanne, THE GARDEN,
             172

1886–1898   François Auguste René Rodin,
             THE KISS, 181

c. 1888   Jacob Riis, BANDIT'S ROOST, 178

1888   Claude Monet, SUNFLOWERS,
             172

1888   Vincent van Gogh, SUNFLOW-
             ERS, 173

1888   Vincent van Gogh, THE SOWER,
             174, color plate 20

1888   Vincent van Gogh after Hiro-
             shige, PLUM TREES IN BLOSSOM,
             174

1890–1891   Louis Sullivan, WAINWRIGHT
             BUILDING, 310

1891–1893   Paul Gauguin, AUTI TE PAPE
             (WOMEN AT THE RIVER), 83

c. 1892   Claude Monet, MORNING HAZE,
             57

1892   Paul Gauguin, AHA OE FEII
             (WHAT, ARE YOU JEALOUS?),
             83

1892   Paul Gauguin, FATATA TE MITI,
             82

1892   Paul Gauguin, TWO NUDES ON
             A TAHITIAN BEACH, 175, color
             plate 21

1892   Paul Gauguin, WORDS OF THE
             DEVIL, 82

1892   Alphonse Legros, HEAD OF A
             MAN, 269

1892   Edvard Munch, KISS BY THE
             WINDOW, 84

1892   Henri de Toulouse-Lautrec, AT
             THE MOULIN ROUGE, 179

1893   Henri de Toulouse-Lautrec,
             JANE AVRIL (oil on cardboard),
             104

1893   Henri de Toulouse-Lautrec,
             JANE AVRIL (lithograph), 105

1894   W. K. Dickson, FRED OTT'S
             SNEEZE, 293

1895   Edvard Munch, THE KISS (dry-
             point and aquatint), 84

1896   Edvard Munch, THE SHRIEK,
             180

1897–1898   Edvard Munch, THE KISS
             (woodcut), 85

1902   Alfred Stieglitz, THE HAND OF
             MAN, 340

1903   Edwin S. Porter, THE GREAT
             TRAIN ROBBERY, 294–295

1904–1906   Paul Cézanne, MONT SAINTE-
             VICTOIRE, 177, color plate 23

1904   Pablo Picasso, A MOTHER
             HOLDING A CHILD AND FOUR
             STUDIES OF HER RIGHT HAND,
             29

1904   Charles Sheeler, FELINE FELIC-
             ITY, 268

1905–1906   Henri Matisse, JOY OF LIFE, 185

1906   Constantin Brancusi, SLEEPING
             MUSE, 183

1906   Claude Monet, WATER-LILIES,
             GIVERNY, 168

1906   Pablo Picasso, SELF-PORTRAIT,
             187

1907–1908   Thomas Eakins, WILLIAM RUSH
             AND HIS MODEL, 37

1907   Pablo Picasso, DANCER, 188

1907   Pablo Picasso, THE YOUNG LA-
             DIES OF AVIGNON, 189

1907 Alfred Stieglitz, THE STEERAGE, 190

1908 Constantin Brancusi, THE KISS, 182, color plate 24

1908 Georges Braque, HOUSES AT L'ESTAQUE, 78

1908 Wassily Kandinsky, BLUE MOUNTAIN, 185, color plate 25

1908 Gustav Klimt, THE KISS, 184

1908 Käthe Kollwitz, THE PRISONERS, 40

1909–1911 Constantin Brancusi, SLEEPING MUSE, 183

1909 Pablo Picasso, THE RESERVOIR AT HORTA DE EBRO, 193

1909 Frank Lloyd Wright, ROBIE HOUSE, 191

1911–1912 Pablo Picasso, GUITAR, 195

1911 Marc Chagall, I AND MY VILLAGE, 81

1911 Piet Mondrian, HORIZONTAL TREE, 204

1911 Pablo Picasso, THE CLARINET PLAYER, 194

1912–1913 Pablo Picasso, SHEET OF MUSIC AND GUITAR, 195

1912 Marcel Duchamp, NUDE DESCENDING A STAIRCASE, #2, 196

1912 Wassily Kandinsky, WITH THE BLACK ARCH, No. 154, 186

1912 Jacques Henri Lartigue, GRAND PRIX OF THE AUTOMOBILE CLUB OF FRANCE, 197

1912 Henri Matisse, NASTURTIUMS AND THE DANCE, 38, color plate 3

1912 Emil Nolde, PROPHET, 281

1913 Pierre Bonnard, DINING ROOM IN THE COUNTRY, 59, color plate 5

1913 Marcel Duchamp, BICYCLE WHEEL, 208

1914–1915 Le Corbusier, DOMINO CONSTRUCTIONAL SYSTEM, 206

1914 Giorgio de Chirico, THE MYSTERY AND MELANCHOLY OF A STREET, 213

1915 Constantin Brancusi, THE NEWBORN, 183

1915 D. W. Griffith, THE BIRTH OF A NATION, 296–297

1916–1917 Kasimir Malevich, YELLOW QUADRILATERAL ON WHITE, 45, color plate 4

1917 John Marin, DEER ISLE — MARINE FANTASY, 275

1917 Egon Schiele, THE FAMILY, 36

c. 1918 Daniel Chester French, ABRAHAM LINCOLN, details of, 52–53

1918 Kasimir Malevich, SUPREMATIST COMPOSITION: WHITE ON WHITE, 93

1919 Marcel Duchamp, L.H.O.O.Q., 209

1919 Paul Klee, SELF-PORTRAIT, 212

1919 Fernand Léger, THE CITY, 198

1919 Kurt Schwitters, CONSTRUCTION FOR NOBLE LADIES, 211, color plate 28

1920 Hannah Höch, THE MULTI-MILLIONAIRE, 210

1921–1954 Simon Rodia, WATTS TOWERS, photograph by Duane Preble, 15

1921 Pablo Picasso, THREE MUSICIANS, 200

1921 Man Ray, THE GIFT, 209

1965   Kenzo Tange, PLAN FOR RE-
        CONSTRUCTION OF SKOPJE, YU-
        GOSLAVIA, 326

1966   Robert Breer, FLOATS, 81

1966   Victor Gruen and Associates,
        METROCORE AND ITS TEN CIT-
        IES, 329

1966   Al Held, GREEK GARDEN, 241

1966   MANHATTAN, 344

1966   Wes Wilson, THE SOUND, 235

1967   Constantinos Doxiadis, DYNAPO-
        LIS, 330

1967   R. Buckminster Fuller, U.S.
        PAVILION, EXPO-67, 314

1967   KALAPALO INDIANS HOUSE, 315

1967   Alice Parrott, RED FORM, 259,
        color plate 35

1967   Carol Summers, CHEOPS, 281,
        color plate 36

1967   Victor Vasarely, UNTITLED, 286,
        color plate 39

November 18,   NASA, THE WORLD, 359, color
1967   plate 42

c. 1968   John D. Kurtz, NINE SEATED
           INFANTRYMEN, 239

1968–1969   Charles Close, FRANK, 274

1968   Elliott Erwitt, HIGHWAYS, 353

1968   M. Paul Friedberg and Associ-
        ates, VEST POCKET PLAYGROUND
        AND NATURE STUDY CENTER,
        348

1968   Dennis Oppenheim, CANCELED
        CROP, 245

1968   Gordon Parks, BOY IN GRASS,
        290, color plate 38

1968   Frank Stella, SINJERLI VARIA-
        TION IV, 242

1969   Bill D. Francis, PEACOCK
        FEATHER, 91, color plate 13

1969   René Gardi, SMITH FROM
        NORTHERN DAHOMEY, 258

1969   Isamu Noguchi, CUBE, 241,
        color plate 40

1969   RIVER WALK, 350

1969   Moshe Safdie, MODEL OF HABI-
        TAT ISRAEL, 327

1970   M. & T. Bass, WOMAN SPIN-
        NING, 258

1970   Max Bill, DOUBLEMENT, 244

1970   Jean Coté, LITTERED LAND-
        SCAPE, 340

1970   LIBRA COMMUNE, photograph
        by Dennis Stock, 257

1971   Sanford Darling, PAINTED KIT-
        CHEN, photograph by Rafael
        Maldonado, Jr., 247

1971   Don Eddy, PRIVATE PARKING X,
        243, color plate 33

1971   Claes Oldenburg, SCULPTURE IN
        THE FORM OF A TROWEL STUCK
        IN THE GROUND, 229

1971   Duane Preble, 101 NORTH, 2

1971   Michael Salzberg, ANTIWAR
        VETERANS IN WHITEFACE, 238

1971   Nora Scarlett, PEACE MARCH,
        239

1971   Toshiko Takaezu, CERAMIC
        POT, 259, color plate 34

April 1971   ANTIAUTO POLLUTION DEMON-
              STRATION OUTSIDE COLISEUM,
              NEW YORK CITY, WHERE THE
              ANNUAL AUTO SHOW WAS ON,
              237

April 1971   APOLLO 16 ASTRONAUTS SALUT-
              ING FLAG ON THE MOON, 298

April 1971   Geoff Manasse, MORATORIUM
              RALLY, 238

Credits

COLOR PLATES

1 Courtesy Christopher Kitson.
2 Kunsthistorisches Museum, Vienna.
3 Pushkin Museum of Fine Arts, Moscow.
4 Stedelijk Museum, Amsterdam.
5 The Minneapolis Institute of Arts. The John R. van Derlip Fund.
6 From THE VISUAL DIALOGUE: AN INTRODUCTION TO THE APPRECIATION OF ART by Nathan Knobler. 2d ed., 1971. Reproduced by permission of Holt, Rinehart & Winston, Inc., New York City.
7 Uffizi Gallery, Florence. Photograph from Editorial Photocolor Archives, Inc., New York City.
8 Courtesy TIME Magazine, New York City.
9 Collection Mrs. Janet S. Fleisher, Elkins Park, Pennsylvania.
10 Photograph by John Webb, London. The Tate Gallery, London.
11 The Museum of Fine Arts, Boston. Bequest of John T. Spaulding.
12 The Smithsonian Institution, Freer Gallery of Art, Washington, D.C.
13 R. R. Donnelley & Sons Company, Chicago.
14 Courtesy Mr. William M. Garland II. Los Angeles County Museum of Natural History.
15 Basel Museum, Switzerland.
16 Editions Arthaud, Paris.
17 Hans Hinz, Basel, Switzerland.
18 Musée Marmottan, Paris. Photo Routhier, Paris.
19 The Louvre Museum, Paris.
20 Collection Vincent van Gogh Foundation, Amsterdam.
21 Honolulu Academy of Arts. Gift of Mrs. Charles M. Cooke, 1933.
22 The Art Institute of Chicago. Helen Birch Bartlett Memorial Collection.
23 Collection Mr. and Mrs. Louis C. Madeira, Gladwyne, Pennsylvania.
24 Österreichische Galerie, Vienna.
25 The Solomon R. Guggenheim Museum, New York City.
26 City Art Museum of Saint Louis.
27 Collection Alfred Roth, Zurich.
28 Los Angeles County Museum of Art.
29 Collection Frau T. Dürst-Haass, Muttenz, Switzerland. Color photograph from Hans Hinz, Basel, Switzerland.
30 The Art Institute of Chicago. Mr. and Mrs. Frank G. Logan Collection.
31 Whitney Museum of American Art, New York City.
32 Commissioned by The Museum of Modern Art, New York City.
33 Contemporary Gallery, New York City.
34 Courtesy of the artist, Honolulu.
35 Ceramics 70 Plus Woven Forms Exhibition, Everson Museum of Art, Syracuse, New York.
36 The Museum of Modern Art, New York City. John B. Turner Fund.
37 From THE PLACE NO ONE KNEW—GLEN CANYON ON THE COLORADO, published 1963 by Sierra Club Books, San Francisco.
38 Courtesy of the photographer, New York City.
39 Courtesy of the author.
40 Photograph by Jerome Feldman, New York City.
41 San Francisco Museum of Art.
42 National Aeronautics and Space Administration, Dallas.

BLACK AND WHITE
ILLUSTRATIONS

1 © 1945 by Saul Steinberg.
2 The Art Institute of Chicago.
3 Courtesy of the author.
4 From LIFE Magazine, © Time, Inc., New York City.
5 Courtesy of the photographer, Oakland,

California.

6 © 1943 by James Thurber. From MEN, WOMEN AND DOGS, published by Harcourt Brace & Co., New York City. Originally printed in THE NEW YORKER.

7 From MAN AND HIS SYMBOLS by C. G. Jung et al., published 1964 by Doubleday & Co., Garden City, New York.

8 Courtesy of the photographer, New York City.

9 From NATIONAL GEOGRAPHIC 136, No. 1 (July 1969): 156.

10 Royal Library, Windsor Castle. Reproduced by gracious permission of H. M. The Queen.

11 Courtesy Al Capp and United Features Syndicate.

12 From A HISTORY OF FAR EASTERN ART by Sherman E. Lee, published 1964 by Prentice-Hall, Englewood Cliffs, New Jersey.

13 On extended loan to The Museum of Modern Art, New York City, from the artist. Permission S.P.A.D.E.M. 1972 by French Reproduction Rights, Inc., New York City.

14 Student metaphor from magazine sources.

15 Courtesy of the author.

16 From CHILDREN OF MANY LANDS, published 1958 by Hanns Reich Verlag, Munich and used with permission of Hill and Wang, a division of Farrar, Straus and Giroux, Inc., New York City.

17 Magnum Photos, Inc., New York City.

18 Reprinted with permission of The Macmillan Company from CREATIVE AND MENTAL GROWTH by Victor Lowenfeld and W. Lambert Brittain. © 1970 by The Macmillan Company, New York City.

19 Reprinted with permission of the Macmillan Company from CREATIVE AND MENTAL GROWTH by Victor Lowenfeld and W. Lambert Brittain. © 1970 by The Macmillan Company, New York City.

20 Drawn by author's son, Jeffrey, at age four.

21 Drawn by author's daughter, Kristen, at age four.

22 From THE PSYCHOLOGY OF CHILDREN'S ART by Rhoda Kellog with Scott O'Dell, published 1967 by CRM Books, Del Mar, California.

23 Courtesy Christopher Kitson.

24 Japanese National Commission for UNESCO.

25 Dumbarton Oaks, Washington, D.C. Research Library and Collection.

26 Ghana National Museum, Accra.

27 Photograph by C. K. Eaton. Reprinted from THE ARTS IN THE CLASSROOM by Natalie Robinson Cole. © 1940, renewed 1968 by Natalie Robinson Cole, with permission of The John Day Co., Inc., Publisher, New York City.

28 National Gallery of Art, Washington, D.C. Andrew Mellon Collection.

29 National Gallery of Art, Washington, D.C. Samuel H. Kress Collection.

30 Museum Berlin, West Germany.

31 On extended loan to The Museum of Modern Art, New York City, from the artist. Permission S.P.A.D.E.M. 1972 by French Reproduction Rights, Inc., New York City.

32 Fogg Art Museum, Cambridge, Massachusetts.

33 Magnum Photos, Inc., New York City.

34 Florence Cathedral. Photograph from Alinari, Florence.

35 The Prado Museum, Madrid.

36 The Frick Collection, New York City.

37 Kunsthistorisches Museum, Vienna.

38 Graphische Sammlung Albertina, Vienna.

39 Uffizi Gallery, Florence. Photograph from Alinari, Florence.

40 Uffizi Gallery, Florence. Photograph from Alinari, Florence.

41 Österreichische Galerie, Vienna.

42 The Metropolitan Museum of Art, New York City. Gift of Louis C. Raegner, 1927.

43 Honolulu Academy of Arts. Gift of Friends of the Academy, Honolulu, 1947.

44 Pushkin Museum of Fine Arts, Moscow.

45 The Baltimore Museum of Art. The Cone Collection.

46 Private collection, Paris. Permission S.P.A.-D.E.M. 1972 by French Reproduction Rights, Inc., New York City.

47 Library of Congress, Washington, D.C.

48 The Museum of Modern Art, New York City.

49 Philadelphia Museum of Art.

50 Magnum Photos, Inc., New York City.

51 Magnum Photos, Inc., New York City.

52 Magnum Photos, Inc., New York City.

53 Stedelijk Museum, Amsterdam.

54 Magnum Photos, Inc., New York City.

55 Courtesy of the photographer, Carmel, California.

56 Archives photographiques de la caisse nationale des monuments historiques et des sites, Paris.

57 Photograph from Holle Verlag, Baden-Baden, Germany.

58 Santa Maria della Vittoria, Rome. Photograph from Alinari, Florence.

59 French Government Tourist Office, New York City.

60   Photograph by Hisao Ohara. From KAT-
     SURA RIKU, published 1972 by Poshobo,
     Japan.
61   Courtesy of the author.
62   From ART TODAY, 5th ed., by Ray Faulk-
     ner and Edwin Ziegfeld, published 1969 by
     Holt, Rinehart & Winston, Inc., New
     York City. All rights reserved.
63   Henry P. McIlhenny Collection, Philadel-
     phia.
64   Original diagrams by Ikki Matsumato.
     Cincinnati Art Museum, Ohio.
65   From DRAWING by Daniel M. Mendelo-
     witz. © 1967 by Holt, Rinehart & Win-
     ston, Inc., New York City. Reproduced by
     permission of publisher.
66   Wadsworth Atheneum, Hartford, Connect-
     icut. Ella Gallup Sumner and Mary Catlin
     Sumner Collection.
67   National Gallery of Art, Washington, D.C.
68   The Minneapolis Institute of Arts. The
     John R. van Derlip Fund.
69   Courtesy of the author.
70   Courtesy TIME Magazine, New York City.
71   Collection Mrs. Janet S. Fleisher, Elkins
     Park, Pennsylvania.
72   Uffizi Gallery, Florence. Photograph from
     Editorial Photocolor Archives, Inc., New
     York City.
73   Private collection. Permission S.P.A.-
     D.E.M. 1972 by French Reproduction
     Rights, Inc., New York City.
74   British Museum, London.
75   The Museum of Modern Art, New York
     City.
76   Photogroph by John Webb, London. The
     Tate Gallery, London.
77   The Museum of Modern Art, New York
     City.
78   Photograph by Phokion Karas, Cambridge,
     Massachusetts.
79   Photograph by Maris. © ESTO, New York
     City.
80   Archives photographiques de la caisse na-
     tionale des monuments historiques et des
     sites, Paris.
81   From JAPANESE HOUSES: PATTERNS FOR
     LIVING by Kiyoyuki Nishihara, published
     1968 by Japan Publications Trading Co.,
     Inc., San Francisco.
82   Ryoko-in, Daitoku-ji, Kyoto.
83   Philbrook Art Center, Tulsa, Oklahoma.
     Samuel H. Kress Collection.
84   The Louvre Museum, Paris.
85   Stanze della Segnatura, Vatican, Rome.
86   Escher Foundation, Haags Gemeentemu-
     seum, The Hague.
87   National Gallery of Art, Washington, D.C.

     Samuel H. Kress Collection.
88   The Metropolitan Museum of Art, New
     York City. Bequest of Benjamin Altman.
89   The Museum of Fine Arts, Boston. Be-
     quest of John T. Spaulding.
90   Bern Foundation, Photographie Giraudon,
     Paris. Permission A.D.A.G. 1972 by French
     Reproduction Rights, Inc., New York
     City.
91   The Smithsonian Institution, Freer Gal-
     lery of Art, Washington, D.C.
92   National Gallery of Art, Washington, D.C.
     Samuel H. Kress Collection.
93   Photographs by Kornblee Gallery and
     Basil Langton, New York City. Courtesy
     Morton G. Neumann, Chicago.
94   Galeria Bonino, New York City.
95   The Museum of Modern Art, New York
     City. Mrs. Simon Guggenheim Fund.
96   National Gallery of Art, Washington, D.C.
     Gift of the W. Averell Harriman Founda-
     tion in memory of Marie N. Harriman.
97   National Gallery of Art, Washington, D.C.
     Chester Dale Collection.
98   The Metropolitan Museum of Art, New
     York City. Rogers Fund, 1921.
99   Pushkin Museum of Fine Arts, Moscow.
100 Oslo Kommunes Kunstamlinger, Munch-
     museet, Oslo.
101 Graphische Sammlung Albertina, Vienna.
102 Graphische Sammlung Albertina, Vienna.
103 The Frick Collection, New York City.
104 National Gallery of Art, Washington, D.C.
     Widener Collection.
105 The Museum of Modern Art, New York
     City.
106 © 1960 by Saul Steinberg.
107 Idemitsu Art Gallery, Tokyo.
108 British Museum, London.
109 Photograph by Quality Graphic Service,
     Honolulu. University of Hawaii Press.
110 R. R. Donnelly & Sons Company, Chi-
     cago.
111 The Museum of Modern Art, New York
     City.
112 The Louvre Museum, Paris.
113 Courtesy Mrs. Cleve Gray, Cornwall
     Bridge, Connecticut.
114 Magnum Photos, Inc., New York City.
115 The Fine Arts Gallery of San Diego, Cali-
     fornia.
116 The Museum of Modern Art, New York
     City.
117 The National Gallery, London.
118 Pitti Gallery, Florence.
119 Marienkirche, Danzig, Poland. Photograph
     from Alinari-Art Reference Bureau, New
     York City.

120 St. Peter's Basilica, Rome. Photograph from Alinari, Florence.
121 The Baltimore Museum of Art. The Cone Collection.
122 The Baltimore Museum of Art. The Cone Collection.
123 From LAUTREC BY LAUTREC by Philippe Huisman and M. G. Dortu, published 1964 by Viking Press, New York City.
124 From LAUTREC BY LAUTREC by Philippe Huisman and M. G. Dortu, published 1964 by Viking Press, New York City.
125 The Museum of Modern Art, New York City.
126 The Louvre Museum, Paris. Photograph from Alinari-Art Reference Bureau, New York City.
127 From ROCK PAINTINGS OF THE CHUMASH by Campbell Grant, published 1965 by University of California Press, Berkeley.
128 Instituto Biblico, Rome.
129 Museum of the American Indian, New York City.
130 Courtesy Mr. William M. Garland II. Los Angeles County Museum of Natural History.
131 Editions Arthaud, Paris.
132 British Museum, London.
133 From MAN AND HIS SYMBOLS by C. G. Jung et al., published 1964 by Doubleday & Co., Garden City, New York.
134 Basel Museum, Switzerland.
135 Musée Cernuschi, Paris.
136 National Museum, New Delhi.
137 From ART IN EAST AND WEST by Benjamin Rowland, published 1954 by Harvard University Press, Cambridge, Massachusetts.
138 The Cleveland Museum of Art. Purchase from the J. H. Wade Fund.
139 From THE WORLD OF CARTIER-BRESSON by Henri Cartier-Bresson, published 1947 by Viking Press, New York City.
140 Koninklijk Museum, Antwerp.
141 Museum for Eastern Asiatic Art, Cologne, Germany.
142 Jingo-ji Temple, Kyoto.
143 Kofuku-hi, Nara, Japan.
144 Idemitsu Art Gallery, Tokyo.
145 Jingo-ji Temple, Kyoto.
146 French Government Tourist Office, New York City.
147 From NARRATIVE OF THE UNITED STATES EXPLORING EXPEDITION 5 by Charles Wilkes, published 1845 by Lea and Blanchard, Philadelphia, republished 1970 by Gregg Press, Upper Saddle River, New Jersey. Drawn by A. T. Agate, engraved by Rawdon Wright and Hatch. Courtesy British Museum, London.
148 George Hulton Photo Researchers, Inc., New York City.
149 Government of India, Archaeological Survey of India, New Delhi.
150 Hans Hinz, Basel, Switzerland.
151 Chateau de Saint-Germain-en-Laye, Yvelines, France.
152 The Metropolitan Museum of Art, New York City.
153 Detroit Institute.
154 The Museum of Fine Arts, Boston.
155 Photograph by Alison Frantz, Princeton, New Jersey. National Museum, Athens.
156 National Museum, Naples. Photograph from Alinari-Art Reference Bureau, New York City.
157 (a) Photograph by A. F. Kersting, London. (b) Photograph by Alison Frantz, Princeton, New Jersey.
158 Olympia Museum, Greece. Photograph from Alinari, Florence.
159 National Museum, Athens. Photograph from Alinari-Art Reference Bureau, New York City.
160 Museo Profano Lateranense, Rome. Photograph from Phaidon Press, London.
161 Palazzo Capitolino, Rome. Photograph from Phaidon Press, London.
162 National Gallery of Art, Washington, D.C. Samuel H. Kress Collection, 1939.
163 Photograph from Alinari, Florence.
164 Editorial Photocolor Archives, New York City.
165 Museo dei Conservatori, Rome. Photograph from Hirmer Verlag, Munich.
166 Bildarchiv Foto Marburg, Germany.
167 (a) From MONASTERY AND CATHEDRAL IN FRANCE by Whitney S. Stoddard, published 1966 by Wesleyan University Press, Middletown, Connecticut. (b) From CIVILISATION by Kenneth Clark, published 1970 by Harper & Row, New York City. (c and d) Archives photographiques de la caisse nationale des monuments historiques et des sites, Paris.
168 Cappela degli Scrovegni, Padova, Italy. Photograph from Alinari, Florence.
169 Photograph from Alinari, Florence.
170 Academia, Venice.
171 Santa Maria delle Grazie, Milan. Photograph from Alinari, Florence.
172 The Louvre Museum, Paris. From LEONARDO DA VINCI: A DEFINITIVE STUDY, published 1956 by Reynal & Co., New York City.
173 Uffizi Gallery, Florence. Photograph from

Alinari-Art Reference Bureau, New York City.

174 Academia, Florence. Photographs from Alinari, Florence.

175 Santa Maria del Popolo, Rome. Photograph from Alinari-Art Reference Bureau, New York City.

176 National Gallery of Art, Washington, D.C. Andrew Mellon Collection.

177 From Elementary Treatise on Physics by E. Atkinson, 1872. George Eastman House Collection, Rochester, New York.

178 From The World of Bernini, 1590–1680 by Robert Wallace and editors of Time-Life Books, published 1970 by Time, Inc., New York City.

179 The Louvre Museum, Paris.

180 The Louvre Museum, Paris.

181 The Prado Museum, Madrid.

182 From Paul Revere's Engravings by Clarence S. Brigham, published 1969 by Atheneum, New York City.

183 Bayerische National Museum, Munich. Photograph from George Eastman House, Rochester, New York.

184 Photograph from the Bibliothèque Nationale, Paris.

185 Stavros S. Niarchos Collection.

186 Verlag M. Dumont Schauberg, Cologne, Germany.

187 Verlag M. Dumont Schauberg, Cologne, Germany.

188 Verlag M. Dumont Schauberg, Cologne, Germany.

189 From Space, Time and Architecture, vol. 5, by Siegfried Giedion, published 1967 by Harvard University Press. Etching, British Crown copyright. Photograph from Victoria and Albert Museum, London.

190 The Louvre Museum, Paris.

191 The Royal Photographic Society Collection, London.

192 The Louvre Museum, Paris.

193 This painting was destroyed during World War II. Formerly in State Picture Gallery, Dresden. Verlag F. Bruckman KG, Munich.

194 National Gallery of Art, Washington, D.C. Gift of Horace Havemeyer in memory of his mother, Louisine W. Havemeyer.

195 Musée Marmottan, Paris. Photo Routhier, Paris.

196 Collection Jocelyn Walker, London. Permission S.P.A.D.E.M. 1972 by French Reproduction Rights, Inc., New York City.

197 The Louvre Museum, Paris.

198 Photograph by Durand-Ruel, Paris. Permission S.P.A.D.E.M. 1972 by French Reproduction Rights, Inc., New York City.

199 George Eastman House Collection, Rochester, New York.

200 George Eastman House Collection, Rochester, New York.

201 The Louvre Museum, Paris.

202 The Metropolitan Museum of Art, New York City. The H. O. Havemeyer Collection.

203 Collection Vincent van Gogh Foundation, Amsterdam.

204 Collection Vincent van Gogh Foundation, Amsterdam.

205 Collection Vincent van Gogh Foundation, Amsterdam.

206 Honolulu Academy of Arts. Gift of Mrs. Charles M. Cooke, 1933.

207 The Art Institute of Chicago. Helen Birch Bartlett Memorial Collection.

208 The Art Institute of Chicago. A. A. Munger Collection.

209 Collection Mr. and Mrs. Louis C. Madeira, Gladwyne, Pennsylvania.

210 Museum of the City of New York. Jacob A. Riis Collection.

211 The Louvre Museum, Paris. Photographie Giraudon, Paris. Permission S.P.A.D.E.M. 1972 by French Reproduction Rights, Inc., New York City.

212 The Art Institute of Chicago. Helen Birch Bartlett Memorial Collection.

213 The Museum of Modern Art, New York City.

214 Musée du Luxembourg, Paris. Photograph from Alinari, Florence. Permission S.P.A.D.E.M. 1972 by French Reproduction Rights, Inc., New York City.

215 Philadelphia Museum of Art. The Louise and Walter Arensberg Collection.

216 National Gallery, Bucharest.

217 Joseph H. Hirshorn Collection, New York City.

218 Philadelphia Museum of Art. The Louise and Walter Arensberg Collection.

219 Österreichische Galerie, Vienna.

220 The Barnes Foundation, Merion, Pennsylvania.

221 The Solomon R. Guggenheim Museum, New York City.

222 Galerie Maeght, Paris.

223 Philadelphia Museum of Art. The A. E. Gallatin Collection.

224 Private collection, New York.

225 Musée de l'Homme, Paris. Collection Congrégation des Orphelines d'Auteuil.

226 The Museum of Modern Art, New York City.

227 Reproduced from CAMERA WORK. The Museum of Modern Art, New York City.
228 Hedrich-Blessing, Ltd., Chicago.
229 The Metropolitan Museum of Art, New York City. Gift of Dr. and Mrs. Franz H. Hirschland.
230 Private collection. Photographie Giraudon, Paris. Permission S.P.A.D.E.M. 1972 by French Reproduction Rights, Inc., New York City.
231 Private collection. Permission S.P.A.-D.E.M. 1972 by French Reproduction Rights, Inc., New York City.
232 Photograph by David Gahr. Permission S.P.A.D.E.M. 1972 by French Reproduction Rights, Inc., New York City.
233 Collection Georges Salles, Paris. Photographie Giraudon, Paris. Permission S.P.A.-D.E.M. 1972 by French Reproduction Rights, Inc., New York City.
234 Philadelphia Museum of Art. The Louise and Walter Arensberg Collection.
235 Courtesy of the photographer, Paris.
236 Philadelphia Museum of Art. The A. E. Gallatin Collection.
237 Courtesy of the author.
238 City Art Museum of Saint Louis.
239 The Museum of Modern Art, New York City.
240 The Museum of Modern Art, New York City.
241 On extended loan to The Museum of Modern Art, New York City, from the artist. Permission S.P.A.D.E.M. 1972 by French Reproduction Rights, Inc., New York City.
242 Munson-Williams-Proctor Institute, Utica, New York.
243 Collection Alfred Roth, Zurich.
244 Fondation Le Corbusier, Paris.
245 The Architects Collaborative, Cambridge, Massachusetts.
246 Joseph E. Seagram & Sons, Inc., New York City.
247 The Museum of Modern Art, New York City.
248 Private collection, United States.
249 The Museum of Modern Art, New York City.
250 Florian Kupferberg Verlag, Mainz/Berlin. From MALEREI FOTOGRAFIE FILM by Lazlo Moholy-Nagy.
251 Los Angeles County Museum of Art.
252 Source unknown.
253 Collection Frau T. Dürst-Haass, Muttenz, Switzerland. Color photograph from Hans Hinz, Basel, Switzerland.
254 Private collection. Photograph courtesy The Museum of Modern Art, New York City.
255 The Museum of Modern Art, New York City.
256 The Prado Museum, Madrid.
257 The Museum of Modern Art, New York City.
258 Collection Mr. and Mrs. Richard K. Weil, Saint Louis.
259 University Art Museum, Berkeley, California. Gift of Julian J. and Joachim Jean Aberbach, New York.
260 Whitney Museum of American Art, New York City.
261 Collection Miss Katharine Ordway, Westport, Connecticut.
262 Museum of Modern Art, New York City.
263 Courtesy Paul Bijtebier, Brussels.
264 Courtesy Mrs. Albert D. Lasker, New York City.
265 East-West Center, Honolulu.
266 The Art Institute of Chicago. Mr. and Mrs. Frank G. Logan Collection.
267 Dallas Museum of Fine Arts. Dallas Art Association Purchase.
268 Archives photographiques de la caisse nationale des monuments historiques et des sites, Paris.
269 (a) Fondation Le Corbusier, Paris. (b) Fondation Le Corbusier. Photograph from G. E. Kidder Smith.
270 Collection Mr. and Mrs. Frank Titelman.
271 Courtesy of the artist.
272 Sidney Janis Gallery, New York City.
273 Derse Advertising Company, Milwaukee, Wisconsin.
274 Photograph by Hannah Wilke.
275 Black Star Publishing Co., Inc., New York City.
276 Kornblee Gallery, New York City.
277 Whitney Museum of American Art, New York City.
278 The National Gallery of Canada, Ottawa.
279 Photograph by Jack Mitchell, New York City. Collection Mr. and Mrs. Tom Wesselmann.
280 Collection Mrs. Ben Cunningham, New York City.
281 The Museum of Modern Art, New York City.
282 Courtesy of the artist, Lagunitas, California.
283 Photograph by David Gahr, New York City.
284 Horst Schafer-Photo Trends, New York City.
285 Courtesy of the photographer, Berkeley, California.

286 Courtesy of the photographer, Washington, D.C.
287 Courtesy of the photographer, Berkeley, California.
288 Courtesy the Office of Chief of Military History, Department of the Army.
289 Collection Samuel Wagstaff, Jr.
290 Photograph by Jerome Feldman, New York City.
291 Andre Emmerich Gallery Inc., New York City.
292 Courtesy Mr. and Mrs. Burton Tremaine, Meriden, Connecticut.
293 San Francisco Museum of Art.
294 Commissioned by The Museum of Modern Art, New York City.
295 Contemporary Gallery, New York City.
296 Galerie Denise René, Paris.
297 John Weber Gallery, New York City.
298 Photograph courtesy of the artist, Brooklyn, New York.
299 Courtesy of the photographer, Santa Barbara, California.
300 From How to Wrap Five Eggs: Japanese Design in Traditional Packaging by Hideyuki Oka, published 1967 by Harper and Row, New York City.
301 Coca-Cola is a registered trademark of The Coca-Cola Company. Coca-Cola Archives, New York City
302 Knoll Associates, New York City.
303 Courtesy of the photographer, Honolulu.
304 Sketch published with permission of Professor Richard I. Felver, Carnegie-Mellon University, and may not be reproduced without his written approval.
305 Isuzu Motors Ltd., Tokyo.
306 American Cancer Society.
307 The EVE label is a registered trademark of Liggett & Myers Incorporated.
308 From Art: Search & Self-Discovery by James A. Schinneller, published 1968 by Intext Publishing Group, New York City. Courtesy of the architect, Milwaukee.
309 Magnum Photos, Inc., New York City.
310 Courtesy of the photographers, Berkeley, California.
311 From African Crafts and Craftsmen by René Gardi, published 1970 by Van Nostrand Reinhold Co., New York City.
312 Honolulu Advertiser, 1972.
313 Courtesy of the artist, Honolulu.
314 Ceramics 70 Plus Woven Forms Exhibition, Everson Museum of Art, Syracuse, New York.
315 Honolulu Advertiser, 1972.
316 Honolulu Advertiser, 1972.
317 Honolulu Advertiser, 1972.

318 Honolulu Advertiser, 1972.
319 Honolulu Advertiser, 1972.
320 Honolulu Advertiser, 1972.
321 Collection Ruth and Hermann Vollmer, New York City.
322 From The Chapel at Ronchamp by Le Corbusier, published 1957 by Praeger, Publishers, New York City. Courtesy Fondation Le Corbusier, Paris.
323 Fondation Le Corbusier, Paris.
324 On extended loan to the Museum of Modern Art, New York City, from the artist. Permission S.P.A.D.E.M. 1972 by French Reproduction Rights, Inc., New York City.
325 On extended loan to The Museum of Modern Art, New York City, from the artist. Permission S.P.A.D.E.M. 1972 by French Reproduction Rights, Inc., New York City.
326 The Metropolitan Museum of Art, New York City. Purchase, 1924, Joseph Pulitzer Bequest.
327 Kröller-Müller Foundation, Wassenaar, Otterlo, Holland.
328 The Smithsonian Institution, Freer Gallery of Art, Washington, D.C.
329 Courtesy of the author.
330 Fogg Art Museum, Cambridge, Massachusetts. Louise E. Bettens Fund.
331 The Metropolitan Museum of Art, New York City. Gift of the artist, 1892.
332 From French Drawing of the 20th Century, edited by Ed. Mermod-Lausanne, published 1955 by Vanguard Press, New York City.
333 British Museum, London.
334 Collection Mr. and Mrs. C. C. Wang, New York City.
335 Milwaukee Art Center, anonymous gift.
336 The Minneapolis Institute of Arts.
337 Honolulu Academy of Arts.
338 National Palace Museum, Taipei, Taiwan, Republic of China.
339 National Palace Museum, Taipei, Taiwan, Republic of China.
340 Albright-Knox Art Gallery, Buffalo, New York. Charles Clifton Fund.
341 The Art Institute of Chicago. Clarence Buckingham Collection.
342 Kunstmuseum der Stadt Dusseldorf, Germany.
343 The Museum of Modern Art, New York City. John B. Turner Fund.
344 The Brooklyn Museum. Gift of Mrs. H. O. Havemeyer.
345 The Metropolitan Museum of Art, New York City, Bequest of Mrs. H. O. Have-

meyer, 1929.

346 The Cleveland Museum of Art. Gift of Ralph King.
347 Courtesy of the author.
348 From ART TODAY by Ray Faulkner and Edwin Ziegfeld, published 1969 by Holt, Rinehart & Winston, New York City, p. 258.
349 From LIFE Magazine, © 1937 Time, Inc., New York City.
350 From LIFE Magazine, © 1954 Time, Inc., New York City.
351 From THE PLACE NO ONE KNEW—GLEN CANYON ON THE COLORADO, published 1963 by Sierra Club Books, San Francisco.
352 Courtesy of the photographer, New York City.
353 Courtesy of the photographer, Massachusetts Institute of Technology, Cambridge.
354 George Eastman House, Rochester, New York.
355 Library of Congress, Washington, D.C.
356 The Museum of Modern Art/Film Stills Archive, New York City.
357 The Museum of Modern Art/Film Stills Archive, New York City.
358 CBS Television Network, New York City.
359 Hirmer Fotoarchiv, Munich.
360 The Museum of Modern Art, New York City. A. Conger Goodyear Fund.
361 Photograph from Alinari, Florence.
362 Courtesy Frank Willett, Evanston, Illinois.
363 From ART: THE REVEALING EXPERIENCE by Kurt Kranz, published 1964 by Shorewood Publishers, Inc., New York City.
364 Galerie Louise Leiris, Paris. Permission S.P.A.D.E.M. 1972 by French Reproduction Rights, Inc., New York City.
365 The Metropolitan Museum of Art, New York City. Fletcher Fund, 1956.
366 Photograph by John Palmer.
367 Galerie Denise René, Paris.
368 Photograph by Eduard Trier, Düsseldorf-Oberkassel, Germany.
369 Whitney Museum of American Art, New York City.
370 Worcester Art Museum, Massachusetts.
371 Hedrich-Blessing, Ltd., Chicago.
372 Ezra Stoller © ESTO, New York City.
373 Courtesy R. Buckminster Fuller.
374 Photograph by Stan Wayman. From LIFE Magazine, © 1967 Time, Inc., New York City.
375 Photograph by M. Sakamoto. From PICTURE HISTORY OF WORLD ART 2 edited by Valentin Denis and T. E. de Vries, published 1965 by Harry N. Abrams, New York City.
376 From ISE: PROTOTYPE OF JAPANESE ARCHITECTURE by Kenzo Tange and Noboru Kawazoe, published 1965 by M.I.T. Press, Cambridge, Massachusetts.
377 Courtesy Kenzo Tange.
378 Source unknown.
379 Techbuilt Corporation, Cambridge, Massachusetts.
380 Cortez Corporation, Kent, Ohio.
381 Photograph by Michael Bass, Berkeley, California.
382 Seattle City Light.
383 Agence Rapho, Paris.
384 Agence Rapho, Paris.
385 Pinacoteca Nazionale, Siena, Italy.
386 Reprinted from ARCOLOGY: THE CITY IN THE IMAGE OF MAN by Paolo Soleri by permission of the M.I.T. Press, Cambridge, Massachusetts. Copyright 1969 by M.I.T.
387 Photograph by Osamu Murai, Tokyo.
388 Doxiadis Associates, Athens, Greece.
389 From THE VISUAL DIALOGUE by Nathan Knobler, 2nd ed., published 1971 by Holt, Rinehart & Winston, New York City.
390 Photograph by Irving W. Bailey (dec.), Professor of Botany, Harvard University. Courtesy of E. S. Barghoon, The Biological Laboratories, Harvard University, Cambridge, Massachusetts.
391 Courtesy Vilma Chiara Schultz, Cardaillac, France.
392 From WHO DESIGNS AMERICA? by Laurence B. Holland, published 1966 by Doubleday & Co., Garden City, New York.
393 From EUROPE FROM THE AIR edited by Emil Egli and Hans Richard Muller, translated by E. Osers, published 1960 by Wilfred Funk, New York City.
394 From CITIES OF DESTINY edited by Arnold Toynbee, published 1967 by McGraw-Hill Book Co., New York City.
395 Courtauld Institute of Art, London. Lee Collection.
396 Church of Santa Maria del Carmine, Florence. Photograph from Alinari, Florence.
397 Courtesy of the photographer, Honolulu.
398 Courtesy of the author.
399 Photograph by Elihu Blotnick, 1971. B.B.B. Associates, Berkeley, California.
400 Courtesy of the author.
401 Courtesy of the author.
402 Chicago Natural History Museum.
403 The Smithsonian Institution, National Collection of Fine Arts, Washington, D.C.
404 Courtesy of the photographer, Carmel, California.
405 STAR BULLETIN, Honolulu.

406 George Eastman House, Rochester, New York.

407 Courtesy of the photographer, Berkeley, California.

408 Courtesy of the photographer, San Jose, California.

409 From LE CORBUSIER: THE MACHINE AND THE GRAND DESIGN by Norma Evenson, published 1969 by George Braziller, New York City.

410 Photograph by Orlando Cababan. From WHO DESIGNS AMERICA? edited by Laurence B. Holland, published 1966 by Doubleday & Co., New York City.

411 The Travelers Insurance Companies, Hartford, Connecticut.

412 The Travelers Insurance Companies, Hartford, Connecticut.

413 Rainbow Plaza Development, Inc. Architects, Anbe, Aruga & Associates, Inc., Honolulu.

414 Architects, Reinhard and Hofmeister, Corbett, Harrison and MacMurray, Hood and Fouilhoux, Harrison and Fouilhoux. From THE STORY OF ART by Ernst H. Gombrich, 11th ed., published 1966 by Praeger, Publishers, New York City.

415 Photograph by Bruce Davidson. Magnum Photos, Inc., New York City.

416 Courtesy of the photographer, Abbott Village, Maine.

417 Whitney Museum of American Art, New York City.

418 Courtesy of the photographer, New York City.

419 M. Paul Friedberg and Associates, landscape architects, New York City.

420 Fondation Le Corbusier, Paris.

421 Zintgraff Photographers, San Antonio, Texas.

422 Loebel Productions, Inc., Sherman, Connecticut.

423 The Oakland Museum, California.

424 Magnum Photos, Inc., New York City.

425 Bay Area Rapid Transit, Oakland, California.

426 Photograph by D. A. Bermann, Oakland, California.

427 Photograph by Eugene Daniels. Black Star Publishing Company, Inc., New York City.

428 © 1954 by Saul Steinberg.

429 From THE COMPLETE BOOK OF NATURE PHOTOGRAPHY by Russ Kinne, published 1962 by Amphoto, New York City. Courtesy Photo Researchers, Russ Kinne, New York City.

430 National Aeronautics and Space Administration, Dallas.

Notes

FRONT MATTER AND INTRODUCTION

1 Ralph Graves, ed., *The Master of the Soft Touch*, LIFE 67, no. 21 (November 21, 1969): 64c.

2 Caroline Thomas Harnsberger, ed. TREASURY OF PRESIDENTIAL QUOTATIONS (Chicago: Follett Publishing Co., 1964), p. 22.

WHY ART?

1 Reid Hastie and Christian Schmidt, ENCOUNTER WITH ART (New York: McGraw-Hill Book Co., 1969), p. 314.

2 C. L. Barnhart and Jess Stein, eds., THE AMERICAN COLLEGE DICTIONARY (New York: Random House, 1963), p. 70.

3 Copyright by Elizabeth-Ellen Long.

4 Don Fabun, THE DYNAMICS OF CHANGE (New York: Prentice-Hall, 1968), p. 9.

5 Henri Matisse, *The Nature of Creative Activity*, in EDUCATION AND ART, ed. Edwin Ziegfeld (New York: UNESCO, 1953), p. 21.

6 Douglas Davis, *New Architecture: Building for Man*, NEWSWEEK 77, no. 16 (April 19, 1971): 80.

7 Luciana Pignatelli and Jeanne Molli, THE BEAUTIFUL PEOPLE'S BEAUTY BOOK (New York: McCall Books, 1971), p. 3.

8 Rudolf Arnheim, ART AND VISUAL PERCEPTION: A PSYCHOLOGY OF THE CREATIVE EYE (Berkeley: University of California Press, 1954), p. v.

9 Carroll Quigley, *Needed: A Revolution in Thinking?* THE JOURNAL OF THE NATIONAL EDUCATION ASSOCIATION 57, no. 5 (May 1968): 9.

10 Amédée Ozenfant, THE FOUNDATIONS OF MODERN ART, trans. John Rodker (New York: Dover Publications, 1952), p. 323.

11 Abraham H. Maslow, TOWARD A PSYCHOLOGY OF BEING (New York: Van Nostrand Reinhold Co., 1968), p. 136.

12 Jim Hicks, *Piet Hein Bestrides Art and Science*, LIFE 61, no. 16 (October 14, 1966): 64.

13 Bergen Evans, DICTIONARY OF QUOTATIONS (New York: Delacorte Press, 1968), p. 340.

14 Courtesy of Watts Towers.

15 Frances S. Kornbluth and Bernard Bard, *Who Kills Your Child's Creativity?* FAMILY CIRCLE (September 1967): 39.

16 John Holt, How CHILDREN FAIL (New York: Pitman Publishing Corp., 1964), p. 167. Reprinted with permission.

17 See quote by Henri Matisse on page 9; see note 5 in this chapter.

18 Susumu Hani, director, CHILDREN WHO DRAW PICTURES (New York: Brandon Films).

19 Marius de Zayas, *Pablo Picasso, An Interview*, in ARTISTS ON ART, ed. Robert Goldwater and Marco Treves (New York: Pantheon Books, 1958), p. 417; originally printed in THE ARTS (New York, May 1923).

20 Henri Matisse, *Notes of a Painter*, trans. Alfred H. Barr, Jr., in PROBLEMS OF AESTHETICS, ed. Elised Vivas and Murray Krieger (New York: Holt, Rinehart & Winston, 1953), p. 256; originally printed as *Notes d'un peintre*, LA GRANDE REVUE (Paris, 1908).

21 Ibid., p. 260.

22 Ibid., pp. 259–260.

23 Herbert Bittner, KAETHE KOLLWITZ DRAWINGS (Cranbury, N.J.: A. S. Barnes & Co., 1959), p. 15.

WHAT DO WE RESPOND TO IN A WORK OF ART?

1 John Cage, A YEAR FROM MONDAY: NEW LECTURES AND WRITINGS (Middletown, Conn.: Wesleyan University Press, 1969).

2 Edward Weston, EDWARD WESTON, PHOTOGRAPHER: THE FLAME OF RECOGNITION, ed. Nancy Newhall (New York: Aperture

Monograph, Grossman Publishers, 1965), p. 39.

3   Ibid., pp. 34, 39.
4   Ibid., p. 22.
5   Ibid., p. 34.
6   Kenneth Clark, CIVILISATION (New York: Harper & Row, Publishers, 1969), p. 50.
7   Albert E. Elsen, PURPOSES OF ART (New York: Holt, Rinehart & Winston, 1967), p. 183.
8   William Mills Ivins, Jr., PRINTS AND VISUAL COMMUNICATION (Cambridge, Mass.: Harvard University Press, 1953), p. 57.
9   Leonardo da Vinci, NOTEBOOKS OF LEONARDO DA VINCI, ed. Jean Paul Richter (New York: Dover Publications, 1970), p. 69.
10   Faber Birren, COLOR PSYCHOLOGY AND COLOR THERAPY (New Hyde Park, N.Y.: University Books, 1961), p. 20.
11   Edgar Cayce, AURAS (Virginia Beach, Va.: A.R.E. Press, 1945), pp. 11–13.
12   Wassily Kandinsky, CONCERNING THE SPIRITUAL IN ART, original trans. Michael Sadleir, retrans. Francis Golffing, Michael Harrison, and Ferdinand Ostertag (New York: George Wittenborn, 1955), p. 58.
13   Elsen, PURPOSES OF ART, p. 437.
14   Leonardo da Vinci, *Perspective of Colour and Aerial Perspective: Of Aerial Perspective (1488–1489)*, in A DOCUMENTARY HISTORY OF ART 1: THE MIDDLE AGES AND THE RENAISSANCE, ed. Elizabeth G. Holt (New York: Doubleday & Co., 1957–58), p. 282.
15   D. T. Suzuki, *Sengai, Zen and Art*, ART NEWS ANNUAL 27, pt. 2, no. 7 (November 1957), p. 118.
16   Henri Matisse, *Notes of a Painter*, trans. Alfred H. Barr, Jr., in PROBLEMS OF AESTHETICS, ed. Elised Vivas and Murray Krieger (New York: Holt, Rinehart & Winston, 1953), p. 259; originally printed as *Notes d'un peintre*, LA GRANDE REVUE (Paris, 1908).

WHAT WAS ART LIKE
IN THE PAST?

1   Marius de Zayas, *Pablo Picasso, An Interview*, in ARTISTS ON ART, ed. Robert Goldwater and Marco Treves (New York: Pantheon Books, 1958), p. 418; originally printed in THE ARTS (New York, May 1923).
2   Hermann Hesse, DEMIAN (New York: Harper & Row, Publishers, 1970), p. 122.
3   Raniero Gnoli, THE AESTHETIC EXPERIENCE ACCORDING TO ABHINAVAGUPTA (Rome: Instituto Italiano per il Medio ed Estremo Oriente, 1956), p. xx.
4   Carl G. Jung et al., MAN AND HIS SYMBOLS (Garden City, N.Y.: Doubleday & Co., 1964), p. 232.
5   Ananda Coomaraswamy, DANCE OF SHIVA (New York: Noonday Press, 1965), p. 78.
6   Goldwater and Treves, eds., ARTISTS ON ART, p. 1.
7   Sinclair Gauldie, ARCHITECTURE (New York: Oxford University Press, 1969), p. 29.
8   Karl Kerényi in Joseph Campbell, THE MASKS OF GOD: OCCIDENTAL MYTHOLOGY (New York: Viking Press, 1964), p. 174.
9   Hellmut Wol, LEONARDO DA VINCI (New York: McGraw-Hill Book Co., 1967), p. 18.
10   Ibid.
11   Ibid., p. 45.
12   Elizabeth G. Holt, ed., A DOCUMENTARY HISTORY OF ART 1: THE MIDDLE AGES AND THE RENAISSANCE (New York: Doubleday & Co., 1957–58), p. 284.
13   Beaumont Newhall, THE HISTORY OF PHOTOGRAPHY (New York: Museum of Modern Art, 1964), p. 11.
14   Acts 9:3–4 HOLY BIBLE, Authorized King James Version (Edinburgh: William Collins Sons & Co., 1956), p. 105.
15   Kenneth Clark, LOOKING AT PICTURES (New York: Holt, Rinehart & Winston, 1960), p. 127.
16   Eugène Delacroix, THE JOURNAL OF EUGENE DELACROIX, trans. Walter Pach (New York: Covici-Friede Publishers, 1937), p. 314.
17   Beaumont Newhall, *Delacroix and Photography*, MAGAZINE OF ART 45, no. 7 (November 1952): 300.
18   Tom Prideaux, THE WORLD OF DELACROIX, eds. of Time-Life Books (New York: Time, Inc., 1966), p. 168.
19   Louis H. Sullivan, THE AUTOBIOGRAPHY OF AN IDEA (New York: Dover Publications, 1956), frontispiece.
20   Henry David Thoreau in THE PORTABLE THOREAU, ed. Carl Bode (New York: Viking Press, 1947), p. 301.
21   Pierre Schneider, THE WORLD OF MANET, eds. of Time-Life Books (New York: Time, Inc., 1968), p. 17.
22   Newhall, HISTORY OF PHOTOGRAPHY, p. 60.
23   Margaretta Salinger, GUSTAVE COURBET, 1819–1877, Miniature Album XH (New York: Metropolitan Museum of Art, 1955),

p. 24.

24 Schneider, World of Manet, p. 68.

25 Vincent van Gogh in John Rewald, Post-Impressionism — From van Gogh to Gauguin (New York: Museum of Modern Art, 1958).

26 Vincent van Gogh, *To His Brother Theo*, in Artists on Art, ed. Goldwater and Treves, pp. 383–384.

27 Ronald Alley, Gauguin, The Colour Library of Art (Middlesex, Eng.: Hamlyn Publishing Group, 1968), p. 8.

28 Ibid., p. 19.

29 Ibid.

30 Ibid., pp. 19, 22.

31 Cézanne and the Post-Impressionists, McCall's Collection of Modern Art (New York: McCall Books, 1970), p. 2.

32 Ibid., p. 5.

33 Ibid.

34 Ibid.

35 Herbert Read, A Concise History of Modern Sculpture (New York: Praeger, Publishers, 1964), p. 14.

36 Alfred H. Barr, Jr., ed., Masters of Modern Art (New York: Museum of Modern Art, 1955), p. 124.

37 William Fleming, Art, Music and Ideas (New York: Holt, Rinehart & Winston, 1970), p. 342.

38 Ibid.

39 Ibid.

40 Wassily Kandinsky, *Reminiscences*, in Modern Artists on Art, ed. Robert L. Herbert (Englewood Cliffs, N.J.: Prentice-Hall, 1964), p. 27.

41 Georges Braque in Roland Penrose, Picasso: His Life and Work (New York: Schocken Books, 1966), p. 125.

42 Helmut and Allison Gernsheim, Concise History of Photography (New York: Grosset & Dunlap).

43 Newhall, History of Photography, p. 111.

44 Colven Tomkins, The World of Marcel Duchamp, eds. of Time-Life Books (New York: Time, Inc., 1966), p. 12.

45 Barr, ed., Masters of Modern Art, p. 86.

46 *Venerable Giant of Modern Sculpture Bares Views*, Honolulu Star-Bulletin, August 24, 1971, p. F–2.

47 Lael Wertenbaker, The World of Picasso, eds. of Time-Life Books (New York: Time, Inc., 1967), p. 130.

48 Herbert Read, A Concise History of Modern Painting (New York: Praeger, Publishers, 1959), p. 160.

49 Goldwater and Treves, eds., Artists on

50 Fleming, Art, Music and Ideas, p. 351.

51 Siegfried Giedion, Space, Time and Architecture (Cambridge, Mass.: Harvard University Press, 1967), p. 617.

52 Hans Richter, Dada 1916–1966 (Munich: Goethe Institut, 1966), p. 22.

53 Barr, ed., Masters of Modern Art, p. 137.

54 Hans Arp in Paride Accetti, Raffaele De Grada, and Arturo Schwarz, Cinquant'annia Dada — Dada in Italia 1916–1966 (Milano: Galleria Schwarz, 1966), p. 39.

55 Barr, ed., Masters of Modern Art, p. 137.

56 Rafael Squirru, *Pop Art or the Art of Things*, Americas 15, no. 7 (July 1963): 16.

57 Kurt Schwitters in Accetti et al., Cinquant'annia Dada, p. 25.

58 Paul Klee, *Notes from His Diary*, in Artists on Art, ed. Goldwater and Treves, p. 442.

59 Barr, ed., Masters of Modern Art, p. 131.

60 Fleming, Art, Music and Ideas, p. 346.

61 Enrico Crispolti, Ernst, Miró, and the Surrealists, trans. Francis H. Keene (New York: McCall Publishing Co., 1970), p. 2.

62 Barr, ed., Masters of Modern Art, p. 174.

63 Three Hundred Years of American Painting, art ed. of Time (New York: Time, Inc., 1957), p. 289.

64 Tomkins, World of Duchamp, p. 162.

65 Barr, ed., Masters of Modern Art, p. 121.

66 Ibid.

67 Tomkins, World of Duchamp, p. 171.

WHAT ARE THE VISUAL ARTS?

1 Marshall McLuhan, Understanding Media (New York: New American Library, 1971).

2 Anthony Blunt, Picasso's Guernica (New York: Oxford University Press, 1969), p. 28.

3 Ichitaro Kondo and Elise Grilli, Katsushika Hokusai (Rutland, Vt.: Charles E. Tuttle Co., 1955), p. 13.

4 André Malraux, Museum without Walls, trans. Stuart Gilbert and Francis Price (Garden City, N.Y.: Doubleday & Co., 1967), p. 12.

5 Henri Cartier-Bresson, The Decisive Moment (New York: Simon & Schuster, 1952), p. 10.

6 Robert M. Sitton, D. W. Griffith: Mas-

TER OF THE MOVIES (Lecture demonstration for film technique, New York: Lincoln
Center for the Performing Arts, 1969).

7   Gene Youngblood, EXPANDED CINEMA
    (New York: E. P. Dutton & Co., 1970),
    p. 259.

8   Louis H. Sullivan, THE AUTOBIOGRAPHY OF
    AN IDEA (New York: Dover Publications,
    1956), frontispiece.

9   UNESCO, ARTS AND MAN (Englewood
    Cliffs, N.J.: Prentice-Hall, 1969), p. 65.

10 Nathan Knobler, THE VISUAL DIALOGUE
    (New York: Holt, Rinehart & Winston,
    1971), p. 430.

11 Kenzo Tange and Noborn Kawazoe, ISE:
    PROTOTYPE OF JAPANESE ARCHITECTURE
    (Cambridge, Mass.: M.I.T. Press, 1965),
    p. 18.

12 Constantinos A. Doxiadis, ARCHITECTURE
    IN TRANSITION (New York: Oxford Uni-
    versity Press, 1968), p. 35.

13 Constantinos A. Doxiadis, THE COMING
    WORLD CITY: ECUMENOPOLIS, IN CITIES
    OF DESTINY, ed. Arnold Toynbee (New
    York: McGraw-Hill Book Co., 1967), p.
    350.

HOW CAN ART SERVE
THE FUTURE?

1   Richard Neutra, SURVIVAL THROUGH DE-
    SIGN (New York: Oxford University Press,
    1954).

2   Walt Whitman in Charles A. Lindbergh,
    The Wisdom of Wilderness, LIFE 63, no.
    25 (December 22, 1967): 8.

3   Rachel Carson, SILENT SPRING (Boston:
    Houghton Mifflin Co., 1962), p. 5.

4   Gen. 1:28 HOLY BIBLE, Revised Standard
    Version (New York: Thos. Nelson & Sons,
    1952), p. 2.

nied Wall, in John Bartlett, FAMILIAR
QUOTATIONS, 14th ed., ed. Emily Morison
Beck (Boston: Little, Brown & Co., 1968),
p. 654b.

6   Richard Lewis, ed., THE WAY OF SILENCE:
    THE PROSE AND POETRY OF BASHO (New
    York: Dial Press, 1970), p. 19.

7   Roderick Nash, ed., THE AMERICAN EN-
    VIRONMENT: READINGS IN THE HISTORY OF
    CONSERVATION (Reading, Mass.: Addison-
    Wesley Publishing Co., 1968), pp. 5–9.

8   Sunset eds., NATIONAL PARKS OF THE
    WEST (Menlo Park, Calif.: Lane Magazine
    & Book Co., 1965), p. 11.

9   Paul and Percival Goodman, COMMUNI-
    TAS (New York: Vantage Books, 1960),
    p. 43.

10 Le Corbusier (Charles Édouard Jeanneret-
    Gris), THE CITY OF TO-MORROW AND ITS
    PLANNING, trans. Frederick Etchells (New
    York: Payson and Clarke, 1929); originally
    printed as URBANISME (Paris, 1924).

11 Ian L. McHarg, MULTIPLY AND SUBDUE
    THE EARTH (Bloomington, Ind.: NET Film
    Service, Indiana University, 1969).

12 Ibid.

13 Henry Alexander, *Lucky You Go Hawaii*,
    BEACON 2, no. 9 (September 1971): 21.

14 Tom Wolfe, THE PUMP HOUSE GANG
    (New York: Farrar, Straus & Giroux,
    1968), p. 240.

15 Peter Blake, *The Ugly America*, HORIZON
    3, no. 5 (May 1961): 6.

16 Donella H. Meadows et al., THE LIMITS
    OF GROWTH (New York: Universe Books,
    1972), p. 196.

17 Ibid.

18 Ibid.

19 Ian L. McHarg, DESIGN WITH NATURE
    (Garden City, N.Y.: Doubleday & Co.,
    1971), p. 7.

Bibliography

FOR GENERAL REFERENCE

A DICTIONARY OF ART AND ARTISTS by Peter Murray and Linda Murray. New York: Praeger, Publishers, 1966.

ART IN AMERICA. Published bimonthly, New York.

CRAFT HORIZONS. Published bimonthly, New York: Museum of Contemporary Crafts.

DOMUS: ARCHITECTTURA, ARREDAMENTO, ARTE. Published monthly, Milano.

ENCYCLOPEDIA OF WORLD ART. 12 vols. New York: McGraw-Hill Book Co., 1960–1969.

FROM ABACUS TO ZEUS: A HANDBOOK OF ART HISTORY by James S. Pierce. Englewood Cliffs, N.J.: Prentice-Hall, 1968.

GREAT MUSEUMS OF THE WORLD, editorial director, Carlo Ludovico Ragghianti, translated and edited by editors of ART NEWS. 15 vols. New York: Newsweek, Inc., 1968–1971.

HORIZON. Published bimonthly, New York.

MCCALL'S COLLECTON OF MODERN ART. 12 vols. New York: McCall Publishing Co., 1968–1970.

REALITES, editor-in-chief, Garith Windsor. Published monthly, New York.

THE COLOR LIBRARY OF ART. London: Paul Hamlyn, 1967.

THE MOTHER EARTH NEWS. Published bimonthly, North Madison, Ohio.

THE POCKET DICTIONARY OF ART TERMS edited by Mervyn Levy. Greenwich, Conn.: New York Graphic Society, 1961.

TIME-LIFE LIBRARY OF ART by editors of Time-Life Books. 28 vols. New York: Time, Inc., 1966–1970.

TIME-LIFE LIBRARY OF PHOTOGRAPHY by editors of Time-Life Books. 17 vols. New York: Time, Inc., 1970–1972.

WHY ART?

ANALYZING CHILDREN'S ART by Rhoda Kellogg. Palo Alto, Calif.: National Press Books, 1969.

ART AND ILLUSION: A STUDY IN THE PSYCHOLOGY OF PICTORIAL REPRESENTATION by E. H. Gombrich. New York: Pantheon Books, 1960.

ART AND VISUAL PERCEPTION: A PSYCHOLOGY OF THE CREATIVE EYE by Rudolf Arnheim. Berkeley: University of California Press, 1954.

ARTS AND THE MAN by Irwin Edman. New York: W. W. Norton & Co., 1939.

ART: THE VISUAL EXPERIENCE by Irving Kriesberg. New York: Pitman Publishing Corp., 1964.

CREATIVITY AND PERSONAL FREEDOM by Frank Barron. Rev. ed. New York: Van Nostrand Reinhold Co., 1968.

CREATIVITY IN THE ARTS edited by Vincent Tomas. Englewood Cliffs, N.J.: Prentice-Hall, 1964.

EYE AND BRAIN by R. L. Gregory. New York: McGraw-Hill Book Co., 1966.

GROWING WITH CHILDREN THROUGH ART by Aida C. Snow. New York: Van Nostrand Reinhold Co., 1968.

INFLUENCE OF CULTURE ON VISUAL PERCEPTION by Marshall H. Segall, Donald T. Campbell, and Melville J. Herskovits. Indianapolis: Bobbs-Merrill Co., 1966.

KAETHE KOLLWITZ DRAWINGS by Herbert Bittner. Cranbury, N.J.: A. S. Barnes & Co., 1959.

MAN AND HIS IMAGES: A WAY OF SEEING by Georgine Oeri. New York: Viking Press, 1968.

MAN AND HIS SYMBOLS by Carl G. Jung et al. Garden City, N.Y.: Doubleday & Co., 1964.

MY WORLD OF ART by Blanche Jefferson and Clyde McGeary. 6 vols. Boston: Allyn & Bacon, 1964. Has teachers' manuals.

PURPOSES OF ART by Albert E. Elsen. New York: Holt, Rinehart & Winston, 1967.

SILENT LANGUAGE by Edward T. Hall. New York: Fawcett World Library, 1969.

THE ARTS AND MAN by UNESCO. Englewood Cliffs, N.J.: Prentice-Hall, 1969.

THE ARTS IN THE CLASSROOM by Natalie Robinson Cole. New York: John Day Co., 1940.

THE CREATIVE PROCESS edited by Brewster Ghiselin. New York: New American Library, 1952.

THE FAMILY OF MAN by Edward Steichen. New

York: Simon & Schuster, 1967.

THE NECESSITY OF ART: THE MARXIST AP-
PROACH by Ernest Fischer. Baltimore: Penguin
Books, 1964.

THE PSYCHOLOGY OF CHILDREN'S ART by Rhoda
Kellogg with Scott O'Dell. Del Mar, Calif.:
CRM Books, 1967.

THE REVEALING EXPERIENCE by Kurt Kranz.
New York: Shorewood Publishers, 1964.

THE SENSES by Wolfgang von Buddenbrock. Ann
Arbor: University of Michigan Press, 1970.

THE VISUAL DIALOGUE by Nathan Knobler. New
York: Holt, Rinehart & Winston, 1970.

WHAT DO WE RESPOND TO
IN A WORK OF ART?

A COLOR NOTATION by Albert Henry Munsell.
Baltimore: Munsell Color Co., 1946.

ART FUNDAMENTALS: THEORY AND PRACTICE by
Otto G. Oevirk et al. Dubuque, Iowa: William
C. Brown Co., Publishers, 1968.

BASIC DESIGN: THE DYNAMICS OF VISUAL FORM
by Maurice de Sausmarez. New York: Reinhold Publishing Corp., 1964.

COLOR: BASIC PRINCIPLES AND NEW DIRECTIONS
by Patricia Sloane. New York: Reinhold Publishing Corp., 1968.

COLOR PSYCHOLOGY AND COLOR THERAPY by
Faber Birren. New Hyde Park, N.Y.: University Books, 1961.

COMPOSITION IN PICTURES by Ray Bethers. New
York: Pitman Publishing Corp., 1962.

DESIGN AS ART by Bruno Munari, translated by
Patrick Creagh. Baltimore: Penguin Books,
Inc., 1971.

DESIGN THROUGH DISCOVERY by Marjorie Elliot
Bevlin. New York: Holt, Rinehart & Winston,
1970.

INTERACTION OF COLOR by Josef Albers. New
Haven: Yale University Press, 1963.

PERSPECTIVE: SPACE AND DESIGN by Louise
Bowen Ballinger. New York: Reinhold Publishing Corp., 1969.

THE ART OF COLOR by Johannes Itten. New
York: Reinhold Publishing Corp., 1961.

WHAT WAS ART LIKE IN THE PAST?

A CONCISE HISTORY OF MODERN PAINTING by
Herbert Read. New York: Praeger, Publishers,
1959.

A CONCISE HISTORY OF MODERN SCULPTURE by
Herbert Read. New York: Praeger, Publishers,
1964.

A DOCUMENTARY HISTORY OF ART 1: THE MID-
DLE AGES AND THE RENAISSANCE edited by Elizabeth Gilmore Holt. Garden City, N.Y.:

Doubleday & Co., 1957–58.

A DOCUMENTARY HISTORY OF ART 2: MICHEL-
ANGELO AND THE MANNERISTS: THE BAROQUE,
AND THE EIGHTEENTH CENTURY edited by
Elizabeth Gilmore Holt. Garden City, N.Y.:
Doubleday & Co., 1957–58.

AFRICAN ART by Frank Willett. New York:
Praeger, Publishers, 1971.

A HISTORY OF FAR EASTERN ART by Sherman
Lee. New York: Harry N. Abrams, 1964.

ANCIENT CHINESE BRONZES by William Watson.
Rutland, Vt.: Charles E. Tuttle Co., 1962.

ART: AN INTRODUCTION by Dale G. Cleaver.
New York: Harcourt Brace Jovanovich, 1972.

ARTISTS ON ART edited by Robert Goldwater and
Marco Treves. New York: Pantheon Books,
1958.

ART, MUSIC AND IDEAS by William Fleming. New
York: Holt, Rinehart & Winston, 1970.

ART SINCE 1945 by Umbro Apollonio et al. New
York: Washington Square Press, 1958.

ASSEMBLAGE, ENVIRONMENTS AND HAPPENINGS
by Allan Kaprow. New York: Harry N. Abrams,
1966.

CHINESE PAINTING by James Cahill. Switzerland:
Skira Art Books, 1960.

CONCERNING THE SPIRITUAL IN ART AND PAINT-
ING IN PARTICULAR by Wassily Kandinsky.
New York: George Wittenborn, 1966.

DADA: ART AND ANTI-ART by Hans Richter. New
York: Harry N. Abrams, 1970.

FOUNDATIONS OF MODERN ART by Amédée Ozenfant, translated by John Rodker. New York:
Dover Publications, 1952.

FOUR ESSAYS ON KINETIC ART by Stephen Bann,
Reg Gadney, Frank Popper, and Philip Stead-
man. St. Albans, Eng.: Motion Books, 1966.

FROM THE CLASSICISTS TO THE IMPRESSIONISTS:
A DOCUMENTARY HISTORY OF ART AND AR-
CHITECTURE IN THE NINETEENTH CENTURY
edited by Elizabeth Gilmore Holt. Garden
City, N.Y.: Doubleday & Co., 1966.

GARDNER'S ART THROUGH THE AGES by Horst de
la Croix and Richard Tansey. 5th ed. New
York: Harcourt Brace Jovanovich, 1972.

GAUGUIN by Ronald Alley. Middlesex, Eng.:
Hamlyn Publishing Group, 1968.

GOYA, THE DISASTERS OF WAR by Xavier de
Salas. Garden City, N.Y.: Doubleday & Co.,
1956.

HISTORY OF ART by H. W. Janson. New York:
Harry N. Abrams, 1969.

HISTORY OF MODERN ART: PAINTING, SCULPTURE
AND ARCHITECTURE by H. H. Arnason. New
York: Harry N. Abrams, 1968.

JAPANESE PRINTS FROM THE EARLY MASTERS TO
THE MODERN by James A. Michener. Rutland,
Vt.: Charles E. Tuttle Co., 1960.

Kinetic Art by Guy Brett. New York: Reinhold Publishing Corp., 1968.

Masters of Modern Art edited by Alfred H. Barr, Jr. New York: Museum of Modern Art, 1955.

Modern Artists on Art edited by Robert L. Herbert. Englewood Cliffs, N.J.: Prentice-Hall, 1964.

Museum without Walls by André Malraux, translated by Stuart Gilbert and Francis Price. Garden City, N.Y.: Doubleday & Co., 1967.

Myths and Symbols in Indian Art and Civilization by Heinrich Zimmer. New York: Harper & Row, Publishers, 1946.

Painting and Reality by Etienne Gilson. Princeton, N.J.: Princeton University Press, 1957.

Painting in the Twentieth Century by Werner Haftmann. New York: Praeger, Publishers, 1965.

Picasso's Guernica by Anthony Blunt. New York: Oxford University Press, 1969.

Primitive Art by Paul S. Wingert. New York: World Publishing Co., 1965.

The Art of the South Sea Islands by Alfred Buehler, Terry Barrow, and Charles P. Mountford. New York: Crown Publishers, 1962.

The Dance of Shiva by Ananda Coomaraswamy. New York: Farrar, Straus & Co., 1937.

The Eternal Present: The Beginnings of Architecture by Siegfried Giedion. Princeton, N.J.: Princeton University Press, 1964.

The History of Photography by Beaumont Newhall. New York: Museum of Modern Art, 1964.

The Painter and the Photographer by Van Deren Coke. Albuquerque: University of New Mexico Press, 1964.

The Story of Art by E. H. Gombrich. 12th ed. New York: Praeger, Publishers, 1972.

WHAT ARE THE VISUAL ARTS?

A Concise History of Photography by Helmut and Allison Gernsheim. New York: Grosset & Dunlap, 1965.

African Crafts and Craftsmen by René Gardi. New York: Van Nostrand Reinhold Co., 1970.

A Poet and His Camera by Gordon Parks. New York: Viking Press, 1968.

Architecture without Architects by Bernard Rudofsky. Garden City, N.Y.: Doubleday & Co., 1964.

Art Career Guide edited by Donald Holden. 2d ed. New York: Watson-Guptill Publications, 1967.

Art from Found Materials: Discarded and Natural: Techniques, Design Inspiration by Mary L. Stribling. New York: Crown Publishers, 1966.

Beyond Habitat by Moshe Safdie. Cambridge, Mass.: M.I.T. Press, 1970.

Ceramics: A Potter's Handbook by Glenn C. Nelson. New York: Holt, Rinehart & Winston, 1966.

Cities by Lawrence Halprin. New York: Reinhold Publishing Corp., 1963

Design of Cities by Edmund N. Bacon. New York: Viking Press, 1967.

Drawing by Daniel M. Mendelowitz. New York: Holt, Rinehart & Winston, 1967. Has companion study guide.

Elements of the Art of Architecture by William Muschenheim. New York: Viking Press, 1964.

Expanded Cinema by Gene Youngblood. New York: E. P. Dutton & Co., 1970.

Experiencing Architecture by Steen E. Rasmussen. Cambridge, Mass.: M.I.T. Press, 1962.

Film as Art by Rudolf Arnheim. Berkeley: University of California Press, 1957.

Focus on D. W. Griffith by Harry M. Geduld. Englewood Cliffs, N.J.: Prentice-Hall, 1971.

Hokusai Sketches and Paintings by Muneshige Narazake. Palo Alto, Calif.: Kodansha International, 1969.

House Form and Culture by Amos Rapoport. Englewood Cliffs, N.J.: Prentice-Hall, 1969.

How to Talk Back to Your Television Set by Nicholas Johnson. New York: Bantam Books, 1970.

How to Wrap Five Eggs by Hideyuki Oka and Michikazu Sakai. New York: Harper & Row, Publishers, 1967.

Ise: Prototype of Japanese Architecture by Kenzo Tange and Noboro Kawazoe. Cambridge, Mass.: M.I.T. Press, 1965.

It's Only a Movie by Clark McKowen and Mel Byars. Englewood Cliffs, N.J.: Prentice-Hall, 1970.

Kindergarten Chats by Louis H. Sullivan. Washington, D.C.: Scarab Fraternity Press, 1934.

Kiss Kiss Bang Bang by Pauline Kael. New York: Bantam Books, 1969.

Masters of the Japanese Print by Richard Lane. Garden City, N.Y.: Doubleday & Co., 1962.

Modern Prints and Drawings by Paul J. Sachs. New York: Alfred A. Knopf, 1954.

Nothing Personal by Richard Avedon and James Baldwin. Toronto: McClelland & Stewart, 1964.

Painting: Some Basic Principles by Frederick Gore. New York: Reinhold Publishing Corp., 1965.

Painting with Synthetic Media by Russell O.

Woody, Jr. New York: Van Nostrand Reinhold Co., 1965.

PHOTOGRAPHERS ON PHOTOGRAPHY edited by Nathan Lyons. Englewood Cliffs, N.J.: Prentice-Hall, 1966.

PHOTOGRAPHS BY HENRI CARTIER-BRESSON by Henri Cartier-Bresson. New York: Grossman Publishers, 1963.

PIONEERS OF MODERN DESIGN by Nikolaus Pevsner. Baltimore: Penguin Books, 1964.

PRINTMAKING by Gabor Peterdi. New York: The Macmillan Co., 1961.

PRINTMAKING TODAY by Jules Heller. New York: Holt, Rinehart & Winston, 1958.

PRINTS AND VISUAL COMMUNICATION by William M. Ivins, Jr. New York: Plenum Publishing Corp., 1969.

PROBLEMS OF DESIGN by George Nelson. New York: Whitney Publications, 1965.

SCULPTURE (Appreciation of the Arts Series 2) by L. R. Rogers. New York: Oxford University Press, 1969.

SPACE, TIME AND ARCHITECTURE by Siegfried Giedion. 5th ed. Cambridge, Mass.: Harvard University Press, 1967.

SYNTHETIC PAINTING MEDIA by Lawrence N. Jensen. Englewood Cliffs, N.J.: Prentice-Hall, 1964.

THE ARTIST'S GUIDE TO HIS MARKET by Betty Chamberlain. New York: Watson-Guptill Publications, 1970.

THE ARTIST'S HANDBOOK OF MATERIALS AND TECHNIQUES by Ralph Mayer. New York: Viking Press, 1968.

THE ART OF DRAWING by Bernard Chaet. New York: Holt, Rinehart & Winston, 1970.

THE ARTS AND MAN by UNESCO. Englewood Cliffs, N.J.: Prentice-Hall, 1969.

THE BEHAVIORAL BASIS OF DESIGN by Robert Sommer. Englewood Cliffs, N.J.: Prentice-Hall, 1969.

THE CAMERA by editors of Time-Life Books. New York: Time, Inc., 1970.

THE CITY IN HISTORY by Lewis Mumford. New York: Harcourt Brace Jovanovich, 1972.

THE CONCERNED PHOTOGRAPHER by Robert Capa et al. New York: Grossman Publishers, 1969.

THE DECISIVE MOMENT by Henri Cartier-Bresson. New York: Simon & Schuster, 1952.

THE EMERGENCE OF FILM ART by Lewis Jacobs. New York: Hopkinson & Blake Publishing Co., 1969.

THE LANGUAGE OF ARCHITECTURE by Niels L. Prak. New York: Humanities Press, 1968.

THE LIVELIEST ART by Arthur Knight. New York: New American Library, 1957.

THE NATURAL WAY TO DRAW by Kimon Nicolaïdes. Boston: Houghton Mifflin Co., 1941.

THE WAY OF CHINESE PAINTING, ITS IDEAS AND TECHNIQUES by Mai-Mai Sze. New York: Random House, 1959.

WATERCOLOR: MATERIALS AND TECHNIQUES by George Dibble. New York: Holt, Rinehart & Winston, 1966.

WHO DESIGNS AMERICA edited by Lawrence B. Holland. Garden City, N.Y.: Doubleday & Co., 1966.

YOUNG DESIGNS IN LIVING by Barbara Plumb. New York: Viking Press, 1969.

HOW CAN ART SERVE THE FUTURE?

AS WE LIVE AND BREATHE: THE CHALLENGE OF OUR ENVIRONMENT by Gilbert M. Grosvenor. Washington, D.C.: National Geographic Society, 1971.

CITY AND COUNTRY IN AMERICA edited by David R. Weimer. New York: Appleton-Century-Crofts, 1962.

DESIGN WITH NATURE by Ian L. McHarg. Garden City, N.Y.: Doubleday & Co., 1971.

GOD'S OWN JUNKYARD: THE PLANNED DETERIORATION OF AMERICA'S LANDSCAPE by P. Blake. New York: Holt, Rinehart & Winston, 1964.

IN WILDNESS IS THE PRESERVATION OF THE WORLD by Eliot Porter. San Francisco: Sierra Club Books, 1967.

MAN-MADE AMERICA: CHAOS OR CONTROL: AN INQUIRY INTO SELECTED PROBLEMS OF DESIGN IN THE URBANIZED LANDSCAPE by Christopher Tunnard and Boris Pushkarev. New Haven: Yale University Press, 1963.

MAN'S STRUGGLE FOR SHELTER IN AN URBANIZING WORLD by Charles Abrams. Cambridge, Mass.: M.I.T. Press, 1964.

MATRIX OF MAN: AN ILLUSTRATED HISTORY OF URBAN ENVIRONMENT by Sibyl Moholy-Nagy. New York: Praeger, Publishers, 1968.

MOMENT IN THE SUN by Robert Rienow and Leona Train. New York: Ballantine Books, 1967.

SURVIVAL THROUGH DESIGN by Richard Neutra. New York: Oxford University Press, 1969.

THE AMERICAN AESTHETIC by Nathaniel A. Owings. New York: Harper & Row, Publishers, 1969.

THE AMERICAN ENVIRONMENT: READINGS IN THE HISTORY OF CONSERVATION edited by Roderick Nash. Reading, Mass.: Addison-Wesley Publishing Co., 1968.

THE AMERICAN LANDSCAPE by Ian Nairn. New York: Random House, 1968.

THE HIDDEN ORDER OF ART by Anton Ehrenzweig. Berkeley: University of California Press, 1971.

THE IMAGE OF THE CITY by Kevin Lynch. Cambridge, Mass.: M.I.T. Press, 1960.

THE LANGUAGE OF CITIES by Franziska P. Hosken. New York: The Macmillan Co., 1968.

THE LAST LANDSCAPE by William H. Whyte. New York: Doubleday & Co., 1968.

THE LAST WHOLE EARTH CATALOG. Menlo Park, Calif.: Portola Institute, 1971.

THE LIMITS OF GROWTH by Donella H. Mead-ows et al. New York: Universe Books, 1972.

THE WAY OF SILENCE: THE PROSE AND POETRY OF BASHO edited by Richard Lewis. New York: Dial Press, 1970.

THIS IS THE AMERICAN EARTH by Ansel Adams and Nancy Newhall. San Francisco: Sierra Club Books, 1970.

Artist and title index

Subject index

Abstract; abstraction
  art, 26, 92, 108, 109, 127, 186
    beginnings of, 111
    definition of, 108
    Early Christian, 140
      representational, combined with, 184
  expressionism. *See* Expressionism, abstract
  geometric, 131, 147, 183
    of human figure, 128
  icon, 146
  images of Christ, 140
  in cubism, 199
  of objects for tools, 109
  painting, 200, 204
  primitive form, 189
  sculpture, 140, 183
  surrealism. *See* Surrealism
  symbolism, 127
    Christian, 140
Academic style, 162–163
  l'École des Beaux Arts and, 163
  rejection of, 170
Acrylics, 242, 275
  effect on painting of, 242
Adam and Eve, 332
Advertising
  art, posters as, 235
  communications, 255
  design, 255, 298
  television, 255, 297, 298
Aerial perspective. *See* Perspective, aerial
Aesthetic; aesthetics, 46
  art, 8
  awareness and environmental crisis, 2
  concern, 323
  decisions, 13. *See also* Beauty; Creativity; Imag-
    ination; Quality; Perception; Ugliness
  definition of, 9
  environmental, 357
  experience, 92
  mobile homes, lack of in, 320
  reality by camera, 287
  traditions
    Buddhist, 116
    Egyptian, 120

    European, 120
    Indian, 120
    Japanese, 120
Africa; African, 201
  Cameroons, 113
  Egypt. *See* Egypt
  Ife Kingdom, casting techniques of, 302
  Nigeria, Benin District, 112
  North, 111
  sculpture, 112
    Ashanti, 25, 26
    influence of, 188
  Tassili-n-Ajjer, Sahara Desert, 111
Afterimage. *See* Cinematography; Color
Age of Reason, 153
  rococo style in, 153
  See also Enlightenment
Alexandria, Egypt, 140
America; American. *See* Indian, American; New
    York City; United States
Anatomy. *See* Human figure
Antioch, 140
Aphrodite, 36, 149. *See also* Venus
Apollinaire, Guillaume, 213
Architecture; architectural, 52, 247, 308–321
  aqueduct as, Roman, 139
  arch
    Gothic pointed, 142
      diagram of, 143
    Roman, 139, 142, 145
    Romanesque, use of, 142
  as functional sculpture, 225
  as shelter, 124
  awareness of, 310
  barns as, 309
  baroque, 153
  Bauhaus, 206, 244, 316
  beauty in, 162, 312
  birthrate and, 318
  Buddhist, 125
  Byzantine, 160
  campus, 321
  cathedral. *See* Cathedrals
  change and, 310
  chapel, 145, 149, 153, 224–225

Scale, 92, 141
    human, 118, 119
        in architecture, 145
Sculpture, sculptural, 52, 202, 299–307
    abstract, 140, 183
    additive. See techniques, additive
    African, 112
        influence of, 188
    aliveness in, 130
    architectural, 307
    architecture and, compared, 48, 125, 225, 308
    armature. See techniques, armature
    Ashanti, 25–26
    assemblage. See Assemblage
    assembling. See techniques, assembling
    Aztec, 24
    balance in, 240
    baroque, 49, 153
    Bronze Age, 128
    Buddha as, 299
        Chinese, 299
        Japanese, 299
        Southeast Asian, 299
    Buddhist, 116
    carving. See techniques, carving
    casting. See techniques, casting
    Chinese, 114, 299
    Christian, 31, 48, 49, 140
    classical style, 131
    color in, 240, 306
    composition in, 100
    cubist, 195, 201
        influences of, 201
    cultural traditions of, 116
    Cycladic, 128
    dada. See Assemblage, dada
    design of, 299
    drapery in, 100
    Early Christian, 140
    Egyptian, 128, 130
        mass in, 64
    era of in Western art, 144
    European
        in-the-round, 48
        sacred, 48, 49
    expressionist, German, 180
    form in
        content and, 48
        linear, 305
        related to technology, 306
    Greek, 130–131, 132, 135, 136, 307
        influence of
            on nineteenth century, 180
            on Renaissance, 150
            on Rome, 137
    Hindu, 48, 49, 117
    human figure in. See Human figure

    impressionist influence on, 180
    individuality in, 137
    Italian, 31, 49, 180
    Japanese, 121, 299
    junk, mechanical, 236
    kinetic, 81, 236, 306, 307
    light, 55
    light in. See materials, light
    mass in, 63, 64, 100, 116
    materials, 301, 302
        air currents, 307
        aluminum, 307
        automation, 54
        color, 306
        electromagnet, 306
        granite, 64
        iron, 307
        laser beam, 55
        light, 54, 306
        marble, 301
        metal, 307
        motorized plastic, 306
        sheetmetal, 307
        steel, 307
        stone, 301
        wire, 305, 306, 307
        wood, 301
    mechanized, 236
    minimal, 64, 240
    mobile, 307
    modeling. See techniques, modeling
    motion. See kinetic
    motion in, 80, 117
    naturalism, 127
    nineteenth-century, 183
    nudity in, 130, 180
    Oceanic, influence of, 188
    painting related to, 233
    pop, 229
    portraits in, 121, 137, 140
    prehistoric, 127, 299
    relief. See Relief
    Renaissance, 31, 150, 307
    representational, 121, 183, 184
    reproductions. See Reproductions
    rhythm in, 306
    Roman, 131
        related to Greek, 137
        in-the-round, 48
    sacred, 48, 49
    simplicity in, 183
    size of, 299
    Solomon Islands, 114
    Southeast Asian, 299
    space, 100
        three-dimensional, 240, 299
    Spanish, influence of, 188
    stabile, 307